Critical Discursive Psychology

Also by Ian Parker

Qualitative Methods in Psychology: A Research Guide (with Peter Banister, Erica Burman, Maye Taylor and Carol Tindall)

Carrying Out Investigations in Psychology (with Jeremy Foster)

Deconstructing Psychopathology (with Eugenie Georgaca, David Harper, Terence McLaughlin and Mark Stowell Smith)

Psychology and Society: Radical Theory and Practice (co-edited with Russell Spears)

Culture, Power and Difference: Discourse Analysis in South Africa (co-edited with Erica Burman, Amanda Kottler and Ann Levett)

Psychoanalytic Culture: Psychoanalytic Discourse in Western Society

Social Constructionism, Discourse and Realism (edited)

Critical Textwork: An Introduction to Varieties of Discourse and Analysis (with the Bolton Discourse Network)

Deconstructing Psychotherapy (edited)

Cyberpsychology (co-edited with Angel Gordo-López)

Critical Discursive Psychology

Ian Parker

Published by
PALGRAVE MACMILLAN
Houndmills, Basingstoke, Hampshire RG21 6XS and
175 Fifth Avenue, New York, N. Y. 10010
Companies and representatives throughout the world

PALGRAVE MACMILLAN is the global academic imprint of the Palgrave
Macmillan division of St. Martin's Press, LLC and of Palgrave Macmillan Ltd.
Macmillan® is a registered trademark in the United States, United Kingdom
and other countries. Palgrave is a registered trademark in the European
Union and other countries.

ISBN-13: 978–0–333–97381–3
ISBN-10: 0–333–97381–X

This book is printed on paper suitable for recycling and made from fully
managed and sustained forest sources. Logging, pulping and manufacturing
processes are expected to conform to the environmental regulations of the
country of origin.

A catalogue record for this book is available from the British Library.

Library of Congress Catalog Card Number: 2002074812

Printed and bound in Great Britain by
CPI Antony Rowe, Chippenham and Eastbourne

For Erica

Contents

Acknowledgements   xi

Notes on Contributors   xiii

1 Theoretical Discourse, Subjectivity and Critical Psychology   1
   Situated knowledge   2
   Theoretical critical distance   8
   Complex subjectivity   14
   Conclusions and openings   18

PART I
Enlightenment, Realism and Power (and their Reverse)   19

2 Against Postmodernism: Psychology in Cultural Context   21
   Postmodern against the modern   23
   A detour: postmodern narrative and Enlightenment
   practice   36
   Four Enlightenment reversals   38
   Conclusion   45

2a Against Against-ism: Comment on Parker
   Fred Newman and Lois Holzman   46

2b Critical Distance: Reply to Newman and Holzman   52
   Knowing something   52
   Knowing nothing   54

3 Against Relativism in Psychology, On Balance   57
   Introduction   57
   For relativism, and against   60
   For critical realism, and against   66
   The separation and reconnection of moral–political
   critique   71

3a Regulating Criticism: Some Comments on an
   Argumentative Complex
   Jonathan Potter, Derek Edwards and Malcolm Ashmore   73
   Introduction   73
   Rhetorical troubles   76

	Recruiting the tortured, oppressed and murdered	77
	Critical realist psychology and critical realism in and against psychology	78
	Trouble in the Parker-complex	80
3b	The Quintessentially Academic Position	82
4	Against Wittgenstein: Materialist Reflections on Language in Psychology	85
	Wittgenstein and psychology	88
	Words, the world and power	92
	Psychology, again	100
	Contexts	103
	Connections and conclusions	104
4a	The Practical Turn in Psychology: Marx and Wittgenstein as Social Materialists	
	John. T. Jost and Curtis D. Hardin	108
	The practical turn	108
	Wittgenstein was not a relativist	111
	(The later) Wittgenstein was not an essentialist	113
	The politics of Wittgenstein	114
	Synthesizing Marx and Wittgenstein	116
4b	Reference Points for Critical Theoretical Work in Psychology	117
	Wittgenstein and Marx	117
	Contradictions	119
	Synthesis	120

PART II
The Turn to Discourse as a Critical Theoretical Resource | 121

5	Discursive Psychology Uncut	123
	Defining 'discourse'	123
	Historical resources: two traditions	125
	Discourse analysis in psychology	128
	Axes of difference in discursive research	132
	Remaining questions	141
6	Discourse: Definitions and Contradictions	142
	Introduction	142
	The turn to language	143

	Criteria	145
	Auxiliary criteria	154
	Reflections and conclusions	157

6a Discourse: Noun, Verb or Social Practice?
*Jonathan Potter, Margaret Wetherell, Ros Gill and
Derek Edwards* 160
   Introduction 160
   Discourse analysis: descriptive and constructive 162
   Reification and intuition 164
   Interpretative repertoires 168

6b The Context of Discourse: Let's Not Throw the Baby Out
   With the Bathwater
   Dominic Abrams and Michael A. Hogg 172

6c Real Things: Discourse, Context and Practice 180
   Object status 181
   Context 182
   Practice 184

PART III
Critical Discursive Research, Subjectivity and Practice 187

7 Reflexive Research and Grounding of Analysis:
   Psychology and the Psy-Complex 189
   Objectivity 191
   Subjectivity 194
   Discursive complexes 197
   The psy-complex 199
   Discussion 202
   Concluding comments 203

8 Tracing Therapeutic Discourse in Material Culture 205
   The material 206
   Analytic steps 208
   Therapeutic discourse, subject positions and power 216
   Concluding comments 219

9 Constructing and Deconstructing Psychotherapeutic
   Discourse 220
   Psychotherapeutic regimes of knowledge 222
   Deconstructing psychotherapeutic knowledge 228

10   Critical Reflections   234
     Discipline   234
     Culture   235
     History   236
     Institutions   237
     Reflections   238

References   241

Index   263

Acknowledgements

Many thanks again for their comments and help to Judith Arrowsmith, Erica Burman, Eugenie Georgaca, Angel J. Gordo-López, Sarah Grogan, Sean Homer, Bernardo Jiménez-Domínguez, Karen Henwood, Ian Law, Rhiannon Lloyd, Terence McLaughlin, Deborah Marks, Richard Mepham, Kevin Moore, Alan Preston, Martin Roiser, John Shotter, Heather Walton and Carla Willig.

Chapter 2 was originally published in 1998 as 'Against Postmodernism: Psychology in Cultural Context', in *Theory and Psychology*, 8 (5), 601–627 (reprinted by permission of Sage Publications Ltd ©); the response by Fred Newman and Lois Holzman was published in 2000 as 'Against Against-ism', in *Theory and Psychology*, 10 (2), 265–270 (reprinted by permission of Sage Publications Ltd ©); and my reply was published in 2000 as 'Critical Distance', in *Theory and Psychology*, 10 (2), 271–276 (reprinted by permission of Sage Publications Ltd ©). Chapter 3 was originally published in 1999 as 'Against Relativism in Psychology, On Balance', in *History of the Human Sciences*, 12 (4), 61–78 (reprinted by permission of Sage Publications Ltd ©); the response by Jonathan Potter, Derek Edwards and Malcolm Ashmore was published in 1999 as 'Regulating Criticism: Some Comments on an Argumentative Complex', in *History of the Human Sciences*, 12 (4), 79–88 (reprinted by permission of Sage Publications Ltd ©); and my reply was published in 1999 as 'The Quintessentially Academic Position', in *History of the Human Sciences*, 12 (4), 89–91 (reprinted by permission of Sage Publications Ltd ©). Chapter 4 was originally published in 1996 as 'Against Wittgenstein: Materialist Reflections on Language in Psychology', in *Theory and Psychology*, 6 (3), 363–834 (reprinted by permission of Sage Publications Ltd ©); the response by John T. Jost and Curtis D. Hardin was originally published in 1996 as 'The Practical Turn in Psychology: Marx and Wittgenstein as Social Materialists', in *Theory and Psychology*, 6 (3), 385–393 (reprinted by permission of Sage Publications Ltd ©); and my reply was originally published in 1996 as 'Reference Points for Critical Work in Psychology', in *Theory and Psychology*, 6 (3), 395–399 (reprinted by permission of Sage Publications Ltd ©). A shorter version of Chapter 5 was originally published in 1997 as 'Discursive Psychology', in *Critical Psychology: An Introduction*, edited by Dennis Fox and Isaac

Prilleltensky, published by Sage. Chapter 6 was originally published in 1990 as 'Discourse: Definitions and Contradictions', in *Philosophical Psychology*, 3, (2), 189–204 (reprinted by permission of Taylor and Francis Ltd, http://www.tandf.co.uk/journals ©); the response by Jonathan Potter, Margaret Wetherell, Ros Gill and Derek Edwards was originally published in 1990 as 'Discourse: Noun, Verb or Social Practice?', in *Philosophical Psychology*, 3, (2), 205–217 (reprinted by permission of Taylor and Francis Ltd, http://www.tandf.co.uk/journals ©); the response by Dominic Abrams and Michael A. Hogg was originally published in 1990 as 'The Context of Discourse: Let's Not Throw the Baby Out With the Bathwater', in *Philosophical Psychology*, 3 (2), 219–225 (reprinted by permission of Taylor and Francis Ltd, http://www.tandf.co.uk/journals ©); and my reply was originally published in 1990 as 'Real Things: Discourse, Context and Practice', in *Philosophical Psychology*, 3 (2), 227–233 (reprinted by permission of Taylor and Francis Ltd, http://www.tandf.co.uk/journals ©). Chapter 7 was originally published in 1994 as 'Reflexive Research and the Grounding of Analysis: Social Psychology and the Psy-Complex', in *Journal of Community and Applied Social Psychology*, 4, (4), 43–66. Chapter 8 was originally published in 1999 as 'Tracing Therapeutic Discourse in Material Culture', in *British Journal of Medical Psychology*, 72, pp. 577–587. Chapter 9 was originally published in 1998 as 'Constructing and Deconstructing Therapeutic Discourse', in *European Journal of Psychotherapy, Counselling and Health*, 1, (1), 77–90.

Notes on Contributors

Dominic Abrams is Professor of Social Psychology and Director of the Centre for the Study of Group Processes at the University of Kent at Canterbury. His books include *Intergroup Relations* (with Michael Hogg) (Psychology Press, 2001). Email: D.Abrams@ukc.ac.uk

Malcolm Ashmore is Lecturer in Social Psychology at Loughborough University. His publications include *The Reflexive Thesis: Wrighting Sociology of Scientific Knowledge* (The University of Chicago Press, 1989) Email: m.t.ashmore@lboro.ac.uk

Derek Edwards is Professor of Psychology at Loughborough Univerrsity. His publications include *Discourse and Cognition* (Sage, 1997). Email: d.edwards@lboro.ac.uk

Rosalind Gill is a Lecturer in Gender Studies and Gender Theory at the London School of Economics. She is author of *Gender and the Media: Audiences, Representations and Cultural Politics*, (Polity Press, in press). Email: r.c.gill@lse.ac.uk

Curtis Hardin is Assisant Professor of Psychology at University of California at Santa Barbara. He has published in a number of psychology journals. Email: hardin@psych.ucla.edu

Alexa Hepburn is Senior Lecturer in Psychology at Nottingham Trent University. She is author of *Critical Social Psychology* (Sage, 2002). Email: alexa.hepburn@ntu.ac.uk

Michael A. Hogg is Professor of Social Psychology at the University of Queensland. His books include *Intergroup* Relations (with Dominic Abrams) (Psychology Press, 2001). Email: Mike@psy.uq.edu.au

Lois Holzman is Director of Educational Programs at the East Side Institute for Short Term Psychotherapy in New York. Her publications include *Schools for Growth: Radical Alternatives to Current Educational Models* (Erlbaum, 1997) Email: LHolzdan@aol.com

John T. Jost is Associate Professor of Organizational Behavior at Stanford University. His publications include *The Psychology of Legitimacy: Emerging Perspectives on Ideology, Justice, and Intergroup Relations* (with Brenda Major, Cambridge University Press, 2001). Email: Jost_John@gsb.stanford.edu

Fred Newman is Director of Training at the East Side Institute for Short Term Psychotherapy and Artistic Director of the Castillo Theatre in New York. His publications include *The End of Knowing: A New Developmental Way of Learning* (Routledge, 1997). Email: esiesc@aol.com

Jonathan Potter is Professor of Discourse Analysis at Loughborough University. His publications included *Representing Reality: Discourse, Rhetoric and Social Construction* (Sage, 1996) j.a.potter@lboro.ac.uk

1
Theoretical Discourse, Subjectivity and Critical Psychology

Where do we start? Often when we are faced with an insurmountable problem or we want to get somewhere when the route looks too rough, we think that it would be much easier if we could start from anywhere but here. I have that kind of thought when I'm working on issues of ideology and power in psychology. The discipline of psychology just does not seem able to tolerate a consideration of those kinds of issues. Or, when it looks like it is taking them seriously the discipline then engages in a thorough assimilative process that the Situationists used to call 'recuperation' (Debord, 1977). The Situationists in the 1950s and 1960s wanted to disrupt the machinery of capitalist consumer culture that they saw operating as a 'society of the spectacle', and so they were particularly sensitive to the recuperation of radical ideas into the spectacle, to the way that threats to power are neutralized and absorbed into the existing rules of the game.

So, psychologists can talk about ideology only when the term applies to belief systems assumed to be collections of attitudes and stereotypes existing as things inside the head, and they will study power only when it refers to the deliberate exertion of one's will over others. Ideas and intentions are compulsively and relentlessly abstracted from social relations in psychological research, they are broken down and then rebuilt so that they will function independently of context. They are then juggled around as researchers try to make them social again by building their own model of society as one into which these kind of things would fit. Theodor Adorno, whose work has suffered exactly this kind of ideological mutilation at the hands of social psychologists working on prejudice, provides a succinct description of this process when he is commenting on the separation of high and low art in Western culture. We could say of the individual and the social in psychology, following

1

Adorno (1967), that 'Both are torn halves of an integral freedom, to which, however, they do not add up.'

The trick is in the tearing, and just as a severed limb is so much more difficult to rejoin to the body when there has been a clean cut, so the bits of mental functioning that have been removed from psychological studies cannot be patched together again properly precisely because they have been so efficiently sliced out of the social. This is also why the Cartesian separation of mind and body which haunts psychology cannot be remedied by those social constructionists who are now starting to talk about 'embodiment' (see Nightingale, 1999). Social constructionists in psychology once thought that the poverty of social explanation in the discipline could be solved by focusing on the way language works to make us human and make a culture (e.g., Harré and Secord, 1972), but they fell straight into the trap that structures mainstream psychology, which divides mental qualities from physical embodiment. You cannot just bring the body back in, as the torn half of the equation, to fill the gap left by a language-based account. If you do, then the result is simply 'bourgeois ideology made flesh' (in a phrase I owe to Terence McLaughlin).

Given this state of affairs – the systematic reduction of cultural and historical phenomena to the level of the individual in the discipline – how do we do 'critical' psychology? What might critical discursive psychology look like? Well, to start, we have to break some of the rules. I'll mention at least three we have to break.

Situated knowledge

The first rule to break is, 'don't talk about yourself'. Now, there are always exceptions to rules of course, and occasions like this do permit even a psychologist to move out of third-person report mode. The problem is that these exceptions often function to confirm what usually goes on, and psychology is well practised at concealing the position of the speaker or writer. Research reports are often so difficult to evaluate because we have a detailed description of apparatus, subjects and procedure, and then a blank space, a kind of absent centre where we would expect one of the key actors in the story to be. This absence has been noticed by qualitative research, which is becoming more important now as a site of critique in the discipline and which encourages us to make the researcher, as a key actor, speak (e.g., Banister *et al.*, 1994; Davies, 2000). A critical psychology should be a reflexive endeavour through and through, and it is often useful to include an account of the moral–political standpoint of the researcher in relation to what they may be observing and changing. We need a way of situating the production of knowledge, and that often means situating it in such a way that we connect biography with history (Young, 1988).

Postmodern themes filtering into the discipline encourage us to be suspicious of grand theory, but I must say that I have never believed psychology, neither the overarching models nor the little findings. Discourse analysis was not around in psychology when I started, but I came into the discipline already reading it from a particular set of positions.

Most psychological studies are carried out on white, male, US American undergraduate students (Sears, 1986), and so it is hardly surprising that the findings from these studies do not translate too well to other populations. The advantage for us here in the UK is that this also makes them a little easier to decode, and we are then alerted to the way culture always frames research. I shared the same kind of cultural privileges as most psychologists in the sense that I am also white and male, but this privilege was mediated and problematized by the obvious hegemony of North American, mainly US, psychology through glossy undergraduate textbooks, and is so all the more now through a peculiar definition in citation counts and funding indices of what counts as an 'international' research journal. It was tempting for a while to react to this by imagining that European psychology was necessarily a progressive alternative to US American varieties (Parker, 1989). That was a mistake, and we need to be sceptical about European research as well as connecting with critical work in US America (e.g., Prilleltensky, 1994; Fox and Prilleltensky, 1997). The opposition between Europe and US America does draw our attention to the fracturing of whiteness into different kinds of power that our Western psychology enjoys (Bulhan, 1981; Howitt and Owusu-Bempah, 1994). We need to be careful not to abstract the psychology we study 'here' from cultural context, and with rapidly increasing globalization that means an international context. We should not abstract it as if it could be torn from the relationship with the psychology of others that helps define it (cf. Sampson, 1993).

Like other academic disciplines, psychology is structured by social class divisions, and this affects who conducts research on those outside the academe and how that research is interpreted and published (Sennett and Cobb, 1972). A kind of lower middle-class background and a first degree in a polytechnic helped sensitize me to how psychological theories were embedded in a way of looking at the world that was at best driven by a liberal concern with helping people to fit comfortably and at worst led by idle curiosity. At the same time, research and publication success are linked to class through systems of patronage and exclusion, something that studies of the fate of resubmitted journal articles from different institutions indicate quite clearly (Peters and Ceci, 1982). There have been some interesting reflections on how this bears on the position of working-class women in higher education which also show how class positions mark the subjectivity of those subjected to them (Walkerdine, 1990).

Something I realized quite recently was that my curiosity about the way that psychology operates is stereotypically male. Men still dominate teaching and research in psychology when most of the students are women (Burman *et al.*, 1995), and men tend to go into it to find out about the mind and behaviour as if these were properties of other people. Women, on the other hand, more often want to learn something about themselves and relationships with others (Kagan and Lewis, 1990). Noticing this is valuable, but there is a danger of romanticizing this willingness to participate body and soul in psychology and, if we did that, we could end up supporting a more efficient recruitment of women and men into the machinery of psychology. Such romanticizing and essentializing of other places that might resist and cure the ills we suffer in psychology appears in many forms. Sometimes it is necessary but it is always risky, and I will return to this issue later.

I studied the stories told about child development, the diagrams of bits of memory and the tales of Americans doing things in groups. I didn't go into psychology to discover the things that psychology thought it was discovering, but to discover how the discipline of psychology itself worked. When you are doing psychology critically, you need to watch the psychologists. In a sense I did choose where to start from, then, but all choices are conditioned by local sets of circumstances that it might be possible to move in and out of, and perhaps even to control, and these sets of circumstances are also woven into cultural–political environments that constitute where it is possible for us to move, and what it is possible for us to think. This 'modern' culture revolves around the illusion of free choice and the fantasy that you can step outside the social to view the world and give a neutral objective account. So, when we look at where we are, we need to be aware of the position and theoretical frame we adopt as we step back. There are two ways of stepping back and looking at the map.

Mapping the ground plan

One helpful critical review by Perry Anderson (1968) of the 'ground-plan' of British culture in 1968 located psychology in an intellectual climate in which empiricism – close observation and correlation – was so ingrained as to be a *style* of research rather than mere methodological preference. The psychologism which underpinned contemporary aesthetics and historical research at that time found a champion in psychology in Hans Eysenck who was one of a number of key conservative *émigrés* from continental Europe who found in Britain a comfortable intellectual home and who were influential in the development of a constellation of academic subjects after the Second World War. These subjects were designed to revolve around what Anderson terms an 'absent centre'; that is, the lack of any *sociology* as a distinct discipline which could reflect upon the cultural totality. Critical psychologists have specific concerns about what our discipline is doing to people but we are nourished by inter-disciplinary research, or trans-disciplinary research (Curt, 1994), and we need to develop our intellectual work now in the context of the human sciences. These human sciences include cultural studies, literary theory and women's studies, and it is difficult to imagine how we could work without those, let alone without social theory.

That academic cultural landscape described by Anderson has been rapidly transformed in the past 25 years partly as a result of the political ferment of the 1960s and 1970s and partly by the growth of higher education, as he acknowledges in a later review (Anderson, 1990a, 1990b). Psychology is briefly dispatched by Anderson in that later review with a reference to the Cyril Burt fraud and Eysenck's dabbling in astrology, but it has seen some extraordinary changes in the late 1980s and since 1990. Psychology does still need to be conceptualized in relation to other academic disciplines, in relation to sociology and cultural studies which now operate as some kind of 'centre'. They provide us with intellectual resources for locating and unravelling accounts of mind and behaviour, even as they still also carry with them normalizing functions which complement psychology (Therborn, 1976).

Psychology is also structured by its relation to philosophy as the study of ordinary language in the British analytic tradition and now as a sustained reflection on what extraordinary metaphorical work language performs in the continental European deconstructive and hermeneutic traditions. It also exists in relation to psychoanalysis which has moved from what Anderson describes as being an exceptional and marginal Kleinian 'technical enclave' in the 1960s to cultural centre-stage. I will return to this picture of the relationship between academic disciplines, and to the role of psychoanalysis later. For the moment, though, we can take from this mapping of disciplines an image of academic psychology as constituted as an empiricist endeavour that thinks it is the centre when it is really trapped between two other absent centres – reflection on society and reflection by the researcher – centres which it repeatedly disavows as it enforces their absence.

Mapping the psy-complex

The other way of mapping psychology is to focus on the relationship between what it says and what it does, the inside and outside of the academe or clinic. I moved into psychology because it saturates Western culture. I remember being told by fellow Marxists that this was a mistake because it was such a quintessentially bourgeois discipline. But is it not so important, I thought, to study it precisely because it is so essential to bourgeois discipline and so powerful in its essentializing naturalizing reduction of problems to the individual?

The years of Thatcherism and Reaganism and the rejuvenated ideology of free enterprise as capitalism rolls over the new markets of Eastern Europe have fuelled postmodern fantasies of unfettered choice and the end of history (Fukuyama, 1992), and they have further fuelled individualism and psychology, and encouraged the delving deep into individuals to find genetic causes, cognitive mechanisms or true selves. It is difficult to avoid all the talk there is around now about people's minds and internal emotional states and relationships. At every turn we meet the practices that specify how we should adapt to problems and reason about them and which govern how we should understand our feelings about others. The therapeutic discourse in magazine advice columns, radio counselling phone-ins and day-time confessional television is producing an emotionally literate public. Some radical activist-therapists would like to encourage such emotional literacy (e.g., Samuels, 1993; Psychotherapists and counsellors for social responsibility, 1996), but we need to ask what regimes of truth that way of talking locks us into (Gordo-López, 2000).

An article in the British Psychological Society house journal *The Psychologist* had the title 'The rising tide of psychology' in which it was celebrating, with no apparent irony despite that rather sinister title, how the numbers studying and practising psychology are still increasing rapidly (Messer, 1996). The dramatic expansion of popular psychology in recent years has been made possible by the accumulation and diffusion of state welfare policies and practices in a variety of institutions from the end of the last century. The careful observation and regulation of mental hygiene in families and schools proceeded through the proliferation of apparatuses of knowledge and self-knowledge such that individual pathology would not only be represented in policy documents and professional training, but that individuals should also be able to represent to themselves how they should be (Rose, 1996). Self-help movements function here as a paradoxical meeting point for tendencies for emancipation and regulation. This process has been usefully described by work on the 'psy-complex'. The 'psy-complex' is the network of theories and practices which elaborate and implement psychological knowledge. The psychiatric system is the most evident and often the most obviously oppressive sector of the psy-complex (Parker *et al.*, 1995), but psychiatry functions as part of a dense matrix of assumptions about normality and abnormality through which psychologists in clinical practice, education and social work observe people and make them speak.

There is a powerful double-bind operating in this matrix, a double function of the psy-complex which so often sabotages the attempts of those psychologists who are trying to empower people by using psychology. This function has been analysed well by Michel Foucault, whose work has inspired studies of the psy-complex (Ingleby, 1985; Rose, 1985; Parker, 1995a). Power cannot be handed over to the subjects of the psy-complex, because power does not exist as if it were in packages that psychologists have a lot of compared with their 'disempowered' clients (Goodley and Parker, 2000). Rather, power operates through the psy-complex by recruiting subjects who will do the work themselves, so that the disciplinary panoptical function of observation that Foucault (1975a) described as operating in most concentrated form in the modern prison system is sustained by the confessional structure of care which incites us to speak and to believe that the more we speak, the freer we will be (Foucault, 1976a). This means that we are the most thoroughly invested subjects of the psy-complex, and what psychotherapists like to call 'psychologically minded', when we learn to look for the truth in ourselves and when we simultaneously understand that we need a real expert to become, as narrative therapists would put it, 'experts on our own lives' (White, 1995).

Confessing my own history and position here is also to participate in the webs of the psy-complex. That is also a risk we take when we encourage researchers to engage in a reflexive analysis, and so we must be clear that we are not trying to uncover unmediated experience but, rather, developing a theoretical reflection on what we are doing. This brings me to the second broken rule.

Theoretical critical distance

The second rule to break is, 'don't work with theory'. Psychology has, as I've noted, been thoroughly empiricist in style, and has developed theoretical models very cautiously, keeping speculation under tight rein as it slowly links together its little findings in different combinations using 'intervening variables' and 'hypothetical constructs' (Hyland, 1981; Parker, 1987). However, a new wave of theoretical work developed toward the end of the 1980s and beginning of the 1990s. In the English-speaking world this is marked by the founding of the journal *Theory & Psychology* in 1990, also by *Feminism & Psychology* which started in the same year, and by *Culture & Psychology* (from 1995). These academic journals have fared better than those published outside mainstream publishing houses in the US, such as *Psychology and Social Theory* and *PsychoCritique* from the 1980s, which have now collapsed, and *PsychoCulture* which started in 1996 as little more than a newsletter. *Psychology in Society* operated as an agitational and theoretical forum for psychologists and other mental health activists in organizations like OASSSA (Organisation of Appropriate Social Services in South Africa) working against apartheid in South Africa, and is still going. *Nordiske Udkast* has also been recently relaunched in Scandinavia as *Outlines: Journal of Critical Social Science* as a forum which continues, in part, the project of Holzkampian Critical Psychology within the broader project of critical social science. In Latin America, *AVEPSO*, published in Caracas, publishes critical theoretical work as well as empirical studies (for a review of these different tendencies, see Parker, 1999a). An influential strand of theory which has sometimes pushed the tolerance of traditional academic psychologists to breaking point has been discourse. There are three crucial aspects of the turn to discourse in psychology. The first is empirical.

Empirical discourse

Discourse-analytic approaches are helpful at the moment because they cue us into looking at how the little findings that the overarching models build upon are constructed, fabricated, narrated (Parker, 1992). Accounts of experiments, for example, are treated as texts which look at first glance like windows onto the world but which we discourse analysts read as screens that hold representations of what a world might be like, and what people and things inside them might be like if the account were true. There was a study, for example, in a Japanese psychology research journal which looks quite interesting called

'Effects of stroking horses on both human's and horses' heart rate responses' (Hama *et al.*, 1996). But instead of picking up the data from this study and putting it alongside other data so that you then imagine you are accumulating facts about physiology, touching and empathy, a discourse-analytic reading would focus on how the facts are storied into being in the descriptions and observations of the body in specific experimental and cultural settings. You have to be sure not to let your eye slip from the text, not to be lured into looking right through it to where you imagine you are really seeing, in this case, horses' heart rate responses. The facts are storied in the text, and we then have to locate the text, culturally and historically.

There is a risk in this close reading of text if we do not locate it, which is that discourse analysis might come to mimic the empiricism of its host discipline. Tendencies in discourse analysis which simply import conversation analysis or ethnomethodology from sociology could reproduce all the conservative functions those approaches served there (Gouldner, 1971). This would then turn discourse research into the helpmate of psychology. This process is most perilous for critical psychologists when there are calls for tightening up transcription conventions in the hope that we would thereby more accurately and directly represent what was really there. These calls are often combined with a hostility to any theoretical account which might override what are thought to be participants' 'mundane reasoning'. Not only is there a danger of reproducing the fantasy of being able to abstract and replicate behavioural regularities, which is a game conversation analysis plays when it pretends to identify formal devices in speech (e.g., Antaki, 1994), but also of making it seem as if a closer, more detailed description really captures each distinct 'accomplishment' in micro-interaction, which is the game ethnomethodology plays in its own peculiar blend of empiricism and relativism (e.g., Edwards and Potter, 1992; Potter, 1996).

Despite these pitfalls, empirical work in discourse analysis still plays a progressive role because it offers a methodological alternative, as part of the broader qualitative research movement in the discipline, which pulls psychologists away from the idea that they are working with an accumulating store of facts about mind and behaviour. Psychologists can then realize why they need to be critical when they see that the stories psychology tells are not true. Critical psychologists have then been able to use discourse analysis empirically in education and clinical work to reveal the 'truth effects' of psychology (e.g., Harper, 1994; Marks *et al.*, 1995). Their own stories, of course, are informed here by a certain view of the conditions of possibility for these truth effects. The second crucial aspect of the turn to discourse for critical work, then, is theoretical.

Theoretical discourse

The most important sources for discourse-oriented critical psychology have been Foucault's work on the history of regimes of truth which form psychological subjects in Western culture, Derrida's deconstruction of the metaphysics of presence which makes psychology unable to comprehend what it makes absent in its theory and practice, and Lacan's description of the work of repression and the unconscious in language as the subject produces and refuses what is absent, what is other to itself. These are the three main writers we often think of as 'post-structuralists'. What critical psychologists call 'post-structuralism' is a mythical school of thought, of course, an invention of English-speaking commentators on a number of historians, philosophers and psychoanalysts working mainly in France (Anderson, 1983; Dews, 1987; Žižek, 1999). A better way of identifying what these writers have catalysed in English-speaking academic culture is provided by the US Marxist literary critic and cultural analyst Fredric Jameson (1991) in his account of the development of what he terms 'theoretical discourse'. Theoretical discourse encompasses the work of these writers and others and provides a conceptual space for addressing how forms of knowledge function in culture, and thus it provides a critical distance from powerful ideological forms of knowledge like psychology.

Theoretical discourse has had a powerful impact on psychology, recruiting and mobilizing at least four different constituencies; a first small band at the end of the 1970s who founded the journal *Ideology & Consciousness* who read and absorbed key French texts as the basis for a more complex theoretical account of the subject and the social (Adlam *et al.*, 1977; Henriques *et al.*, 1984; Rose, 1985; Hollway, 1989; Walkerdine, 1990); a second group who took up these ideas combining them with micro-sociology and analytic philosophy, finding in them criticism of traditional psychology and the hope that it could be improved (Potter and Wetherell, 1987; Edwards and Potter, 1993; Billig, 1987; Harré and Gillett, 1994); a third group, which is where I identify myself, who used the ideas tactically as a lever against psychology without such an investment in them as an alternative or complementary truth (Parker and Shotter, 1990; Burman, 1994; Curt, 1994; Burman *et al.*, 1996; Levett *et al.*, 1997); and a fourth group which is the large mass of traditional psychologists who do not understand but know that they do not like these ideas, and who react to them in such a way as to make the discipline seem even more foolish than it does normally (e.g., Morgan, 1996; Furnham, 1997). Leaving aside that fourth group, which is quite rattled by the growth of theoretical discourse in psychology, I should say that this way of splitting the differences between different critical writers would be contested by most of them, and we have all tended to move from one position to another as we deal with psychology and as psychology deals with us.

Again, there is a risk of the recuperation of theoretical discourse generally by the discipline, and the success of new academic journals publishing discourse research is evidence of that risk. There is much attention to postmodernism in marginalized strands of psychology recently, for example, and some important critics of the discipline from the 1970s have been attracted by the idea that a 'postmodern psychology' might provide an alternative to reductionist old-style research and help us move with the spirit of the times (e.g., Gergen, 1991; Shotter, 1993). Wittgenstein is advertised here as one of the writers who could help us abandon the search for deep Truth, and instead locate psychological processes in ordinary language so that we might encourage and celebrate a diversity of ways of speaking. If that were possible, we could leave these language-games exactly as they are because we would have also realized that there is no measure for how oppressive they might be. This just won't do, of course, for although the modern grand narratives of understanding and emancipation have been dissolved in some sectors of contemporary society, the resulting postmodern condition is, as Jameson (1984a, 1991) argues, but part of the 'cultural logic' of late capitalism. We must remember that Jean-François Lyotard (1979) wrote the book *The Postmodern Condition* as, the subtitle tells us, 'a report on knowledge', for the Canadian government to assess investment opportunities in the field of new information technologies. Both the phenomenon and the attempts to grasp it are still rooted in capitalism.

Attempts to grasp the nature of oppression in theoretical discourse are not by any means exhausted, and feminist theory still operates as a key site of critique and reflexive interrogation of the work of Foucault, Derrida and Lacan in such a way as to keep that radical dynamic going. Although an attention to gender in psychology did look for a moment as if it might collapse into discourse analysis, we are now seeing discourse research become a site for the elaboration of feminist analyses of psychology generally (e.g., Wilkinson and Kitzinger, 1995). Postcolonial theory has also helped us to step back and situate modern knowledge and its postmodern mutations in a global context, and to explore and deconstruct the process of othering that constitute this culture and its forms of discipline (Spivak, 1990). In addition, queer theory opens up the nature of oppression and the fantasies of human nature that underpin it. As part of the terrain of theoretical discourse, queer theory disturbs gender categories that structure psychology as it makes a mockery of most psychological research studies which revolve around the attempt to establish 'sex differences' (Butler, 1990). Not only do we want to study the truth effects of psychology, then, we want to bring about disturbing and transformative effects in psychology. The turn to discourse has a third aspect, then, which is where it connects with politics.

Political discourse

One thing I did know when I started studying psychology was that my political position was very different from that which seemed to be presupposed by the discipline. I was attentive to the crucial role that psychology plays in the state apparatus and ideological machinery of capitalism. Since I was a revolutionary Marxist (see Mandel, 1978, 1979), I was not impressed by the way psychology and psychiatry was used in the Soviet Union, and knew that we also needed to understand how it really did operate as a form of discipline there. It still does. The educational psychology service in Russia, for example, is run by the police. One of the lessons of Stalinism should surely be that 'Marxist psychology' is an oxymoron, as well as being conceptually incoherent and often dangerous. I say this with deference to those trying to construct an historical materialist science of the subject (Tolman and Maiers, 1991; Tolman, 1994) or to reconstruct personality theory around a notion of the labouring subject as 'an ensemble of social relations' (Sève, 1978), as well as to the variety of well-intentioned radical behaviourist, cognitivist or ecological Marxists who are still struggling to understand and resist bourgeois psychology (see Parker and Spears, 1996).

It seems to me that Marxist psychologists are trapped in an impossible double paradox. On the one hand, they must work within the range of terms for defining action and experience which are available to us in bourgeois culture and which reproduce the individual in this culture. Any attempt to escape, or to work askew or in diametric opposition to those terms is doomed to failure because those attempts are still then mapping themselves into one of the fantasy spaces that bourgeois culture constructs as the 'other' to itself. On the other hand, Marxist psychologists are trying to produce an account of the way this kind of subject that we are now works as a self-regulating individual with the kind of second nature that binds it to capitalism, while trying to imagine a time when even the Marxist theory they use will be a relic. Marxism is one of the few theoretical systems that accounts for its own production as a dialectical function of particular economic and cultural conditions (Mandel, 1971, 1986), and so it holds open the promise of a time when the categories it employs will be out of date. That must mean at least the end of Marxist psychology (Parker, 1999b).

Adorno's comment on high and low art in Western culture as being 'torn halves of an integral freedom' is relevant here, for although psychology likes to think of itself as a science, it is actually one of the high arts which draws upon and drips into but still disparages everyday psychology, its low art. It would not solve the problem to sentimentalize common-sense psychology, for it is the *relationship* between the two and the fact that they cannot add up again to an integral freedom that is the problem. This is why groups like 'Psychology Politics Resistance', which was founded in 1994 as a network of academics, professionals and users of psychology services working to challenge the use and abuse of power by the discipline, are so important (Reicher and Parker, 1993). Psychology Politics Resistance, and its voice, *Asylum* magazine, are only one of many initiatives which have challenged psychology outside or from inside the discipline (e.g., Billig, 1978, 1979). Psychology Politics Resistance does not have a line on which bits of psychology might be true, but it mobilizes people against theories and practices that are false, false because they are mystifying and oppressive. The issue here is not whether one believes in a real world outside discourse or not, and we have wasted much time in psychology recently arguing round in circles on that one with some fairly objectionable claims about what we might doubt about the history that bears us (Edwards *et al.*, 1995). Rather, the issue is how one locates oneself in certain kinds of practice. Critical realism did seem to provide a theoretical anchor here (Bhaskar, 1989; Collier, 1994), but an appeal to any kind of 'real' will fail when the debate is conducted in an academic practice which is structured around the abstraction of knowledge from the real and around the enforced absence of reflection on society or reflection by the researcher on their position in society. What a group like Psychology Politics Resistance provides for those of us in psychology is a reference point and a practice where the question is *how* one will talk about the world. It then also forces us to ask why someone in psychology should ever imagine that it might be possible not to do so. To understand why psychology should be so successful in banishing reflexive analysis, we need to turn to psychoanalysis, and so to the third broken rule.

Complex subjectivity

The third rule to break is that we should not address psychoanalysis, for there is an incredibly powerful prohibition that psychology students learn very early on, which is that anything Freudian is nonsense or non-science. This is extraordinary if one looks at the close connections that many of the most revered historical figures in psychology had with psychoanalysis. That there should be no reference in psychology textbooks to Piaget's membership of the International Psychoanalytical Association or to Luria's role in founding the Russian Psychoanalytical Society (Roudinesco, 1990; Miller, 1998), and that there should be such gross misrepresentation of Freud's ideas in psychology (Richards, 1989), are surely evidence of some peculiar process of denial that might lead us to imagine that psychoanalysis is indeed the 'repressed other' of psychology (Burman, 1994). This repression does not at all mean that psychoanalysis is a progressive alternative to psychology. Psychoanalysis is one of the fantasy spaces constituted by this culture, but it does function as a form of knowledge in this culture which combines reflexivity with theory in a way that most psychologists find unthinkable.

We also need to take psychoanalysis seriously because, if critical psychologists are to situate psychological knowledge and their own activity in cultural context, they now have to face up to the way that psychoanalysis saturates Western culture. You do not have to like any tenet of Freudian theory to admit that psychoanalytic notions about the unconscious, repression, what children know and what they remember are all around us. Psychoanalytic theory and practice are kept at bay by some sectors of the psy-complex and encouraged by other sectors, and it circulates outside the clinics in advertising, films and television. Psychoanalytic discourse, then, structures cultural phenomena and provides certain kinds of subject positions for participants. Kleinian analysis is treated as a 'technical enclave' by Anderson in his 1968 review of the intellectual landscape and then as moving to cultural centre-stage by 1990, but we need to look at how this form of psychoanalytic knowledge functions in culture (Parker, 1997a).

For example, the accounts given by people who believe that they have been followed by UFOs or abducted by aliens are structured by images of bodies being opened and penetrated and the merging of oneself into omnipotent controlling entities that a Kleinian analyst would not find surprising. I would argue that this is not because Kleinian theory is true, but because psychoanalytic notions of projective identification, splitting and the image of the mind as a kind of container filled with destructive objects circulates through culture and through the talk about alien abductions to make sense of it, and then reproduce motifs of invasion and control. This arena for the reproduction of psychoanalytic subjectivity then has consequences for images of conspiracy and war. Although cultural phenomena like this may seem trivial, then, they sediment political ideologies and relations of power in forms of psychology that are real to the inhabitants. There is a dangerous paradox though, which is that the psychoanalytic subject positions that structure this psychoanalytic discourse can only be displayed by using psychoanalytic theory (cf. Hollway and Jefferson, 2000). Why take the risk, when it would be possible to simply denounce psychoanalysis as pathologizing ideology and as plain wrong (Millet, 1977; Timpanaro, 1976)? We need to answer this in two slightly different, dialectically interconnected ways.

Cyberpsychology

First, as far as psychology is concerned, we surely have the task of drawing upon forms of knowledge that we have available to us to use as levers against what is oppressive. We need an antithesis, if you like, to the ideological theses of psychological technology. We have something like that in 'cyberpsychology', as one example, in the forms of strange dispersed subjectivity that we live as we live in cyberspace (Gordo-López and Parker, 1999). Postmodern sectors of contemporary culture have been made possible by the rise of information technology and the emergence of the service and entertainment industries after the Second World War (Jameson, 1984b; Mandel, 1974), and there is now, as a function of the global network of computer systems, a cyberspace which operates as an environment where subjectivity slips the nets of psychology. Here conventional psychology will not work. Interaction does not follow the rules identified by social psychologists, biographies do not follow the narratives traced by developmental psychologists, and memory is not accessed in the ways cognitive psychologists would expect. This is not even psychoanalysis as psychologists understand it. If anything, it is closer to some of the notions of the unconscious, deferred action and the real that we find in 'postmodern' psychoanalysis in the Lacanian and post-Lacanian tradition. At the same time as we use psychoanalysis against psychology, then, we need to find a way of fragmenting psychoanalysis and locating it as a materially effective science fiction in late capitalism (Parker, 1997a).

Second, as far as psychology's relationship with culture is concerned, we have the task of connecting with forms of culture which challenge rather than confirm psychology's strange model of the world as built up out of self-contained individuals. Here, the sub-cultural antithesis to psychological technology is to be found, but again as only one example, in the broader sense of cyberspace, and in the queer dispersed subjectivities that inhabit cyberia as a place which brings together electronic and ecstatic sub-cultures–that is, in the crossover between those using new software to surf and those using new designer drugs to dance. Again, we should see these as thoroughly material practices both in the sense that the bodies are wired into the net and in the sense that the interconnection in the clubs is facilitated by activating serotonin uptake inhibitors (Rushkoff, 1994). Now the sense of interconnection with others is through symbolic space not through some infantile narcissistic merging with the mother, and all the old verities of psychoanalysis as well as those of psychology are dissolved in a Lacanian and post-Lacanian meditation on subjectivity as fragmented, and in relation to others rather than as something essential and fixed. Again, theoretical discourse helps us conceptualize how psychoanalysis operates as a fantasy space which is constituted by material practices, in the 'discursive hardware' if you like, and so it allows us to use it and to unravel it (cf. Burman *et al.*, 1996).

Repression and cynicism

It could be argued that the paradox that faces psychoanalysis is rather like that faced by Marxists who want to develop a theory which serves certain functions in certain economic conditions, but without making claims to universal truth. Given that psychoanalysis structures subjectivity now, would it not be a hopeless fantasy to wish that we could start from anywhere but within psychoanalysis?

I need to emphasize again, I think, that psychoanalysis is not true. It is *constituted* as the repressed other of psychology and as the place in culture where subjectivity is structured and unravelled. When psychology imagines that it is the centre and source of a neutral and objective empirical examination of individuals, it makes reflection on society and reflection by the researcher into something incomprehensible and irrational, repressed and unconscious, into absent centres. It enforces their absence, and ensures that they can then only be decoded by psychoanalysis which functions as a site of resistance. And then when the psy-complex incites the individual to imagine that they are the centre and source of cognition and perception, memory and fantasy, it makes all the collective processes of thinking into alienated symbolic material that can only be recovered using psychoanalysis. The move we need to make here to understand this is very like that made by Slavoj Žižek (1989, 1999) in his Hegelian interpretation and mutation of Lacan, of the way the repressed is constituted as such by the very process of repression. Like the commodity in Marxist analysis, a symptom cannot be understood by discovering what it *really* represents. Rather, the task is to discover how it has been made into what it is. Psychoanalysis itself then operates as a symptom, and we need to understand how it has been constituted in order to make it work for us.

Of course it is tempting to imagine that the solution to all the ills of psychological technology lies hidden fully-formed somewhere else, and that all we have to do is to find it and liberate it. Some Marxists imagine that it lies in a 'Marxist psychology', some social constructionists now see it in 'the body' or, in a strange alliance with humanists, insist that it is 'the self'. Some feminists think that they know what women really are like and that they simply need to be given a voice (e.g., Gilligan, 1982), and there are, of course, a host of orientalists waiting inside and outside Jungian circles who think they know that the truth lies in other mysterious and exotic cultural practices.

The two-fold production by exclusion of psychoanalysis is compounded by the immediate and obvious presence of psychoanalytic concepts around us in culture. Again, Žižek (1996) captures this nicely with his observation that ideology now operates in a more open cynical way with an additional layer of surplus enjoyment which holds us to it when we know we are weaving it, and it confounds the hopes of those who thought that making it evident so that people could reflect upon it should be enough to dissolve it. This is the playful cynical relativism of the postmodern condition which invites racists to talk like social workers and talk about their family background when they are asked to account for why they behave the way they do and which incites individuals to sieze on any fundamentalist notion that takes their fancy as something that needs no justification. Now our reflection on false consciousness has to be theoretically informed, and an appeal to the truth won't do the trick. It is the production of the problem that has to be unravelled. Psychoanalysis too can operate as a fundamentalism in this cultural climate, and there are no guarantees that it would not then be worse than mainstream psychology. It should also be said that in some other cultural settings, such as Argentina, psychoanalysis is not at all the 'repressed other' of psychology and it efficiently represses anything that does not correspond to a mainly Lacanian orthodoxy. Theoretical resources such as these always need to be used tactically and culturally situated.

Karl Kraus, a Viennese journalist and vituperative opponent of Freud, had a nice line when he wrote that 'Psychoanalysis is the disease of which it pretends to be the cure' (cited in Gay, 1988), and we do have to think dialectically about how forms of knowledge that may be useful to us might actually be useful. It is the *relationship* between psychology and psychoanalysis that is the key, and they are both perhaps then, in Adorno's words 'torn halves of an integral freedom, to which, however, they do not add up'.

Conclusions and openings

This might all simply be assisting the recuperation of radical ideas into the spectacle, of course. A collection of Situationist writings was published in the 1990s with sandpaper covers so that it destroyed the books next to it on the shelf. Psychoanalysis, and any kind of reflexive analysis of the place of subjectivity in psychological research for that matter, should be like that kind of book. Theoretical discourse generally is determined to rub psychology up the wrong way, and it helps us use and locate forms of knowledge that psychology cannot bear. Critical psychology works with these abrasive allies to pursue its task of making the psychology that feels so familiar to us look strange so that we can then ask what it is doing to us. These are strange bedfellows, and a critical psychology that uses theoretical discourse to explore subjectivity calls for strange metaphors that started anywhere but here in psychology, but they are now here too.

Part I

Enlightenment, Realism and Power (and their Reverse)

This Part of the book brings together three related polemics. These are interventions which have the aim of sharpening critical reflection on theoretical resources that are often employed by discursive researchers in psychology now – postmodern arguments about the nature of the world in which we conduct our debates, relativist refusals of the kinds of truth assumed by psychologists, and Wittgensteinian notions of language and language games. Critical psychology is, among other things, a battle of ideas, and this Part captures the intensely polemical argumentative nature of what has been happening in the discipline in conferences, seminars and the pages of journals in recent years.

The interventions in Chapters 2, 3 and 4 include an argument *for* a 'critical' use of postmodernism, relativism and Wittgenstein, but the argument in each case, is also *against* the conservative implications of each of these theoretical resources. This polemical aspect of the chapters had the useful effect of provoking a response from those critical writers who are most enthusiastic about what they have to offer. The exchanges thus have the virtue of including some of the key players in the debates. A common thread running through my initial interventions is the argument that we need to assess theoretical positions *dialectically*. This means that we need to evaluate in what ways they function for and against critical perspectives in psychology *and* we need to locate the way they have emerged now as part of a broader historical view of psychology and critical movements within it. My replies to those who were kind enough to respond to my arguments are designed to show how the one-sided nature of the positions they take undermine the progressive purposes they champion. And, in line with a dialectical analysis of their arguments, the positions they take are revealed to be untenable *even on their own terms*.

2
Against Postmodernism
Psychology in Cultural Context

Postmodern writing has forced psychology to confront a series of problems pertaining to the nature of human consciousness, personal integrity and language. It invites us to re-think notions of undivided and unitary self-hood that have underpinned much orthodox empirical research and theory in the discipline, and it does so in the story-worlds of Progress, Reflection and Opportunity. At the same time as it performs a dispersion of psychological concepts, postmodernism has encouraged a spirit of deconstructive critique and challenge to the modern academic and professional apparatus of the 'psy-complex'. However, 'the postmodern', as a movement of sustained playful theoretical reflection linked to an account of a new cultural context for theoretical research, has now outlived its usefulness. Even the story of 'the modern' that postmodernists pitch themselves against misleads psychologists, traditional and critical. The progressive potential of postmodernism has been exhausted, and those who engage in critical theoretical work in psychology need to attend to the ideological assumptions it carries about social relations and structures of power that threaten a radical political agenda in the discipline. The dangers that flow either from an optimistic naive adoption of postmodern nostrums (relativism, amoralism, collectivism or autonomy) or from a pessimistic disappointed embrace of the alternative visions it incites (scientism, fundamentalism, individualism or organicism), need to be urgently addressed.

What psychologist will be subtle enough to explain our morose delight in being in perpetual crisis and in putting an end to history? Why do we like to transform small differences in scale among collectives into huge dramas? (Latour, 1991: 114)

Writers in psychology have adopted a rhetoric about 'postmodernism' in recent years that presents it either as an internal critique of the discipline allied to a radical agenda or as a full-blown alternative way of conducting research. Early (unpublished) drafts of the introduction for the collection *Texts of Identity*, which Gergen co-edited with John Shotter (Shotter and Gergen, 1989), called for a 'postmodern psychology', and it is emblematic of the postmodern endeavour that it should home in on self-contained separate notions of self-hood, precisely on 'identity' as a central support for old modern ways of being, thinking and doing. That work has continued apace (e.g., Gergen, 1991, Kvale, 1992a), and research in this most ambitious postmodern line of work has provided psychology with a series of problems for our recieved notions of human consciousness, personal integrity and language.

The term 'postmodern' has also, in the process, come to stand in for a variety of approaches including some which deliberately drew upon 'post-structuralist' theories of the subject (e.g., Henriques *et al.*, 1984) and others which are closer to Critical Theory (e.g., Billig *et al.*, 1988). Different forms of discourse analysis and studies of rhetoric have, in the process, come to be seen as promoting a common cause of fragmentation and confusion about the nature and possibility of psychological knowledge. The postmodern turn, which has sharpened the epistemological edge of the linguistic and then discursive turn in psychology, has forced a re-thinking of notions of undivided and unitary self-hood, notions that have underpinned much orthodox theory and empirical research in the discipline. At the same time as it has permitted some re-working of psychological concepts, postmodernism has encouraged a spirit of deconstructive challenge to the academic and professional apparatus of the 'psy-complex' seen as a quintessentially *modern* practice (e.g., Ingleby, 1985; Rose, 1985).

Political processes and social structures in the Western world have undergone a transformation of sorts, and *some* characteristics of contemporary discourse outside psychology are indeed 'postmodern'. Innovative theoretical work in psychology which employs postmodernist rhetoric has opened up connections to political critique (e.g., Ibáñez, 1990). Postmodern psychologists know that modern psychology is oppressive, and that is why their writings often serve as forms of implicit ideology critique. They are able to show how human action always escapes any grid of behavioural regularity, operates in surprising fluid ways, is embedded in networks of social relations and can only be understood contextually.

Psychology needs to take note of the culture which surrounds it, and to develop accounts which connect the discipline with cultural processes, whether they are sympathetic to postmodernism or not. However, if we do *not* live in a postmodern culture or have never even lived in a *modern* culture, critical work in psychology that draws on postmodern writing needs to be more nuanced. What is needed is a critique of postmodernism that values the task of self-understanding situated in some notion of historical progress, a dialectical critique. Although it is caricatured or repressed by 'modern' psychology and further blocked or mocked by postmodernists, Marxism is still a useful resource here, and its role in the argument will be displayed as we proceed.

I argue in this chapter that although postmodern writing has forced us to rethink notions of human consciousness, personal integrity and language and has challenged assumptions of undivided and unitary self-hood that underpin much orthodox and empirical research in psychology, postmodernism has now outlived its usefulness. In the second part of the chapter I argue that postmodernism not only holds certain serious dangers for critical work in and against the discipline but also paves the way for something more worrying. But first, I am going to briefly review what postmodernism is, how we might account for its appearance in psychology, what resistance it has met so far, and why the story it tells about theoretical activity and cultural context is wrong.

Postmodern against the modern

The postmodern stories are about *deconstruction* and *dispersion*. Postmodernism is difficult to define because it performs this deconstruction and dispersion in relation to other stories *and* its internal shape is uncertain and unstable. This means that when it recruits subjects to its narrative structure they find themselves participating in a number of competing, overlapping narratives about what it is and where it comes from. This is part of its attraction to radical reflexive psychologists, of course, because they are turning to postmodernism to challenge or escape a discipline which tries to fix things into a grid of observable movement and to find essential underlying properties which can be reduced to the level of individual separate and undivided units. The trope of *deconstruction* in postmodernism operates through undermining the privilege given to any term in the hierarchically organised systems of concepts which govern texts and practices and through unravelling the ways dominant terms attempt to master the world. The trope of *dispersion* comes into play through the opening out of concepts into mutating networks of relations so that horizontal connections replace vertical ones and in order that spatial metaphors dissolve temporal ones. This undermining and unravelling activity with a view to the proliferation of a multiplicity of horizontal and spatial little narratives is acid in the works of psychology, a corrosive and exhilarating activity of critique as we eat away what had almost consumed us and hallucinate new forms of life beyond close-guarded disciplinary boundaries.

Three postmodern story-worlds

Despite the deconstruction and dispersion of boundaries between itself and others, between inside and outside or between 'us' and 'them', and the promised dissolution of internal boundaries to release us from fixing, trapping or 'knowing' what it *is*, it is still helpful to distinguish between three stories about postmodernism. If we do this, we can understand better what it might mean and where it might be going. This terrain is marked by potholes, quicksands and seismic shifts which change where you thought you were as you try to map it, and postmodern psychologists travel around these three domains using different reference points for different audiences at different times. I call these places *Progression, Reflection* and *Opportunity*.

Progression. Postmodernism is an aspect of a distinct historical period which succeeds old modernity. According to this definition, postmodernism can be viewed as a function of the growth of information technology and the service sector after the Second World War. While modernity had been governed by grand narratives of progress, scientific reason and self-understanding, the postmodern condition is characterised by many little narratives which are limited, and suspicious of any over-arching conceptual framework which promises to find truth under the surface or in the future. For Lyotard, then, 'the status of knowledge is altered as societies enter what is known as the post-industrial age and cultures enter what is known as the postmodern age' (Lyotard, 1979: 3). Lyotard's claim in *The Postmodern Condition* is that people have even lost their nostalgia for the grand narratives and given up the hope of grounding their experience in a theoretical explanation of the functioning of social systems or the movement of history. In this story-world, Marxism is well beyond its sell-by date and psychoanalysis is gazing back into an unconscious world that no longer exists. Here, postmodernism can be conceptualised as 'the cultural logic of late capitalism', and seen as the latest in a series of stages in economic development (Jameson, 1984a, 1984b, Mandel, 1974: cf. Callinicos, 1989). The surplus of signification that Lyotard describes can be treated as a form of information overload which accompanies the third technological revolution in machine-production from 1940 to 1965.

Lyotard's 'report on knowledge', which was commissioned by the Canadian government to assess infrastructural investment opportunities in information technology, argues that 'the direction of new research will be dictated by the possibility of its eventual results being translatable into computer language' (Lyotard, 1979: 4). It is this pragmatic evaluation of computerization that leads Lyotard to suggest that 'We may thus expect a thorough exteriorization of knowledge with respect to the "knower", at whatever point he or she may occupy in the knowledge process' (ibid.: 4). If you treat postmodernism in this kind of way, then it is possible to loop it back into a notion of progress that is quite antithetical to the full-blown postmodern programme that has hit the human sciences in recent years, and even, as Jameson (1991) tries to do, to fold it into a version of Marxism (and psychoanalysis). It is also possible then to augment and counter Lyotard's descriptions with an account of the overall shape of contemporary capitalist culture (e.g., D. Harvey, 1989), or to restrict the scope of the description to those parts of culture that are structured around the exhorbitation of information. The peculiar fluidity of experience that inhabitants of cyberspace or readers of certain styles of science fiction experience, for example, might then be considered as 'postmodern', but these distinct delimited arenas for postmodern subjectivity are possible because of material conditions of production and the specific architecture of electronic environments (Parker, 1997a). Lyotard (1979) himself is cautious enough in *The Postmodern Condition* to warrant this move, saying of his account of 'language games' and 'communication circuits' which define the social bond in the postmodern age that he is 'not claiming that the *entirety* of social relations is of this nature' (ibid.: 15).

Psychologists who live in Progression see postmodernism as a great leap forward for the discipline, and many supporters of the postmodern revolution can only be recruited to this narrative on the basis that it takes them to what they have always striven for. This is where postmodernism continues in the tracks of the 'new paradigm' rhetoric of the 1970s (e.g., Harré and Secord, 1972). Whereas the argument then was that the discipline of psychology was undergoing a scientific paradigm shift and this warranted a new psychology which would treat people as human beings rather than as objects, we are now invited into the much more grandiose idea that the whole world is changing and so we really have to leap on board (e.g., Gergen, 1991; Newman and Holzman, 1997). This is where postmodernism is able to offer a new lease of life to humanists struggling to make psychology a more comfortable place for human beings. Despite the structuralist and post-structuralist critiques of humanism outside psychology in the 1970s and inside in the 1980s (e.g., Henriques *et al.*, 1984; Parker, 1989) to the point where experience seemed to some to be reduced to a mere effect of language, postmodernists are now reassuring humanists that they value experience more than modern writers ever had (e.g., Kvale, 1992b; McNamee and Gergen, 1992a). There is the promise, in one account for example, of 'a radical restoration of a reverence for human relations' (Young, 1992: 144). This is also where traditional psychologists are promised that they can continue what they were doing before as long as they give their practices and interpretation of the results a little ironic shine. While radical psychologists once demanded a complete overhaul of concepts and methods in the discipline (e.g., Armistead, 1974; Reason and Rowan, 1981), now we are told that 'psychologists should not be dissuaded by postmodernism from forging ahead with technological developments' and that 'there remains an important place for sound prediction and personal skills within various practical settings' (Gergen, 1992: 26).

In Progression, then, Lyotard is seen as one of the analysts who has helped us to understand the shape of culture and where it is going, and postmodern psychologists who are inspired by this diagnosis and prognosis are happy to forget that this kind of picture of underlying structure and dynamics of the social world is exactly what they scorn the old moderns for trying to make. We should also note that although Jameson has tried hard to make Lyotard fit this story-world outside psychology, he does not really belong here. He belongs in the next one.

Reflection. Postmodernism is an intensification of a reflexive shift which accompanied the beginning of modernity. In this second story-world, postmodernism does not come at the end of the modern but it was there at its birth, there as a precondition for modern citizens to question who they were and what they might become. As we trace our way back through artistic and cultural movements which seem to anticipate postmodernism – from Dada and Surrealism in the twentieth century to Laurence Sterne in the eighteenth – we find that they have been *necessary* to the process of modernization. As Lyotard (1979) puts it, 'In an amazing acceleration, the generations precipitate themselves. A work can become modern only if it is first postmodern. Postmodernism thus understood is not modernism at its end but in the nascent state, and this state is constant' (ibid.: 79). Postmodernism is, then, 'a part of the modern' (ibid.: 79) and it is expressed in moments of fluidity amidst the congealing of the modern around certain set ideas, in the moments of triviality which disrupt serious unreflective life, and in sustained reflection around the contours of culture.

Descriptions of the experience of modernity which sidestep definitions of the postmodern as something distinct have also linked it to consciousness under capitalism: 'it pours us all into a maelstrom of perpetual disintegration and renewal, of struggle and contradiction, of ambiguity and anguish. To be modern is to be part of a universe in which, as Marx said, "all that is solid melts into air"' (Berman, 1982: 15). Berman's hope, in his book which borrows Marx's phrase for its title, is that this cultural context of ambiguity and uncertainty might then re-frame Marxism itself: 'A fusion of Marx with modernism should melt the too-solid body of Marxism – or at least warm it up and thaw it out' (ibid.: 122). Here we arrive at a crucial difference between those who look to reflexivity as the acceleration of a dialectic between truth and change, and those who see reflexivity as an activity independent of historical consciousness. Even Lyotard (1979: 74) points out that 'capitalism inherently possesses the power to derealize familiar objects, social roles, and institutions to such a degree that the so-called realistic representations can no longer evoke reality except as nostalgia or mockery'. The political consequences he draws from this, however, are very different, and very much more conservative than those drawn by Berman.

Psychologists who live in Reflection include those who have taken up the account of modernism and modernization that Berman develops to perform a two-fold analysis of what it permits and what it prohibits. In explorations of 'identity crises' in modernity, there is a dialectical notion of truth and change that modernism opens up and also an attempt to capture something of the dialectic between self and other. Here, reflection is quite carefully boundaried, and thoroughgoing postmodern transgression is viewed with some suspicion. For Frosh (1991), for example, modernity

is made up of fragments, of contradictory forces, elements and groups of elements. Progressive solutions to the crisis of identity recognise this, absorb the reality of contradiction and conflict, and provide kernels of identification and challenge that encourage and support people to face this reality.

(ibid.: 195)

Postmodernism throws this out of balance at the very moment when it emphasises what is most exciting and liberating about it while forgetting its dangers, and it presents a threat of psychotic breakdown at the very moment that it destabilises fixed fast-frozen forms of identity to offer unlimited possibilities of change. A very similar move, but one which is less queasy about using the term 'postmodern' to characterise this acute reflection on the relationship between self and other and the progressive potential of such reflection is to be found in the work of Sampson (e.g., 1993; cf. Condor, 1997). Even for some writers who contrast the postmodern to the modern, there is an attempt to decouple the 'postmodern turn' from a historical shift, and to see the postmodern as opening up wider possibilities for reflection under the general rubric of 'uncertainty' (Michael, 1994).

For some psychologists, 'uncertainty' is one of the defining characteristics of what it is to know without knowing in the postmodern. Either this is 'knowing of a third kind' from within a position that is qualitatively different from knowing 'how' or knowing 'that' (Shotter, 1993), or it is a form of activity or performance which is postmodern because it requires 'the end of knowing' (Newman and Holzman, 1997). Reflection is thus celebrated *and* redefined, made central *and* dispersed. Postmodern psychology in Reflection is an activity that was always there, and it now comes into its own. While its self-ironizing exploration of knowledge and subjectivity means that it always opens up new spaces for reflection, it also adjoins a third postmodern world which tries to take advantage of those spaces and settle there.

Opportunity. Postmodernism is an opportunity to break out of the polarities which govern modern representations of the world. Sometimes lists of diametric opposites – such as design–chance, distance–participation, hierarchy–anarchy, paranoia–schizophrenia, presence–absence, purpose–play, transcendence–immanence – are presented (-re-presented) to characterise the difference between modern and postmodern thought (e.g., Hassan, 1987). However, the moral is invariably that we now have a chance to deconstruct and disentangle ourselves from these oppositions altogether. At the same time, we are reassured that we will not be left with nothing. When

Lyotard (1979: 41) argues that 'Most people have lost the nostalgia for the lost narrative', of scientific progress, for example, he is quick to point out that 'It in no way follows that they are reduced to barbarity' (ibid.). Instead, there are new opportunities: 'What saves them from it is their knowledge that legitimation can only spring from their own linguistic practice and communicational interaction' (ibid.). Here, then, there is a surprising voluntarist twist to the structuralist and post-structuralist narratives about the constitution of subjectivity in language, and postmodernism now appears not so much as a continuation of these conceptual critiques of individual autonomy as the saviour of the self.

One of the curious paradoxes of postmodernism is its emphasis on community and conversation between equals on the one hand – and this is the line which is taken by Rorty (1989) and then by Gergen in psychology – and the argument on the other that, as Lyotard puts it, 'Consensus has become an outmoded and suspect value' (1979: 66). In this land of opportunity it does also sometimes seem as if radical hopes for social change which underpinned the activities of French intellectuals have been abandoned for a North American vision of change as a function of individual choice. What breaking down the old metanarratives of modernity leads to is the possibility of opening up many little narratives, and anyone can play.

Psychologists who live in Opportunity are the most enthusiastic about what postmodernism can do to the discipline and to the world. This is where the rhetoric of 'new vistas' in the discipline flourishes. Indeed, it seems that one of the main problems of old modern psychology was that it halted the progressive movement forward of human understanding and prevented us from siezing opportunities and forging ahead: 'in postmodern perspective, we find the culture in constant danger of objectifying its vocabularies of understanding, and thereby closing off options and potentials' (Gergen, 1992: 26). Again, traditional psychologists are welcomed in, and told that 'there is nothing about postmodern thought that argues against continuing research, for example, on gene splicing, depression, or the effects of day care programs on developing children' (Gergen, 1994a: 414). The most important defining characteristic of postmodernism in this guise is that all may seize the new possibilities that are opened by the climate of uncertainty in the discipline and that innovations may bloom.

One recent stake for postmodernism as Opportunity in British social constructionist psychology has been canvassed under the heading of a

'climate of problematization' (Curt, 1994) or (later) 'the climate of perturbation' (Stainton Rogers *et al.*, 1995). Metaphors of tectonic shifts in
the discursive landscape proliferate in this account, and these shifts
open up places for new varieties of talk. In some North American
accounts, postmodernism seems almost equivalent to a pre-revolution-
ary situation in which the old order is breaking down and where there
is an openness to new ideas but where there is as yet no clearly formulated alternative (Newman and Holzman, 1997). Here the stakes seem
to be able to keep the field as open as possible. Postmodernism in psychology, then, is a beleagured field of opportunity that needs to be
defended while we regroup.

There is a paradox in each of these story-worlds, that themes of progression, reflection and opportunity are also supposed to be key
defining features of modernity. More accurately, these themes – the
notion that humanity is moving forward with an exponential accumulation of material and conceptual resources, that this is faciliated by
the dualistic separation of transcendental ego from empirical ego so
that we think we view our progress from an external vantage point,
and that we need to assess the costs and benefits of different courses of
action before we choose the best option at the best moment – are key
defining features of *capitalism*.

Reactions to postmodernism in psychology

Although postmodernism has been taken up quite fast in psychology,
it has also met some resistance. Some psychologists are keen to hold
onto the old discipline and to defend it against this new threat (e.g.,
Furnham, 1997). This is because they genuinely believe that psychology is benevolent and beneficial. 'Modern' psychologists are mobilizing to discredit postmodern arguments, and they are quite happy to
lump all critical work under the heading of 'postmodernism' now
because it is then easier to attack. Some of these arguments, though by
no means all, would actually be endorsed by those critical researchers
who are less enchanted with the discipline. The contextual arguments
that Smith (1994) makes, for example, that the term 'postmodern' is
misleading, with a more accurate descriptor being 'late modern', and
that the malaise in contemporary society which does lead people to
give up trying to find a true account is treated by postmodernists as if
it were an 'intrinsically valid' position (ibid.: 408), are fairly uncon-
tentious (though we will turn to problems with that 'late modern'
characterization in a moment). His assertion that postmodernism is

characterised by 'antiscientific relativism' (ibid.: 408) begs at least two different key questions, however; critical psychologists may want to ask either what is wrong about antiscientific relativism given the oppressive masquerade of scientific truth that the discipline has performed up to now, or to ask whether psychology so far has any right to lecture others about what is scientific given its failure so to discover any universal covering laws or underlying mechanisms for thought or behaviour. In similar vein, Morgan asks, 'Would a post-modernist like to explain how a "discourse" causes blue flowers to look lighter than red ones as twilight falls, a fact that is explained by the difference in spectral sensitivities between cone and rod pigments?' (1996: 32). This is a neat little trap, and we would only be able to answer it by taking each of the terms Morgan locks together and looking at what work they do. This would be a discourse analysis, perhaps, but it would not necessarily be a 'postmodern' answer to the question.

It seems that even though he is one of the brighter well-intentioned critics, Smith (1994) cannot resist reducing many of the problems he finds to psychological variables; as in the claim that postmodernism is the perspective of 'alienated writers from the humanities' (ibid.: 410) or that it is 'the experience of the Euro-American elite that is evoked when we apply the label "postmodern" to our present predicament' (ibid.: 406). Both of these claims, which could have been framed in a more constructive contextual way, neglect the way that postmodern rhetoric has filtered through various scientific disciplines and into the 'Third World'. Even less helpful are claims that postmodernism amounts to 'the abandonment of hope to find a secure foundation for beliefs and values' (ibid.: 408), or that 'There is an ingredient of resentful envy in the postmodern stance' (ibid.: 409). Critical psychologists should be allies of the postmodernists when they expose the pretensions of psychology to be a science and to trivialize the claims psychologists make about 'facts' they think they have discovered and when postmodernists are being pathologised as individuals in ways the discipline is most practised at.

For radicals in psychology, the problem is two-fold. Not only do they now have to counter the claims of the discipline to help people and resolve social problems, but they are faced with an enthusiastic postmodern friend in their struggle who claims to be more benevolent and beneficial but is equally keen to freeze out any claims to historical progress or self-understanding. While modern psychologists are busy defending their territory as natural science and guarding the facts from those who would seek to dissolve them into historical context and social relations, postmodern psychologists are busily recruiting all those who have suffered from arrogant exclusion by the discipline (e.g., McNamee and Gergen, 1992b). Family therapists, for example, have been keen to rally to postmodernism, with a number of different consequences that it is beyond the scope of this chapter to assess (McKenzie and Monk, 1997; Parker, 1999b).

It sometimes seems as if almost every variety of psychology is being brought together under the postmodern umbrella, with Vygotsky and Gibson (Shotter, 1993), and Mead, Wundt and Skinner (Kvale, 1992c) being enrolled at various points. These psychologists would usually be thought of as being very *modern*. The problem is that those who characterise themselves as 'postmodern' are defining themselves against and within the terms of the debate laid down by the moderns. This prepares a two-way trap as postmodernists flee into something that is a very rickety construction and from something that is no less conceptually shaky.

Postmodernism and 'the modern constitution'

In much 'postmodern' writing in psychology there is confusion about the precise referent for the term 'postmodern'. It may be argued that this confusion about reference is in the postmodern spirit, and we should not really worry too much about the relationship between words and those imaginary 'things' which some suppose to lie outside the words. This type of defence is symptomatic of a problem in postmodern writing, that at the very point where we look for clarity over concepts we find terminological slippages which prevent critical reflection. The postmodern is certainly, as some theorists in psychology have pointed out, marked by 'uncertainty' (Michael, 1994), and that uncertainty, while enjoyable for some, can prevent others from coming to grips with it as a psychological or cultural phenomenon.

Postmodernism makes a virtue of its ambiguity and uncertainty. There is a double ideological effect here, for on the one hand the resistance to attempts to define postmodernism make it more difficult to identify points of similarity with other progressive and retrogressive movements and to be able to assess what would be helpful and what harmful, and on the other hand the slipperiness leads us to believe that we *do* know what it is and to make some serious mistakes about the categories we are using to make sense of it. We need to reflect on the two sides of the problem; the ubiquity of 'the postmodern' in recent ideology, and the limitations of 'the modern' as a conceptual device to understand how ideology in contemporary culture works.

Here we have to locate psychology and the psy-complex in wider ideological debates.

We have always been postmodern. First, the argument that we have
moved 'beyond' something that was once oppressive into a quite different cultural condition where all parameters of critical analysis no
longer apply is an old ideological ploy. In many cases the argument is
explicitly used to warrant an abandonment of Marxist analysis, with
an early example being Burnham's (1941) *The Managerial
Revolution* after his break from Trotskyism, or to shift attention to the
sphere of 'intellectual technology', with a key example being Bell's
(1973) *The Coming of Post-Industrial Society* to discredit analyses of ideology as outmoded. Lyotard's (1979) postmodern story now comes in a
latest more ambitious wave of work which insists that all the old categories are inappropriate. Fukuyama (1992), writing from the US State
Department is keen to claim that this is even because we have wit-
nessed the end of history. What each of these writers particularly want
to erase is the idea that some dramatic change might now be possible
or necessary, for all the possible or necessary changes have already happened (e.g., Baudrillard, 1983). These writers have had some success in
focusing the debate on change as a continually flowing process rather
than as meeting resistance and involving structural breaks.

This is what has led some critical writers to also be wary of the adjectives 'constant', 'uninterrupted' and 'everlasting' which are extracted
by Berman (1982) from Marx's description of the development of the
commodity form under capitalism – 'constant revolutionizing of production, uninterrupted disturbance, everlasting uncertainty and agita-
tion' (Marx and Engels, 1848) – and extrapolated to the condition of
modernity. Anderson points out that these terms 'denote a *homoge-
neous* historical time, in which each moment is perpetually different
from every other by virtue of being *next*, but – by the same token – is
eternally *the same* as an interchangeable unit in a process of infinite
recurrence' (1984: 101). While this description accurately captures the
character of the life of commodities under capitalism, it obscures the
way in which the capitalist mode of production is discontinuous from
preceding and, for Marxists, succeeding modes of production.
Anderson draws the conclusion that the category of 'modernity' is
vacuous, and that it leads cultural analysts and activists to bring
together a variety of different practices under one heading and then to
imagine that the process of radical change is a continual rather than a
punctual process. Since we are changing all the time we cannot and

need not think about how to bring about certain kinds of structural transformation, and so Marxism is effectively paralysed and ironized under cover of a generous extension of narratives of 'change' (Callinicos, 1995; Norris, 1990).

There seems to be a compound-ideological process operating, then, in which there is not only the perpetual illusion that we have passed *beyond* the modern, with the 'postmodern' being a particularly successful expression of this, but also an equally powerful idea that bewitches us, which is that what we are being pulled forward from is something that was *modern* to start with.

We have never been modern. There is a powerful discursive frame around our accounts of the modern and the postmodern, and we need to step outside that frame to be able to understand how it has gripped us. We have been trapped within the terms of a certain kind of debate which invites postmodern psychologists to think that they need to find an alternative to modern thought and incites mistaken and well-meaning traditional psychologists to retreat into modern assumptions when they are confronted by the postmodernists.

Bruno Latour (1991) points out in his little book *We Have Never Been Modern* that we use the term 'modern' at our peril, for it underpins a series of conceptual mistakes about the way in which scientific knowledge is produced and protected. For Latour, that which we think of as being 'modern' is not a state of affairs or a cultural condition into which we have moved but rather a series of contradictory practices of 'translation' and 'purification'. The work of translation is accomplished through the mixing together of hybrid forms in varieties of networks which allow categories to be broken down and rebuilt anew. The work of purification operates through the strict separation of categories, of culture from nature and of human from nonhuman. Latour (ibid.: 112) is willing to accept that this strict separation might be a real defining mark of 'the modern': 'Moderns do differ from premoderns by this single trait: they refuse to conceptualise quasi-objects as such. In their eyes, hybrids present the horror that must be avoided at all costs by a ceaseless, even maniacal purification.' What Latour calls the modern 'Constitution' is bound by guarantees that it is indeed possible to keep culture and nature, human and nonhuman separate. However, this continual conceptual cleansing also reinforces the strict distinction between what we imagine we are as 'moderns' distinct from those cultures who have also *always* engaged in processes of translation and purification, and so 'The moderns have a peculiar propensity for understanding time that passes as if it were really abolishing the past behind it' (ibid.: 68).

While Latour's work has been attractive to some postmodern psychologists because it appears to celebrate disruption, hybridification and transgression (e.g., Michael and Kendall, 1997), he takes pains to distance himself from postmodernism. He says of the postmodernists that 'It is of course impossible to conserve their irony, their despair, their discouragement, their nihilism, their self-criticism, since all of those fine qualities depend on a conception of modernism that modernism has never really practised' (Latour, 1991: 134). His assessment of the contribution of postmodern writers is more nuanced, and he particularly wants to prevent the mistake that postmoderns make about the nature and culture of the modern Constitution: 'Take away from the postmoderns their illusions about the moderns, and their vices become virtues – nonmodern virtues' (ibid.: 134).

Postmodern psychology mistakenly defines itself against a certain kind of cultural–historical backdrop that it calls the 'modern', and it is all the easier for *psychologists* to fall into this trap because the discipline of psychology has constituted itself in such a way that it produces a caricature of historical progress and a repression of self-understanding which justifies what it is doing precisely on the basis that it is modern. This means that postmodern psychologists are racing off down a cul-de-sac to find something better, with the idea that the postmodern is either more progressive, that it is able to open up a space for critical reflection or that it offers opportunities for change. It also means that when some of us who were tempted to join them then turn back and try to get out when we realize something is wrong we are faced once again with 'the modern' as our only point of reference (e.g., Parker, 1989, 1992; Roiser, 1991, 1997).

Latour makes a surprising statement at one point in his book which makes some helpful links with an alternative tradition, Marxism, that he otherwise has little time for;

> We can keep the Enlightenment without modernity, provided that we reintegrate the objects of the sciences and technologies into the Constitution, as quasi-objects among many others – objects whose genesis must no longer be clandestine, but must be followed through and through, from the hot events that spawned the objects to the progressive cool-down that transforms them into essences of Nature or Society.
>
> (Latour, 1991: 135)

Although Latour is not writing as a Marxist here, the way he situates 'the modern' and 'the postmodern' as theoretical forms and scientific practices as part of an historical process is compatible with Marxism. Here, his account can be read within Marxism, as a Marxist narrative, and it is worth pointing out (once again) that Marxism has rarely viewed itself as a 'metanarrative' (Montag, 1988). Marxism in a number of traditions has viewed itself as a *situated* Enlightenment narrative which *only* makes sense within a *certain* kind of political–economic system, and with a conception of change *within* that system which identifies stress points and collective agents who facilitate or inhibit emancipatory action. To put Marxism in the modern Constitution, as Lyotard insists on doing, is to peform exactly that work of translation and purification that Latour describes as being the practice of those who think they are modern.

A detour: postmodern narrative and Enlightenment practice

One of the important charges levelled against postmodernism is that it reflects preoccupations of the post-industrial 'First World', and that it then arrogantly reads out a specific cultural malaise onto the whole planet. Smith's (1994) comment about it being the perspective of alienated writers from the humanities or that of the Euro-American elite is of this kind. It is important to be clear about whether this charge should be allowed to stick, not so that we may then rescue postmodernism but that we may better assess its advantages and disadvantages. It does *not* seem true for two reasons.

First, the simultaneous integration and disorganization of capitalism on a world scale, its globalization, do seem to bring to the fore exactly the kinds of processes postmodernists are concerned with. This is evident in the emerging strand of 'postcolonial' writing which continues the deconstruction and dispersal of imperialist ideology and identity that postmodernism champions, but viewed as 'discrete cultural systems' (During, 1987) or as an effect of 'cultural mimesis' (Richard, 1987). Second, the political advantages of a 'postmodern' position of critique and styles of mobilization seem to be recognised by activists in the 'Second' and 'Third' worlds, the parts of the world formerly inhabited by the bureaucratised workers states and the third world – that is, in each domain once characterised by revolutionary Marxists as 'the three sectors of world revolution' (Mandel, 1979). We can see how this plays itself out, and then assess the value and limitations of this strategy in political discourse, before turning back to postmodernism in psychology.

First, in relation to the bureacratised workers states, particularly in the Soviet Union and former Yugoslavia, there have emerged forms of political critique which depart both from traditional entrepreneurial market ideology and from Stalinism.

It is striking that the most disturbing 'postmodern' accounts to emerge are those that go all the way in breaking not only from 'the modern' but also from the Enlightenment, looking instead to the break-up of Yugoslavia, for example, as the positive site of struggles on an explicitly interpersonal and individual basis (e.g, Meštrovič, 1994). Those 'postmodern' accounts which have developed from Eastern Europe which retain some sense of collectivity, egalitarian goals and reasoned argument are, on the other hand, seen as a continuation of the Enlightenment (e.g., Burbach *et al.*, 1996).

Second, in relation to movements in Latin America that have been characterised as 'postmodern', the label is sometimes used simply to write off guerilla movements, such as the Peruvian Tupac Amaru as replaying the past in caricature (e.g., Gott, 1996). The term 'postmodern' is also used to apply to the Mexican Zapatistas, though, to condemn them for departing from a strict economic analysis of the relationship between classes and between the Mexican state and imperialism; 'The EZLN views the class struggle in an idealised fashion' (K. Harvey, 1995: 14). The term has been used predominantly, however, to congratulate them for breaking from hierarchical forms of organization and political goals; 'The Indian uprising in Chiapas that burst upon the world scene in January is a postmodern political movement ... it is not bent on taking power in Mexico City, nor is it calling for state socialism (Burbach, 1994: 113).

Apart from the formal programme of the Zapatistas. and widespread reports that more computer disks have been seized in raids on the Lacandon jungle than guns – something which serves the cyberpomo image of the movement – their public proclamations do seem designed to subvert 'modern' forms of politics (Esteva and Prakesh, 1997). Metaphors of history are very rarely employed, for example, and there is instead a shift to metaphors of place and space, of the 'penthouse', 'ground floor' and 'basement' levels of Mexico that a visitor might enter (Marcos, 1995a). Responses to moves by the Mexican government are often framed in multiple ways rather than through a single correct line, with, for example, 'three interpretations' being offered of the election results (e.g., Marcos, 1995b). Masked Zapatistas often claim that they are all 'Marcos' with Marcos himself as only a 'subco-mandante' cipher of a collective decision-making process, and there is a proliferation of 'bases' all given the same name, such as 'Aguascalientes', or used to confuse visitors, as in the choice of 'La Realidad' (i.e., 'Reality') for the July 1996 Intercontinental Encounter (Scott-Fox, 1997).

It would be tempting to forget that the uprising in Chiapas in January 1993 was against the North American Free Trade Agreement (NAFTA) which imposes imperialist power deeper on the Mexican people, with quite real material poverty increasing as a result, and the 'postmodern' rhetoric is a *strategic* part of a struggle embodied in Enlightenment hopes for justice and rights to speak. Postmodernism of a kind is present, then, but if the postmodern motif is overplayed, then we lose sight of the material context within which it *functions* so effectively. There is a corresponding conceptual inflation among the beneficiaries of NAFTA, to the point where once-critical terms become meaningless, when, for example, *Newsweek* can describe Bill Clinton as 'A Postmodern President'; 'He has created a chaotic White House, but a very postmodern one, where management is more horizontal than hierarchical' (Klein, 1994: 22).

The way through this, then, is not just to denounce 'postmodernism' as a fully formed ideological reaction to Marxism or as the cause of the strategic mistakes right-wing Croatians or left-wing Zapatistas might make (Hearse, 1994; North, 1995; Tunney, 1991, Walsh, 1995a, 1995b), but to understand how specific forms of postmodern rhetoric open up or close down a dialectical movement of truth and change. Here we also have a recognition not only that postmodernism is het-erogeneous but that Marxism must also be heterogeneous. To insist that Marxism, or radical political movements more generally, be prop-erly 'modern' would be to betray what was most seriously and playfully progressive about them, and to insist that critical psychology be prop-erly modern would be just as restricting to those who want to open up the discipline to wider social and historical processes and to have some sense of where it is possible to move forward to, where we are going and whether we want to go in that direction.

Four Enlightenment reversals

If we step back and view the emergence of stories of the modern and the postmodern as occurring within the wider context of the Western Enlightenment then we can get a better grasp on what exactly is on offer from these different stories and what the ideological stakes are. Postmodern psychologists will immediately recognise two key characteristics of the Enlightenment – the relationship between truth and change and that between self and other – as their own, and this is partly because postmodernism has been attractive to many of them precisely because it trades on very unpostmodern themes of progression, reflection and opportunity. What will be a little more difficult to persuade them of, but we must try, is the kind of relationship between those terms that is important to take into account, and the political consequences for the way we situate ourselves historically.

The relationship between truth and change and between self and other is *dialectical*, and that means that we both open up the tension between the terms deconstructively, unravelling the privilege given to one over the other, and we try to understand how that tension is socially constructed as part of a wider network of relationships of conceptual privilege and power. In this sense dialectics performs the deconstruction and dispersion that postmodernists celebrate. Cultural phenomena are not static not only because they have come *from* somewhere, but because they are also evolving and mutating and *going* somewhere.

Just as it is possible to find the roots of postmodernism in the rise of information technology and the service sector and to identify aspects of the crisis in psychology and the turn to language which provoked the postmodern turn in the discipline, so it is possible to trace out what might come *next*. If we want to ask what the conditions of possibility for postmodernism in psychology are, we have to account not only for how it came to be but also what it is becoming. What might the postmodern turn into? Here a dialectical account is helpful.

A dialectical account is able to pick up some of the transformations within postmodern rhetoric and is able to identify the various discursive shapes that are emerging in and against it. A dialectical account is attentive to the way that postmodernism incites certain responses, the way that it constitutes the field for those cultural movements that are struggling to be first past the post. In this kind of account we can see not only what dangers there are in postmodern psychology, but also how it bears some responsibility for the dangers that follow it, dangers that may be more difficult to deal with. This is why I trace the following defining characteristics of postmodernism as the four Enlightenment reversals. Elements of the argument so far and the four reversals are displayed in Table 2.1.

Table 2.1   Times and transformations

Enlightenment	Modernity/ Psychology	Postmodernism	Next
truth and change dialectic	regularity	relativism 'uncertainty'	scientism (internal backlash)
truth and change dialectic	essentialism	amoralism 'beyond'	fundamentalism (e.g., identity politics)
self and other dialectic	reductionism	collectivism 'relationality'	individualism (e.g., assertiveness)
self and other dialectic	individualism	autonomy 'choice'	organicism (contextual backlash)
Enlightenment dialectic: historical progress self-understanding	caricatured repressed	paralysed ironized	suppressed parodied

Relativism and scientism

There has been much argument outside and inside psychology about relativism and its dangers (Gill, 1995), and there seems little point in labouring the arguments against relativism again here. It should be pointed out, however, that for many critical psychologists, the argument that the problem in postmodernism is 'unscientific relativism' (Smith, 1994: 408) is not one they would want to adopt. Rather, the problem concerns what happens to critical positions that have relativised psychology and rendered it unscientific only to find that their own position of critique is eaten away just as fast (Burman, 1990). There are political problems with relativism, and postmodernism efficiently dissolves any claims we might make about the ideological role of psychology by seeding doubt into those claims and uncertainty into the community of radical psychologists. The point at issue here, though, is what happens when that relativism also nourishes its opposite.

One of the symptoms simultaneously of the influence and crisis of postmodernism is the increase in crass appeals to science as a reaction to what is often characterised as the new dominant irrational spirit of the academe. Recent examples in the British press are by writers who have crossed the border over to science from the arts, but rather than this inspiring a critical reflection on scientific procedures, it has seemed to provoke all the more awe: Regis (1995), for example, a philosopher who is now a science journalist, reviewing Paul Feyerabend's autobiography, complains that a '"storytelling" interpretation is now highly popular among philosophers of science', and comments 'Scientists may wonder how his brand of irrationalism ever managed to escape from the ranks of the medieval demonology with which it ought to be classified' (ibid.: 26). This stance has also been expressed by those taking their cue from the Gross and Levitt's (1994) book *Higher Superstition*, which targets the 'academic left' as the source of what they term, in the subtitle of a companion edited volume, the postmodern 'flight from science and reason' (Gross *et al.*, 1996). The sociology of scientific knowledge that inspired discourse analysis in psychology is then decried as a 'crazy programme' which feeds postmodernism, and as 'conspiratorial nonsense' in a 'new empire of absurdity' (Forbes, 1995: 13).

The return to science in forms of virulent scientism which are as irrational as the irrationality they try to escape cannot, I would argue, simply be written off as a reaction to postmodern relativism. This scientism is an *internal* backlash which delights postmodernists, and which sometimes seems to be deliberately provoked by them (even when they may claim to intend a more moderate assessment of science), much in the same manner as ultra-left groups who mistakenly believed that the repressive state apparatus could only be defeated if its violence was unleashed, and so made clearer to the masses (e.g., Stoke Newington 8 Defence Group, 1972). If there is any truth in the postmodern argument that us-and-themism constitutes the 'them' as all the more powerful, then its exemplary form would be the way that patently unreasonable attacks on all forms of science makes all those who think they are scientists behave unreasonably.

Amoralism and fundamentalism

The relativism in some discursive psychology and in postmodern approaches has often been treated by its critics as equivalent to amoralism (e.g., Gill, 1995), and although the epistemological relativism that even critical realists would see as central to their account of science is sometimes distinguished from moral relativism (e.g., Widdicombe, 1995), there is often a slide from one into the other. This is the kind of attitude that led two separate papers about postmodernism in psychology in the same issue of *Theory and Psychology* in 1997 to cite with approval Nietzsche's assertion that we should seek to go 'beyond good and evil' (Greer, 1997: 97; Kendall and Michael, 1997: 12). Once the grounds for distinguishing between good and evil have been eaten away, then there is no reason why one should not opt for one or the other.

However, as with relativism, the problem does not lie only with what postmodernism celebrates but with what it *prepares* as an all too certain moral response. This preparation is structural rather than individual or intentional. There are two aspects that are worth noting. The first is the emergence of what Žižek (1996) terms 'postmodern racism' in which neo-Nazi skinheads in Germany account for violence toward foreigners by citing increasing insecurity, diminishing social mobility and the breakdown of paternal authority. That is, the stories that were once told to 'explain' racism are now being used to warrant it. It is as if these postmodern racists have done their discourse analysis and now *perform* it. In the process, of course, they reveal some of the limitations of discourse analysis, postmodern or otherwise, that make it seem that by showing us the warranting character of language it had done all the critical work necessary. The second aspect is the way 'cynical distance' incites participants to fix upon any idea they find attractive, and to refuse to justify it in relation to other possible ideas. As Žižek points out, 'This accounts for the paradox that today cynically "enlightened" intellectuals who are no longer able to believe in any social Cause are the first to fall prey to "fanatical" ethnic fundamentalisms' (ibid.: 210). Criticism of any cultural practice is thus made impossible at the very same moment as the cultural practice is essentialised and naturalised, given warrant; in this postmodern world such practices as female circumcision or suttee 'must be understood in context, as a part of the cultural whole' (Marglin and Marglin, 1990: 234). As has been pointed out, 'A questioning of Eurocentric values soon leads to a suspension of all moral judgements' (Mitter, 1994: 103), and this is why the role of postmodernists has been as malign as the essentialists in their commentaries on communalism in India (Vanaik, 1997).

Moving back closer to psychology again, we could view the 'identity politics' that postmodern psychologists worry about as an *effect* of the postmodern. Rather than being an expression of 'modern' essentialist notions of self-hood in psychology, identity is a form of fundamentalism that is provoked by the amoralism of postmodern argument.

Collectivism and individualism

For some writers, including those who are sympathetic to Marxist ideas (e.g., Newman and Holzman, 1997), postmodernism invites a form of relational politics which embeds 'selves' in social context and encourages collective action. There is a problem, though, with their collectivist vision of an 'end of knowing' which automatically discredits those who would think that it must be possible to find a place to step back and assess things. Although it is true that Marxism can itself warrant notions of cognition which contradict and undermine its image of the person as 'an ensemble of social relations' and we need to be wary about this, there are ways of reading Marx which produce an account of cognition as located in social practices (Reed, 1996). It seems that Newman and Holzman (1997) risk celebrating that very absence of 'critical distance' which Jameson (1984a) identified as a problem in postmodernism (and mistakenly tried to rectify with an appeal to 'cognitive mapping'). The pitfalls of collectivism in postmodernism pale into insignificance, however, when we discover what it has spawned, in a powerful strain of individualism.

The rhetorical trick which appears time and again through the celebration of open dialogue in postmodern discourse is that when everything is up for grabs, those who are strongest will be the winners, and those who appeal to consensual taken-for-granted starting points in analysis, historical understanding or moral standpoint are positioned as those who are susceptible to what Nietzsche (1977) called 'slave mentality'. There are plenty of postmodern psychologists who value dialogue, but when the ground rules for the dialogue are repeatedly eroded, all that is left is a battle of wills. This discourse thus incites individualism, smuggling it in through the backdoor while it appears to simply celebrate perspectivism and appeals to the motif of uncertainty. The certainties which are provoked here are an expression of one of the central themes in Nietzsche's (1977) work which have reappeared in postmodern thought, 'the supersession of "modernity" by a harder, less wimpish form of subjectivity' (Lovibond, 1989: 19). In some ways, the twist that underlies this ostensibly 'open' and 'rhetorical' postmodern, postpolitical questioning of historical truths is of a piece with the fantasy of being a postmodern, and, as one feminist critic of that tradition has pointed out, 'in reading postmodernist theory we should be on the watch for signs of indulgence in a certain collective fantasy of masculine agency or identity' (ibid.). The obsession with 'assertiveness' functions in this way, with a reduction to the behaviour emanating from the self as locus of change combined with a cognitivist parody of self-understanding.

Autonomy and organicism

The individualism which is provoked by relational rhetoric in postmodernism is slightly different from the image of autonomous free choice that some postmodern psychologists have been keen to champion. In this case, the motif of autonomy also seems to be flipping over

into its diametric opposite, something which might be best characterised as a form of organicism. We see this in the increasing number
of appeals to 'nature' among postmodernists and among those who
have been drawn into the orbit of postmodernism and who are trying
to find their way out. The motif of ecology is repeatedly incanted as a
solution to pitfalls of postmodernism, even among its friends (e.g.,
Kendall and Michael, 1997). New Age movements do, at first sight,
appear to be postmodern in their suspicion of traditional medicine or
scientific knowledge and in their playful engagment with a variety of
contradictory ideas and practices. However, the motif of nature reappears as something which grounds the *truth* of those practices.

In psychological traditions outside the discipline of psychology, most
importantly the Jungian movement, we not only have a celebration of
nature but also its mystification as something which cannot be appre-
hended by reason but as something which holds humanity together in a
collective unconscious – albeit in a collective unconscious which Jung,
who flirted a good deal with racist ideas, fractured into distinct forms of
racial unconcious (Dalal, 1988). One of the first appointments to a profes-
sorship in analytical psychology in the UK recently, Renos Papadopoulos,
was reported as predicting that 'with the waning of Post-Modernism as
the creed for every self-respecting intellectual, it will be replaced by
Jungianism (albeit in Post-Modernist garb)' (Hugill, 1995: 11). I must
say that I am inclined to agree, but would see this as a baleful effect of
postmodernism in psychology rather than a rich legacy.

The organicist thematic can also be seen in the appropriation of
postmodern rhetoric in versions of narrative therapy. The family
therapy tradition was always susceptible to recuperation by organic
metaphors and notions of what a natural healthy living system should
look like (Fowers and Richardson, 1996).

Organicism, as a powerful player in the contextual backlash against
postmodernism, is particularly dangerous when it is legitimated by scientism, as the internal backlash inside psychology, and it feeds forms
of fundamentalism and individualism as solutions to social problems.
These four aspects of the reaction which is seeded and nurtured by
postmodernism as part of a dialectical process are themselves dialectically interrelated but any further movement is suppressed at the same
time as any further self-understanding which would help us to escape
them is ruthlessly parodied. This is not a simple repetition of themes of
regularity, essentialism, reductionism and individualism in 'modern'
psychology, but a ratchet up into a qualitatively more irrational and
unpleasant version of each.

Conclusion

Postmodern writing has provided a resource for radical psychologists, both as a theory of subjectivity and language and as a point of critique directed at the possibility of adequate theory in the discipline. The postmodern turn has thrown the project of psychology and its associated disciplinary apparatuses into question. However, postmodernism threatens a radical political agenda in the discipline, and can only be comprehended by locating psychology in wider social and historical context. Now we need to address two kinds of danger that flow from postmodern writing. The first comes with an enthusiastic adoption of postmodern nostrums, and is particularly pernicious in its embrace of relativism and amoralism, and naive in its paradoxical blend of collectivism and autonomy. The second comes from a pessimistic and disappointed adoption of the various alternative visions postmodernism incites as it goes into crisis, and stimulates scientism, fundamentalism, individualism and organicism. Now, it would seem that the costs are too great. Postmodernism, as a movement of sustained playful theoretical reflection, and postmodernity, as a cultural background for theoretical research, have now outlived their usefulness. They are already now inciting and encouraging some dangerous tendencies in psychology. Furthermore, unless a radical agenda for research is developed which is able to comprehend how cultural preoccupations enter into and condition psychological research, the 'postmodern' turn in psychology will turn into something worse.

2a
Against Against-ism
Comment on Parker

Fred Newman and Lois Holzman

This comment on Parker's 'Against Postmodernism: Psychology in Cultural Context' contextualizes Parker's 'against-ism' (critical) stance. Parker characterizes postmodernism as theoretical play that has gone too far. Having exhausted its progressive potential, it's become a breeding ground for reactionary ideas now threatening psychology and a radical political agenda. Parker, recognizing that what he fears postmodernism has spawned are products of modernism, employs 'dialectical critique' to historically contextualize postmodernism and its dangers. As postmodernists Parker takes to task, the authors argue that the relevant points of difference between him and them have more to do with their differing institutional locations and conception/practices of dialectics than with postmodernism.

The homely image evoked for us by Parker's erudite contribution 'Against Postmodernism: Psychology in Cultural Context' is that of the panicky working-class mother trying to get the children to stop enjoying themselves at play because the authoritarian Daddy is about to come home and he will be even more abusive than usual if he sees them having fun. As 'a movement of sustained playful theoretical reflection', postmodernism is exhausted, and Parker dutifully chastizes this corrosive and exhilarating activity' that celebrates 'deconstruction and dispersion', incites and provokes certain reactionary responses, and even delights in some, for example the backlash of scientism. The real danger of postmodernism, Parker seems to be saying, is not in what it is but in what it will produce. Curiously, here he invokes dialectics (mis-understood, especially by academic Marxists, to mean 'dialectical critique') to *predict* (*retrodict*) the reactionary consequences of too much play, that is, postmodernism. Parker asks, 'What might the postmodern tum into?' and answers, 'Here a dialectical account is helpful'.

If, as Parker suggests, postmodernism as self-reflexive criticalness has always been a part of modernism – and we would agree that it has – then surely the reactionary consequences of postmodernism (thus understood) have always been there also. And they have. Indeed, this 'scientific' sleight of hand (foolishly called 'dialectics') is traditionally employed by academic Marxists to predict what is already there, that is, known/believed to be inevitable.

Parker is our good friend and a very bright one. We are postmodernists. Parker is 'Against Postmodernism'. Is he therefore against us? We think not. We are surely not against him. We are, if this metaphor is to prevail, 'Against Against-ism'. Or is that too playful? But what we are for is, perhaps, far more important than what we are against. And, as Marxist postmodernists, we are for dialectics, not as a pseudo-science of predicting (retrodicting) what is already known, but as a practice (a practical-critical tactical activity) for moving forward developmentally given that little or nothing is any longer knowable.

It is not on postmodernism that we and Parker disagree – it is on dialectics.[1] For, on our account, what postmodernism must become if it is to playfully engage the reactionary consequences of modernism is *revolutionary activity* – that playful, practical–critical, developmental performance[2] which is, without doubt, a wonderful component of modernism but which has, in modernism's senility, been constantly conspired against. It is the joy of modernism, the emancipatory joy of its self-reflexivity and revolutionariness (its historical anti-religiosity), that postmodernism attempts to salvage – from capitalists and academic Marxists alike. Obviously, capitalists and academic Marxists are not the same. But they do, inadvertently, conspire in their joyless rejection of genuine dialectics (revolutionary activity). Parker, our friend, wants to have his cake (institutionalized knowing) and eat it too (institutionalized Marxism). And, we guess, he can. But as Marxists (or, on Parker's revealing formulation, 'writers ... who are sympathetic to Marxist ideas',), we want our share of the dialectical pie (or pudding).

Dialectics is the form of understanding required to go forward given the necessary and tactical abandonment of knowing. The point, the early Marx made plain, is not to interpret the world but to change it. Goodbye knowing. But Marxists (like capitalists and, indeed, the later Marx himself) get caught up in systemization and knowing how capitalism works as a precondition for going forward. Systemization is the name of the Daddy who comes home and requires that Mommy stop the kids from playing. Late capitalism's senile systemization is, in some

ways, even more overbearing than religiosity (its systematic predeces-
sor), for religion at least offered hope of a joyous afterlife. Late capitalist systemization offers no hope; if we take the revolutionary joy (the
practical–critical activity) out of modernism, then we are left with
religion without hope.

Dialectics is, for us, the understanding (not the cognitive) component of play – it is play without rules. It is the play of childhood, of
development, of becoming. And, yes, play can outlive its usefulness
but it never outlives its importance. For if we stop playing, who cares if
life is useful? Can we playfully suggest that it seems strangely appropriate that our British friend Parker take on the role of cooling out his
French and American post-modernist playmates? Yes, Ian, we know
this is serious business. That's precisely why we must play. Dialectics
and revolutionary activity are simply too important to take themselves
so seriously.

As we see it, taking oneself too seriously is an occupational hazard of
an academic location (the seat of institutionalized knowing). It can
and frequently does rob one of the joy of self-reflexivity, for example
the impact that being granted authority as an official knower has on
how one sees and understands. Critique (dialectical and otherwise)
becomes the name of the game. Parker's characterization of our work
and play embodies just this kind of non-reflexive, institutionalized
bias. He treats us as if we, too, have an academic location and are in
the business of knowing and critiquing, that is, he treats us entirely too
seriously.

For twenty-plus years, we have been practicing dialectics as method,
playing without rules, as one small *unsystemized* effort to transform
human relations and make psychology relevant to people's lives. Along
with hundreds of others, we have brought into existence and nurtured
a community and its various institutions which are not funded, con-
trolled or validated by any government institution or university. They
were built not with government grants or taxpayers' money, but
through years of standing on street comers and knocking on doors,
asking ordinary people to support independent, progressive psychology, culture and politics. People learned about our work not in a
college text or university lecture, but from our community organizing.
Our institutions don't function according to the authoritarian, hierarchical structure of traditional institutions. Our training center, the East
Side Institute, gives no grades, degrees or tenure. Our therapy centers
do not diagnose and we have no rules (implicit or explicit) against
clients socializing with other clients or therapists. The All Stars Talent

Show Network, our youth development organization, produces talent shows at which everyone who auditions gets into the show. Virtually everyone connected with the Castillo Theatre, including the actors, producers, set designers, and so on, serves on the house staff when the house is open. The radically democratic collectivity we have built emerged as an inseparable part of what we were building, and it continues to evolve. Rooted in the dialectic relationship being/becoming, our 'business' is creating becoming. Surely, it doesn't follow from our intentions or practice that we've succeeded in overcoming authoritarianism, but it does follow that any honest analysis of our work needs to take our history into account. But Parker is in the business of critiquing and predicting what is already known, and he failed to note that we happen to be a group of people who self-consciously tried to create an emancipatory environment that nurtures the play of development instead of replicating an authoritarian environment that insists on the serious business of knowing.

Parker is against postmodernism because he fears it is a breeding ground for reactionary ideas and practices. We agree that it can be, but we disagree that it is therefore problematic. Should parents stop children from playing because they might get hurt in that developmental process? Should we legislate against physical exercise because some might use their strength to engage in socially destructive behavior?

Parker's institutional location distorts his vision of postmodernism's 'playful theoretical reflection' on collectivism and our community's collectivism in particular. He says:

> For some writers, including those who are sympathetic to Marxist ideas (e.g. Newman and Holzman, 1997), postmodernism invites a form of relational politics which embeds 'selves' in social context and encourages collective action. There is a problem, though, with their collectivist vision of an 'end of knowing' which automatically discredits those who would think that it must be possible to find a place to step back and assess things. ... It seems that Newman and Holzman (1997) risk celebrating that very absence of 'critical distance' which Jameson [1984a] identified as a problem in postmodernism ...

Parker is correct. We do risk celebrating the absence of critical distance if what it entails is stepping back to the authoritarian structure of the university and systemizing emergent developmental activity. Far from an academic issue for us, collectivism has been integral to our practice of dialectics, that is, our postmodern play (absent both Mommy and Daddy). We don't understand collectivism as simply people coming together, as Parker implies; its complex tactical forms over the years have emerged along with creating what we have created.

Parker goes on to, paradoxically, implicate postmodern collectivism in the production of another reactionary *modernist* tendency – individualism:

> The rhetorical trick which appears time and again through the celebration of open dialogue in postmodern discourse is that when everything is up for grabs, those who are strongest will be the winners, and those who appeal to consensual taken-for-granted starting points in analysis, historical understanding or moral standpoint are positioned as those who are susceptible to what Nietzsche (1977) calls 'slave mentality'. There are plenty of post-modern psychologists who value dialogue, but when the ground rules for the dialogue are repeatedly eroded, all that is left is a battle of wills. This discourse thus incites individualism, smuggling it in through the back door while it appears to simply celebrate perspectivism and appeals to the motif of uncertainty.

Here we disagree, once again, with Parker's dim view of postmodern play without rules. For isn't it the case that everything *is* up for grabs and the stronger (the more authoritarianly situated) *are* the winners in our current highly rule-governed world culture? And while we don't agree that a battle of wills is *inevitable,* we much prefer that risky byproduct of open dialogue to the authoritarian control of the ground rules of institutionalized knowing. As postmodern Marxists, our concern with power is as a practice-reconstruction, as far as we can tell, is the activity of people exercising power in the creating of something new.

Over the past few decades, we have created many new things involving tens of thousands of people. New things, of course, are not necessarily good things, but the self-conscious awareness of the manifest human capacity to create new things is profoundly developmental. Our efforts have been to produce new human organization (from talent shows to therapy groups to political caucuses) which do not fetishize the product. It is this continuous effort to create without commodification that, we've come to believe, is joyously emancipatory.

No small part of our critique of knowing (Newman and Holzman, 1997) is that knowing is a form of understanding which requires an object and/or a product, namely the Known or Truth. Hence all knowing is fetishized. No doubt fetishized understanding was the near perfect epistemology for alienated capitalism. Marx, it seems to us, makes this plain. But if we are to journey beyond capitalism (to who knows where!) we must at least begin to abandon knowing. Such experiments (journeys) will not grow in the sterile environment of the bourgeois university. Our theoretical writings emerged after 25 years of continuous practical–critical organizing activity. To relate to them as the alienated product of that work and, moreover, as what is truly valuable in it is a grave distortion. Our recently realized (in some circles) theoretical analytical respectability is a validation of the practical criticalness of our day-to-day, hour-to-hour, year-to-year, decade-to-decade organizing – not the other way around. To objectify it into theoretical positions misses the point (pointless though it may be!). To the extent that we have contributed to Parker's confusion on these matters by our publications, we apologize. Our writings are inadequate progress reports on work in progress. Nothing more. Nothing less. A theoretical consequence is of no consequence at all unless, as Marx makes plain, it contributes to changing, not interpreting, the world.

Notes

1 Parker, our friend and colleague, knows and respects this difference. Indeed, one of us (Newman) recently authored an essay on dialectics at Parker's invitation, appeared in the first edition of the new journal *Annual Review of Critical Psychology*.

2 For discussions of *revolutionary activity*, both its roots in Marx (1845) and Vygotsky (1978, 1987) and its contemporary practice in our work, see Holzman (1997, 1999) and Newman and Holzman (1993, 1996, 1997). We note here only that by 'revolutionary activity' we do not mean the activity of 'making the Revolution' (whatever that might mean), for that is but one quite specific revolutionary activity in which human beings engage.

2b

Critical Distance
Reply to Newman and Holzman

Fred Newman and Lois Holzman's comment on my 'Against Postmodernism: Psychology in Cultural Context' neatly displays the very dialectical processes they want to deny. Their refusal of 'critical distance' exemplifies postmodern avoidance of a political assessment of theories and practices (academic or otherwise), and their complaints about the institutional location of critiques of postmodernism draw attention to their own trajectory into the sphere of academic argument and into the arms of mystifying and depoliticizing postmodern ideology.

Knowing something

Despite many protestations to the contrary, Newman and Holzman know something. In fact, they know a lot about Vygotsky and why revolutionary Marxism is still relevant today, why Wittgenstein might be useful to 'complete' Vygotsky, and why postmodernism needs to be stirred in to stir up complacent 'understanding' or misunderstanding of what the stakes are in these theoretical debates (Newman and Holzman, 1993, 1996, 1997). They also know how to disarm criticisms of their theoretical and practical projects by denying that it is possible any longer to know anything and by encouraging critics and supporters of their work to 'abandon knowing' altogether (cf. Nissen *et al.*, 1999). Postmodernism is a useful ideological tool in this strategy, and I included some references to Newman and Holzman's (1997) refusal of knowing and of critical distance from what they were up to in my critique of postmodernism in psychology. I was right, perhaps. At any rate, we do have to know something about postmodernism and the cultural conditions that feed it if we are to be able to assess its effects and respond to the threats it poses to critical work.

My 'dialectical critique' of postmodernism in psychology traced the actually existing dialectical process by which ideological forms under capitalism function to delegitimize critical work. Capitalism and now late capitalism comprise complex interlocking economic and cultural conditions which alienate workers from their labour and disenchant political activists who try to change things. Repeated ideological assaults on any and all visions of a better world have had the effect, generation by generation, of encouraging adherents of Marxism (for example) to recant and to agree that their interpretations of the world were wrong and prospects for change impossible. Postmodernism has been one of the most recent attempts to persuade us to give up on our old bad ways and to become, instead, more realistic 'post-marxists' (or 'Marxist postmodernists'). The danger is twofold. On the one hand, know-nothing relativism and its Wittgensteinian warrant is effective enough in shifting people from radical politics onto the terrain of academic debate about language (Parker, this volume Chapters 3 and 4). It is not necessary to be part of an academic institution to participate in such dispiriting and futile alienated activity. (By the same token, it is possible to be in an academic institution and argue against such things if one has political reference points outside.)

On the other hand, and this is where my comment on the importance of 'critical distance' with reference to Newman and Holzman's theoretical and practical work was relevant, postmodernism is a cultural formation which is part of a dialectical historical process which provokes certain ideological responses – outright hostility to Marxism, for example, in the claim that all forms of knowledge are now levelled out to the extent that no knowledge claim could ever be thought better than any other – *and* incites ideological responses which are the diametric opposite – for example, a subscription to individual strength of will as the only arbiter of what will be thought to be a correct interpretation or what is to become a dominant knowledge claim. I thus drew attention to the way postmodern collectivism incites individualism (and also to the way its relativism, amoralism and simplistic image of individual choice incite scientism, fundamentalism and organicism, respectively).

One key step in the argument to drive once-radical academics into such a self-alienating maze of anxiety about the impossibility of knowing about the world that they give up trying to change anything is the gross exaggeration of the claim that 'all knowing is fetishized'. By itself this is hardly a novel claim as far as Marxism is concerned. Capitalist society distorts each and every understanding we might construct about it, and the fate of various authoritarian sects and stalinist states is sorry evidence of the way forms of distorted understanding laced into oppressive relationships are able to reproduce themselves inside ostensibly radical movements. But this does not at all mean that 'little or nothing is any longer knowable', and revolutionary Marxists have always struggled, in the midst of the most disastrous historical events, to understand, to interpret, to learn so that in the future things may be different (e.g., Trotsky, 1936; Mandel, 1979).

To make academic Marxists, or any other Marxist for that matter, take steps away from knowing anything Newman and Holzman engage in a deliberate mis-quotation and mis-reading of Marx to make him say that the point 'is not to interpret the world but to change it'. This is to make it seem as if Marx were setting interpretation and change in contrast to each other, and to wilfully gloss over his claim in the same text that 'All mysteries which lead theory to mysticism find their rational solution in human practice and in the comprehension of that practice' (Marx, 1845: 423). 'Comprehension of that practice' is a crucial part of Marxist activity, but Newman and Holzman seem keen to forget this, and to depict any attempt to *comprehend* cultural practices and ideological forces rather than those practices and forces themselves as the main danger.

'Critical distance' does not at all entail, as they profess to fear, 'stepping back to the authoritarian structure of the university and systematizing emergent developmental activity'. Nor does it mean that we must be in favour of 'the authoritarian control of the ground rules of institutionalized knowing'. To set up alternatives in this way – utterly undialectically (tactically, no doubt) – is to close off the possibility of engaging in any kind of dialogue about how we might interpret and change the world. Perhaps they do not intend this. Who knows? What is clear though is that the function of their work, and that of many less canny writers, is that postmodernism prefers mysteries to theories and it is more likely to lead us into mystification than away from it.

Knowing nothing

A dialectical paradox appears in Newman and Holzman's comment, or rather, more precisely in the *relation* between their comment and my article. The paradox is as follows.

On the one side, in order to write my critique of the dynamic of postmodernism in psychology I had to step back from psychology and locate it in a broader cultural context, which included, of course, its historical and political context. Dialectics is only fully applicable and operative on the terrain of historical materialism. When dialectics is applied to 'natural' phenomena it merely captures the reflexive activity of dialecticians as they attribute, usually unwittingly, certain idealized sequences of contradiction and synthesis to things outside the human world. My critique of postmodernism in psychology only makes sense because postmodernism exists in contradictory 'story worlds' inside and outside the discipline, and because the discipline itself exists in a variety of contradictory theories and practices – usually abusive and ideological, hence my acknowledgement at the beginning of the chapter that postmodernism inside psychology is, among other things, a progressive 'corrosive and exhilarating activity'. The brief excursus in the middle of my chapter into an account of the inspiring employment of postmodern rhetoric in the Zapatista resistance to NAFTA in southern Mexico, for example, was designed to illustrate, again, two things. First, how progressive postmodernism can be when it is used tactically (a practice that is really 'practical–critical tactical activity'), and, second, how we can only use postmodernism tactically when we have some notion of *critical distance* from it.

On the other side, in order for Newman and Holzman to write their comment on my critique, they had to step into psychology and abandon even the possibility of reflexive awareness of the cultural locatedness of these arguments. Sure, there is their aside that it is telling that my critique of postmodernism is from someone 'British' addressing ('cooling out') the French and Americans, and, sure, Newman and Holzman make much their activities (in the East Side Institute or the All Stars Talent Show Network) which are outside mainstream psychology. But these are but ploys in an argument which drives them all the more into the domain of academic critique, a trajectory which becomes most evident when they proudly point to their 'recently realized (in some circles) theoretical analytical respectability'.

Newman and Holzman complain that I treat them as if they have an academic location. This is disingenuous. I drew attention to their claim to have reached the nirvana of an 'end of knowing', and pointed out that this 'automatically discredits those who would think that it must be possible to find a place to step back and assess things'. I noted that this claim risks celebrating an absence of critical distance and here I did reference one of their 'academic' texts (Newman and Holzman, 1997). Because their recent work has been deliberately targeted at an academic audience I think it was right to direct the reader to one of those of their texts (and this is something, I assume, at some level they will feel happy about if they really want 'theoretical analytical respectability'). However, my reference also indexed their activities *outside* academic institutions (like the East Side Institute or the All Stars Talent Show Network). I do not think critical comment on these activities necessarily constitutes cult-baiting (as they have suggested elsewhere), and I am good enough friends (I think, and so they say) with them for an assessment of what they do to be a serious part of our theoretical–practical differences (Holzman, 1995; Parker, 1995b). The key question here is not so much where they are coming from though, as where they are heading and where they seem to speaking from in their comment on my article. For even when they refer now to their 'community organizing' as ammunition against my article they do it as a moral warrant from *within* an academic location.

The paradox, then, is that at the very moment they inveigh against seats of 'institutional knowing' we are crossing paths; I am developing an argument which strikes a distance from academic institutions and which attempts to comprehend various ideological ruses to demobilize critical work, while they are heading deeper into academic locations to participate in one of the most popular current ideological gambits, to persuade people they can know nothing. 'Goodbye knowing' indeed; this is where 'Marxist postmodernists' fall for the lure of (US American) Forrest Gump politics.

I keep my distance from what they do and what they say, from academic institutions that do not take them seriously and academic institutions that take them too seriously, and from the postmodernism in psychology that they unfortunately celebrate. Would that our problems were all down to 'capitalists and academic Marxists'. Powerful forces inside and outside academic life seem very friendly at the very moment that they crush the life out of our emancipatory joyful reflexive dialectical critical activities. And postmodernism is one such ideological movement which legitimates academic institutions in contemporary culture at the very moment that it threatens to derogate critical distance in favour of an 'end of knowing'.

3
Against Relativism in Psychology, On Balance

Relativism in psychology unravels the truth claims and oppressive practices of the discipline, but simply relativizing psychological knowledge has not been sufficient to comprehend and combat the discipline as part of the 'psy-complex'. For that, a balanced review of the contribution and problems of relativism needs to work dialectically, and so this chapter reviews four problematic rhetorical balancing strategies in relativism before turning to the contribution of critical realism. Critical realism exposes positivist psychology's pretensions to model itself on what it imagines the natural sciences to be, and it grounds discursive accounts of mentation in social practices. The problem is that those sympathetic to mainstream psychology are also appealing to 'realism' to warrant it as a science and to discredit critical research which situates psychological phenomena. Our use of critical realism calls for an account of how psychological facts are socially constructed within present social arrangements *and* for an analysis of the underlying historical conditions that gave rise to the 'psy-complex'. Only by understanding how the discipline of psychology reproduces notions of individuality and human nature, a critical realist endeavour, will it be possible to transform it, and to socially construct it as something different.

Introduction

The argument in this chapter cuts across and against one of the most progressive recent movements in psychology. Different forms of relativism have inspired imaginative theoretical refusals of ideological motifs in the discipline, even when many of its adherents eschew theory (e.g., Gergen, 1994b; Newman and Holzman, 1997). It has fuelled useful methodological critiques of pretend-science in the discipline, even when its practitioners avoid a commitment to any particular method (e.g., Shotter, 1993; Stainton Rogers *et al.*, 1995). Much contemporary critical psychology draws sustenance from relativist writing (e.g., Fox and Prilleltensky, 1997; Ibáñez and Íñiguez, 1997). Critical psychology is heterogeneous process of critique and auto-critique in the discipline which focuses on the way psychological theory and practice operate to reduce social phenomena to the level of the individual and to normalise certain kinds of behaviour and experience (Parker, 1999a). In this strand of work, the study of power and ideology in the maintainance of oppressive relationships by psychology is often facilitated by relativism. Relativism includes a broad array of social constructionist, discursive and postmodern re-readings of psychological texts which serve to 'deconstruct' them and to reveal their status as *stories* about the mind, so critical psychologists, among others, will ask *why* we now need to mark our distance from it.

To address this question, our use of critical realism needs to look to an account of how psychological facts are socially constructed within present-day social arrangements (e.g., Curt, 1994; Harré, 1983) *and* for an analysis of the underlying historical conditions that gave rise to psychology and the 'psy-complex'. The 'psy-complex' is the dense network of theories and practices to do with the mind and behaviour which divide the normal from the abnormal in order to observe and regulate individuals (Ingleby, 1985; Rose, 1985). Understanding how the discipline of psychology reproduces notions of individual cognition and human nature, a critical realist endeavour, will enable us to transform it, and to socially construct it as something better, perhaps. In the process, relativism also needs to be understood and situated both as a useful tool for ideology-critique *and* as an ideological form which increasingly evens out the cutting edge of critical work in psychology. Critical realism takes a step beyond positivist attempts to establish regularities between cause and effect 'to recognise that there are enduring structures and generative mechanisms underlying and producing observable phenomena and events' (Bhaskar, 1989: 2). Such a step requires a view of an enduring 'intransitive' dimension which for some authors, provides 'the most promising basis for securing the status of critical theory in relation to the sciences as a whole' (Morrow with Brown, 1994: 77).

To follow this step in psychology, and against relativism in the discipline, I need to trace my way through ten different ways 'balance' is constituted and negotiated in psychology. In this first introductory section of the chapter I give due credit to social constructionist writing in psychology (Balance I) and my arguments against relativism and for critical realism in the rest of the chapter should be read in the context of the overall progressive effect of relativism in the discipline so far. I will then describe the way relationships between opposites are usually conceived in psychology (Balance II), and draw attention to a way of understanding these dialectically. In the main sections of the chapter I explore problematic characteristics of relativism in psychology (which I organize around four themes of balance) before turning to the contribution of critical realism, and an acknowledgement of problems that this may pose for critical psychologists (which I also organize around four themes of balance). I then draw together these issues to complete the argument that relativism in psychology plays a profoundly ideological role which critical realism can comprehend, and that relativism tears morality from epistemology, something which critical realism can repair.

Balance I: for relativism

The turn to language in psychology in the 1970s and to discourse in the 1980s, together with the use of notions from post-structuralist writing, encouraged us to reflect on developmental psychology and clinical psychology as parts of the powerful 'psy-complex' in modern culture which helps constitute and regulate subjectivity (Burman, 1994; Parker *et al.*, 1995). Relativism in psychology corrodes the truth claims of a discipline which functions as a key ideological apparatus in Western culture, and it also opens the way to anti-racist and feminist critiques of its pathologizing gaze and practice (Henriques *et al.*, 1984; Burman *et al.*, 1996). Our debt to relativist approaches does need to be acknowledged, then, for without that work a genuinely critical psychology would not be possible. Readers in the human sciences outside psychology do not always appreciate how important it is for us to have a vibrant community of researchers who are ready to challenge the discipline's claims to have 'discovered' this or that essential and universal characteristic of mental functioning and then pathologise those who do not then display it. The balanced account of relativism in psychology in this chapter should be read in that context.

Balance II: on contradiction

Although some writers have emphasised the role of contradiction in dialectical processes of interrelationship and change (e.g., Reason and Rowan, 1981), in many cases psychological and social categories are left intact. Despite the queasiness shown by post-structuralist writers toward dialectics in psychology (e.g., Henriques *et al.*, 1984; Kendall and Michael, 1997), the attention to *power* in that strand of work does alert us to aspects of dialectics that are usually ignored in the discipline. Dialectics attends to the dynamic ever-changing nature of reality, to the way it is torn by opposing forces, and to the way the logic of change is marked by contradiction and the transformation of things into their opposites (e.g., Novack, 1971). To say that activity is dialectical is to appreciate something of the synthetic work that the performance of contradiction always accomplishes. That synthesis is often collusive and mystifying, and here opposites are brought together and balanced in the service of ideology so that contradiction is suppressed. But against this false synthesis there is always resistance, and a dialectical account looks to contradiction at the heart of apparent consensus, to laws of motion which underlie that which appears fixed.

Dialectics is marked by motion and fixity, and it is governed, reflexively we might say, by a dialectic *between* motion and fixity such that the one is only possible by virtue of its envelopment and transformation by the other. So, what counts as truth is relativised in so far as it stands in relation to other accounts, and change proceeds through marking itself against a truth to be challenged and subverted. Critical realism acknowledges the 'social construction' of reality, the reality described by discourse analysis, but embeds such descriptions of relatively enduring structures of talk, conceived of as the interlacing of power and ideology, in a Marxist account of relatively enduring structures of economic exploitation (Bhaskar, 1989) amenable to analysis, explanation and change. (It is in *this* sense the Marxists too are social constructionists, Parker and Spears, 1996.) Critical realist versions of a dialectical account will be explored further below, and used to open up relativism in psychology as a form of ideology.

For relativism, and against

There are serious risks in the social constructionist reworking of psychological concepts. Four rhetorical balancing strategies which exemplify relativist attempts to obscure or avoid the issue are evident. However, as we shall see, in each case the balance between opposing positions also involves the privileging of apolitical individualism and the suppression of an alternative position which would attend to political and social context.

Balance III: minding the gap

One powerful strategy is to pretend that if we were to speak differently about it, then discord between relativists and realists would dissolve. The debate is characterised as an infantile war of position which constructs an 'us' and 'them' in which neither side can win (e.g., Gergen, 1998). The stakes seem so high simply because we have been unable to recognise that they are socially constructed stakes, a view that is in line with the comment that 'The real Gulf war is the gulf between absolutes and relativism' (Brian Eno, *The Guardian*, 20 October, 1995: 11). This strategy displaces our attention from a difference about what it is possible or necessary to know about the world – a contradiction between attempts to provide an account of the real and an avoidance of any such accounts – to a mere difference between narratives, in which we can balance 'realist' and 'relativist' narratives in a common conversation. This strategy is generous enough to include *any* story we might tell about the world, but only on condition that we accept that saying something 'about' something is itself *only* a story.

Attempts to dissolve accounts of power into a spectrum of different personal stories now appear in psychology in pleas that we should all try to span 'absolutes' and 'relativism'. These include claims that this involves 'knowing of a third kind' which gives up reference to things outside language (e.g., Shotter, 1993) and that we should embrace the 'end of knowing' where we are or where we are going (e.g., Newman and Holzman, 1997). While such rhetorical strategies call on us to recognise that the polarity between relativism and realism is a function of discourse, then, they also suppress any account which tries to locate the debate in relations of power and ideology.

Balance IV: undecidability

At the same time as advocates of social constructionism cut away the positivist ground from beneath traditional psychology and relativise their claims about the world, they also accuse critics of leaping too soon to a conclusion about what is bad about the discipline and what may be done about it. They thus relativise the truth claims of the critics and wittingly or unwittingly sabotage principled resistance to the discipline. This is a rhetorical strategy which revolves around the motif of 'undecidability', and it reduces discussions about discourse and the real to a range of turns in a conversation in which we could not ever know which was the correct position. One notorious recent example of this is in the discussion of conversational turns by which anti-relativist appeals to 'death' and 'furniture' try to bring an end to the argument and the relativist courageously keeps the conversation going by insisting that things can never be settled in such a final way (Edwards *et al.*, 1995). The reference to 'death' in this case is to the 'bottom line argument' that anti-relativists make when they summon the example of the Holocaust and defy relativists to suggest that historical events of that kind are socially constructed. The 'furniture' is the table that the anti-relativist bangs on when they demand that we all agree that things like that exist outside language. This call for the permanent suspension of judgement about things that lie outside the text is advertised as being closer to the open reflexive spirit of the best social science – 'relativism is social science *par excellence*' (Edwards *et al.*, 1995: 42) – though later defences of the position pull back to offer a more moderate defence of what is going on (as we shall see below when we come to Balance VI). Despite the call for an abandonment of all assumptions about the world, existing theoretical frameworks are mobilised to encourage us to look before we leap into action, just to look. Ethnomethodology has been enrolled in this way to the cause of relativism in psychology recently (e.g., Potter, 1996; Edwards, 1997).

Ethnomethodology has long been viewed as a reductionist current of thought in sociology (Gouldner, 1971), and now it is one of the components of the backlash against politically-engaged social constructionism and discourse analysis in psychology. In one example, ethnomethodology and conversation analysis are counterposed to 'trendy' 'poststructuralist discourse analysis' which, we are told, enables researchers to make 'sweeping political claims' (Widdicombe, 1995: 106). The author of this complaint positions herself as sympathetic to radical politics in psychology, and the motif of perpetual hesitation over politics is introduced cautiously and reasonably at first; 'by elevating their own political agendas as the pre-established analytic frame, researchers may actually undermine the practical and political utility of the analyses they make' (ibid.: 111). After a detailed conversation analysis of an interview transcript, however, we arrive at the ideological core of the argument, when she argues that 'the most effective way of marketing particular political aims is likely to be through appealing to personal choices and decisions rather than by appealing to collective identities or shared oppression' (ibid.: 124). It is telling here not only that there is a reduction to the individual (again), but that politics is conceived of as something that can only be distributed, 'marketed', as if it were separate from other aspects of social activity.

Indecision is portrayed here as active, and is counterposed to those who think they know – with the claim that 'it is the realists who are frozen in motion, because as soon as they move, they represent' (Edwards *et al.*, 1995: 34) – but this activity is like that of a floating voter in a liberal democracy, unable to decide and unwilling to commit to any position. It also presumes that refusing to take a position is not also itself a position (Willig, 1998). Again, then, there is an exclusion of politics, as something that will always try to arrive *too soon*, and relativism is championed as the most pluralistic place in psychology. It thus constructs an apolitical constituency of those who will *not* decide one way or another, a homologue of the much-beloved collection of hesitating individuals which comprise the bourgeois polity.

Balance V: perspectivism

Relativism presents itself as the most tolerant participant in a conversation when it argues that all claims need to be heard alongside counter-claims; for every position, it is possible to imagine that someone may want to argue for an opposing position. This extension of relativism to the point of perspectivism, in which different realities can never be rationally assessed and freedom of opinion is rendered equivalent to toleration of anything being said, is currently popular in bourgeois culture generally. It underpins conceptions of 'balance' in broadcasting. The BBC television programme *Points of View*, for example, which is designed to air viewers' complaints and praise about the channel, broadcast a letter in early July 1997 asking why the BBC never screened 'positive views of Hitler and Nazi Germany' (reported in *Guardian Media Review*, 14 July 1997: 7).

Once relativists have committed themselves to the idea that 'anything goes', it is difficult for some of them to be able to respond to revisionist histories, of war-crimes, for example, for these are simply 'other perspectives' which we must refrain from condemning as dangerous or wrong. Lyotard's inability to address the claims of the neo-Nazi revisionist Faurisson – that we can have no knowledge about what happened at Auschwitz because there are no surviving witnesses to provide first-hand accounts – is a case in point. Instead, as Norris (1996) points out, we have a feeble appeal by Lyotard to acknowledge the narrative *'differend'* between Faurisson's version and ours. This sorry case also illustrates problems of relativism in 'postmodern' writing, and the dangers of postmodernism in psychology generally should not be underestimated (Parker, this volume, Chapter 2).

The claim that the examples offered in the Edwards *et al.* (1995) 'death and furniture' paper are no more than a 'turn' in a conversation entails a refusal to acknowledge the way perspectives are embedded in narratives which are, in turn, embedded in an historical process which *can* be represented in such a way as to challenge claims about the past and assess attempts to rewrite it. When academic arguments are treated simply as various perspectives which are deployed as turns in a conversation, the construction and *functions* of those arguments are lost sight of. To problematise the 'reality' of certain historical events reproduces and reinforces, often unwittingly, deliberate attempts to relativise them, and to draw attention to the social construction of other events, in contrast, may serve to make visible aspects which have been hitherto obscured.

To understand how arguments operate in this way, out of the direct control of speakers, we need to take into account the wider political context and operations of ideology. When, for example, the Holocaust is re-constructed by relativists as a 'bottom line argument' used against them (as in Edwards *et al.*, 1995) it treats it, at that moment in the argument, as a 'social construction', *as if* it is merely a turn in a conversation which we *must* now doubt in the same way as we playfully doubt the existence of tables. Such re-construction would delight revisionist historians such as Faurisson and the many other neo-Nazi activists who want us to doubt and then deny that the Holocaust happened (Seidel, 1986). Alternatively, when the image of Iraqis murdered on the Basra road at the close of the Gulf war are conjured into the argument (Potter, 1997), it serves to remind us, perhaps, of something which was 'constructed' and which we should now assess as something very real. Those who stay only in the tracks of perspectivist rhetoric, though, *cannot* step back and assess how different doubtful claims function as certainties in certain contexts and how they interlock with other arguments.

Psychologists may be particularly susceptible to this mode of argument because they have been schooled in and subject to a paradoxical rhetorical practice in the psy-complex over the years in which there is, on the one hand, a multiplicity of different incompatible theoretical and methodological frameworks where claims to truth are continually deferred, and, on the other, a series of practices concerned with assessing the way people develop and think in which the psychologist must be *certain* that what they see is *really* there. This series of disciplinary practices does not extend to the views that users of psychology services might have of what psychologists do (an issue that we pick up below in the discussion of Balance VII).

While the toleration of a multiplicity of perspectives seems to be the most democratic response to objectionable opinions, then, it actually levels down the truth claims of oppressor and oppressed such that the oppressed lose one of the few resources available to them; as Geras (1995: 110) argues,

> ... if truth is wholly relativised or internalised to particular discourses or language games or social practices, there is no injustice. The victims and protestors of any *putative* injustice are deprived of their last and often best weapon, that of telling what really happened.

The *de facto* exclusion of certain views (of power and ideology) within the kaleidoscope of images of the world relativism promises also debars collective cumulative memory of historical events, and instead all that is permitted is a collection of individual moment-by-moment perspectives.

Balance VI: extravagance and caution

Relativism sometimes presents itself as an 'extreme' position designed to shock complacent naïve believers in the real, but critics of this position in the wider human sciences have observed that it often retreats into commonplace pleas for tolerance of diversity when it is put under pressure (Geras, 1995).

Even when relativists have been intent on discrediting 'bottom line arguments' because these appeal to a reality that we take for granted, they then pull back and reassure us that it does not mean that they refuse to accept *any* reality. On the one hand, then, there is an extravagant refusal of any 'on-trust stuff'; 'Realism deploys but disguises all this on-trust stuff, asks us to take the table-hitting as an existence of proof for tables-as-such (and much more), while relying on the audience's cooperation in commensensically ignoring how it is done' (Edwards *et al.*, 1995: 29). On the other hand, we are invited to take certain forms of knowledge for granted and to recognise certain claims as 'preposterous'; 'Claims for the unreality of the Holocaust are, like all preposterous claims, like all claims of any sort, examinable for how they are constructed and deployed' (Edwards *et al.*, 1995: 35). Even here, however, it seems that an assessment of the reality or unreality of such claims is confined to a study of how they are 'constructed and deployed'. The question is interminably shifted from what lies outside language to the way 'out there' is constructed (e.g., Potter, 1996).

This rhetorical balancing, in which extravagant outrageous assertions are retracted and more cautious fairly commonplace claims substituted, is also seen in the presentation and responses to descriptions of 'bottom line' arguments. While the authors of the 'death and furniture' paper asserted there that they were advancing the most sustained radical approach in the social sciences (Edwards *et al.*, 1995), the position was later defended on the grounds that it was merely responding to attacks by those hostile to relativism, that it was merely the 'third turn' in a conversation (Potter, 1998).

Such a rhetorical balancing act – minding the gap between absolutes and relativism, refusing to decide, tolerating a variety of perspectives and making and retracting extreme arguments about unreality – is a mixed blessing for critical psychology. Psychologists who are enthusiastic about relativism and insistent that it is the most consistent radical approach can then resort to a democratic ethos to challenge abuses of power in psychology, and ally with radicals to warrant their arguments as thoroughly critical. However, while this balancing of all accounts presents itself as more open than those who want to stop conversations, it systematically conceals its own contradictoriness, and, once again, it is up to each individual to negotiate their way through a conversation about reality claims bereft of historical – political reference points.

There is an alternative to this individualist relativism in critical realism.

For critical realism, and against

Critical realism provides a way of comprehending the rhetorical balancing acts that hold relativism in psychology in place. It both exposes positivist psychology's pretensions to model itself on what it imagines the natural sciences to be, and it grounds discursive accounts of mentation in social practices whose underlying logic and structure can, in principle, be discovered (Manicas and Secord, 1983). Harré and Secord (1972) – advocating a turn to language but also arguing as *realists* – argued way back that, first, psychology should be faithful to its object of study, and that objects of science are complex structured things with powers to act which are not always necessarily realised. A crucial part of the argument here is that different practices produce different forms of knowledge, and so realism (and critical realism) in psychology (perhaps all the more so) needs to remember that it also adheres to the principle of 'epistemic relativism' (Bhaskar, 1989). Realism thus provided a point of critique against psychology as a pretend-science in the early 1970s, and critical realism can now help us to comprehend some of the consequences of the 'turn to language' and 'turn to discourse' in the discipline in the 1980s.

However, different varieties of 'realism' are already being mobilised by those sympathetic to mainstream psychology to warrant it as a science and to rebut social constructionist critiques, to discredit research which situates psychological phenomena as reproduced and transformed in specific cultures and historical moments. The main problem for critical psychologists is that there are researchers who are quite happy to assume that the things they study are 'real', and more than happy to move beyond an over-cautious empiricism which warned them that their observations did not necessarily refer to anything under the surface of behaviour or inside the head. Realism then gives them a warrant to be all the more certain about the existence of mental representations or cognitive structures or wired-in behavioural sequences. Sometimes it is assumed that a 'realist' approach to research necessarily entails our participation in the accumulation of a corpus of knowledge in the discipline and of at least some of the 'facts' psychologists think they know about individuals and culture (e.g., Greenwood, 1989, 1991). Then psychologists can resume their well-rehearsed laboratory-experimental procedures for normalising behaviour and detecting errors in thinking (e.g., Rantzen, 1993). The following sections review specific problems in the up-take of realist arguments in psychology.

Balance VII: moderation about experimentation

There is a risk now that if 'science' is to develop, then it may be at the cost of humanist values and visions of personal–political transformation, and that critical realists may be led to accept that some of the things 'discovered' by scientific psychologists may be true, fixed and immutable. Collier argues, for example, that

> I am certainly not claiming that it is impossible to work in a scientific way with the data provided by non-psychoanalytic practices in psychology. The 'facts' of the 'empirical' psychologies are as good as the 'facts' of psychoanalysis. But the *tendency* of psychological disciplines whose data are of a non-pathological nature is to theorise them in a non-realist, empiricist way.
>
> (Collier, 1981: 15)

Perhaps it would be better, though, to say that the 'facts' of the empirical psychologies are as *bad* as the 'facts' of psychoanalysis (and more on this below, in Balance IX). Collier (1981) also points out that the 'practice' of psychoanalysis is different from that of psychology, and that this gives rise to certain kinds of 'fact'. This is a good argument, and one that is deployed by him in other defences of critical realism where he argues that different kinds of relationship to practice are likely to encourage a philosopher or scientist to believe that activity in the real world does or does not matter (e.g., Collier, 1994, 1998). That is, discussions, for example, about realism and relativism that are conducted in academic seminars are able to spiral around in playful self-reflexive circles as if the world could be dissolved into ironic banter and as if study of the world could be replaced by the study of talk (e.g., Ashmore, 1989; Edwards *et al.*, 1995). We can take Collier's argument further, to ask whether forms of knowledge which were developed in a practice which involved the objects of study, people, as participants and users of psychology services would be different (cf, Parker *et al.*, 1995; Reicher and Parker, 1993). It may be, but it would, at any rate, provide a different context for the discussion of whether or not there was a real world outside language.

Discussions of 'embodiment' in psychology situate studies of discourse in the materiality of beings who are able to use discourse follow a parallel line of argument (Nightingale, 1999; Yardley, 1996). Now, if this is, as the authors claim it to be, 'an invigorated social constructionism' which refuses, as they claim, any 'subjectivist relativism', then critical realism in psychology as I have described it so far would also be *this* kind of social constructionism (Stenner and Eccleston, 1994; Nightingale and Cromby, 1999).

Balance VIII: what non-psychologists want

The use of realism to confirm 'discoveries' and 'facts' that critical psychologists have spent so much energy trying to combat is compounded by the kinds of inter-disciplinary alliances psychologists are keen to make – and, ironically, critical psychologists are affected more than traditional psychologists here. Critical psychologists draw on different theoretical frameworks outside the discipline to contextualise what they are doing and to unravel psychology's 'subject' as a self-enclosed separate entity. Unfortunately, they often encounter fantasies in other disciplines about what 'psychology' can offer to plug the gap there or to provide an account of the individual which is missing (often for very good reasons) from political or sociological theoretical frameworks. As Condor (1997: 140) points out,

> to the extent that historians, social anthropologists, feminists, linguists or social theorists want 'us' as collaborators, they want 'us' *as psychologists*. For they also look beyond the bounds of their disciplines for the solution to their own theoretical stalemates and disciplinary crises of authority. Ironically, the constructs they grasp at as potential solutions (e.g. 'cognition', 'personality') are often just those aspects of Psychology which we are committed to rejecting.

While critical psychologists are trying to develop accounts of 'cognition' and 'memory' as culturally-specific and socially-mediated (e.g., Harré and Gillett, 1994; Middleton and Edwards, 1990), for example, even critical literary theorists and philosophers are sometimes appealing to old reductionist cognitive psychology and 'structures of cognitive-semantic representation' to halt the free play of interpretation or indeterminacy of meaning (e.g., Norris, 1996: 76). What is at issue here is a wider problem to do with the way disciplines like psychology and sociology tear apart the psychological and the social and construct accounts in such a way that it is then impossible to put the two halves together again to make a complete picture (Adorno, 1967). We have to take care, then, that critical realism does not provide a warrant to 'connect' the sciences in such a way as to buttress the power of the psy-complex, and for our allies in other disciplines to unwittingly undo some of the critical deconstruction of psychological concepts we have been carrying out in this discipline.

Balance IX: psychoanalysis as a psychology

The lure of psychoanalysis is also a specific variant of the problem of interdisciplinary attempts to make psychology plug the gap by coming up with a science of the subject to complement the work of other human sciences. This also affects psychologists who imagine that psychoanalysis provides a complete alternative system of thought, and something that will come up with 'real' psychology. Critical realism has already been deployed to support the claims of psychoanalysis in general (e.g., Collier, 1994), and to support particular versions of psychoanalysis (e.g., Rustin, 1987).

We should also note that an effect of such critical realist reappraisals of psychoanalysis is also to distort psychoanalysis itself, and to make it more like experimental psychology (e.g., Stern, 1985). Psychoanalysis may be a powerful cultural form, used as a form of explanation about development and inner states to understand ourselves, but it does not mean that it is not culturally and historically specific, and the task of a critical realist should be to understand how psychoanalysis operates as a form of knowledge rather than to put it on a scientific footing. Psychoanalysis 'works' (and so does much psychology), but we need to understand how it has been constructed as an ideological apparatus of Western culture rather than assume that it is universally true (Parker, 1997a).

Balance X: the rules of scientific debate

Realism can also be a risky rhetoric when it participates in the system of language games of a scientific community and wants to be taken seriously. Although critical realist work in the natural sciences (e.g., Bhaskar, 1978, 1986) has been invaluable to critical psychologists, who have then been able to point out that the discipline of psychology does not operate at all like the natural science it wishes it was (e.g., Harré and Secord, 1972), it can also lead us to idealise what the natural sciences actually do and to forget that they too are ideologically structured regimes of knowledge. One example here is Harré's (1986a) even-handed, fair-minded claim about the probity of the scientific community. This is then taken up by relativists who claim that *they too* are playing by the rules, that 'Relativism is the quintessentially academic position, where all truths are to-be-established' (Edwards *et al.*, 1995: 37). This 'quintessentially academic position' is then allied with science, and counterposed to religion (in whose orbit, by a deft sleight of hand, realism is positioned); 'Those who maintain that their truths are best preserved by protecting them from inquiry are followers of a religious ethic, not a scientific one' (Edwards *et al.*, 1995: 40).

We have to take care, then, to distinguish between a 'critical realist psychology' which serves those who want to rescue the discipline from the wave of critiques in the last thirty years, and 'critical realism *in* psychology' – a critical realism in and against psychology – which focuses on what psychology does to people and challenges each and every claim to truth that is deployed to make it more efficient. It is not surprising, in this light, that the depoliticising effects of relativism have been an unwelcome ally for feminists, for example, who have been battling against psychological 'science' with a political agenda (for the valuing of women's 'real' experience, for example) for years (Gill, 1995).

Critical realist psychology would temper objections to most psychology so far, provide an account of the 'individual' subject to complement work in other disciplines, offer comfort to psychoanalysis as if it were the lost truth, and respect the rules of scientific debate in the psychological community as if it were not riddled with political agendas. Critical realism in psychology, in contrast, is (as the rubric for one of the gatherings of radical psychologists in post-apartheid South Africa put it) 'a spanner in the works of the factory of truth' (Terre Blanche, 1996).

The separation and reconnection of moral–political critique

Relativist arguments in psychology are structured by a series of balancing acts which also serve to protect the apolitical individualism that the discipline usually trades in. These arguments also conceal a more dynamic dialectical contradiction between the surface of the argument (which supports relativism) and underlying stakes (which call for a realist understanding). Here it becomes clearer still how relativism operates as a form of ideology. Edwards *et al.* (1995: 37) claim that theirs is the quintessential academic position, they are actually quite right; they reproduce rather than challenge dominant bourgeois conceptions of academic knowledge as in principle *separate* from the world and as *independent* of moral-political activity. This deeply ideological position presupposes an ability to *separate* moral–political judgement from the stories we tell, and it celebrates Western culture as that which has been able to tell stories *and* step back so that we can acknowledge that they may each be valuable before choosing which one we might prefer. This rests on a Cartesian fantasy – the separation of the individual from the social and of facts from values – that critical realism helps us to understand *and* counter. A critical realist account, in contrast, examines the circumstances under which a form of misleading knowledge *requires* that misleading knowledge as a condition for those circumstances to obtain.

Critical realism helps us to see how important it is to connect moral–political positions with our knowledge about the world, and about the academic disciplines we work in. It enables us to see that relativism is, in this respect, one of the most conservative forms of knowledge in the human sciences, and psychologists who, quite rightly, argue for the importance of reflection upon the 'moral–political' stance of the researcher (e.g., Harré, 1979) play with it at their peril. Although relativism does allow us to open up psychology and show that it consists of a variety of discourses about people's minds, we have to look to the underlying social conditions and the development of the discipline as part of the 'psy-complex' to gain a more critical realist and dialectical understanding of the interests that relativism also serves. Relativism is *both* progressive *and* reactionary in psychology, and a critical realist attention to historically constituted structures of power and the ideological forms of knowledge they require allows us to grasp this dialectically.

Many relativist arguments in psychology claim to escape dominant assumptions in the discipline, but they seek to discredit realists because all of the world is not always immediately evident, ready to be summoned to show that it 'really' exists. Far from defying psychology, then, we see here the revenge and triumph of empiricism. Relativists will object that the argument in this paper is employing a variety of rhetorical devices to construct a difference between relativists and realists and to refer to things 'out there' to settle accounts. Much chapter has been wasted to pursue this line of argument, tediously tracing through these rhetorical devices, of which there must be many, of course, so giving the impression that close description is sufficient to rebut critique (e.g., Edwards *et al.*, 1995; Potter, 1996). Drawing attention to their rhetorical device of reading the text rather than addressing the argument is itself a rhetorical device, and I point this out now (another rhetorical device, of course) to save us all the trouble of engaging in a further spiral of avoidance and textual solipsism. Here we have been pointing to some of the internal logics and structures of the relativist argument, and what they conceal when they claim to reveal everything that there is, or all that can be said about the world (cf. Parker, this volume, Chapter 4). This entails an understanding of the role these arguments play in regimes of power and ideology.

Relativists may also object that what appears to be closed at different points in the argument can always be opened up again, but this too is a poor excuse for not engaging with the argument itself. Critical realists themselves insist that knowledge that we have about the world is provisional, and that we do indeed need to subscribe to 'epistemic relativism' to be scientific. The crucial difference here is that critical realism allows us to comprehend the historical, institutional context within which the human sciences operate, the ideological apparatus which provides the conditions of possibility for psychology and the moral–political interests that are served by those who pursue only relativism.

3a

Regulating Criticism
Some Comments on an Argumentative Complex

Jonathan Potter, Derek Edwards and Malcolm Ashmore

This commentary identifies a range of flaws and contradictions in Parker's critical realist position and his critique of relativism. In particular we highlight: (1) a range of basic errors in formulating the nature of relativism; (2) contradictions in the understanding and use of rhetoric; (3) problematic recruitment of the oppressed to support his argument; (4) tensions arising from the distinction between working in and against psychology. We conclude that critical realism is used to avoid doing empirical work, on the one hand, and to avoid scholarly interdisciplinary engagement, on the other.

Introduction

For some time now Ian Parker and colleagues have been developing a distinctive and complex position in psychology. It has become something of a discrete perspective in critical psychology, with its own publications, workshops, courses and now a house journal. In his critique of relativism Parker has done us a useful service by providing what is, intentionally or not, a synoptic position on the epistemological features of his programme. This attack on relativism has highlighted a range of contradictions and tensions that are worthy of comment. Indeed, the sheer *trouble* Parker has with relativism provides a pointer to trouble with his whole programme. This trouble is displayed in the argument style, which consists of a collage of assertions; it is displayed in a systematic and persistent misreading of the nature of relativism; and it is displayed in the tensions and fissures that crisscross the text. We have space for no more than a sketch of that trouble here, but it seems to arise from an intellectual trajectory that encompasses Foucault, Derrida, discourse analysis, social construction, psychoanalysis, critical realism and traditional Marxism. It incorporates power, ideology, discourse and constructionism as theoretical *and* analytic concepts. These concepts are themselves formulated in a range of contrasting ways. Parker is deeply critical of empiricism and, apparently, empirical work of all kinds, yet has produced straight methodological texts. Some of these tensions are apparent in the current article and others are features of the larger *œuvre*.

Where Parker draws on Rose and Freud in his critique of the 'psy-complex', we wish to draw a reflexive parallel to his project by drawing attention to some elements of what we will call the 'Parker-complex'. Following from his definition of the 'psy-complex', by 'the Parker-complex' we mean his dense network of theories and arguments to do with politics, philosophy and psychology that divides the 'radical' from the 'reactionary' in order to regulate the conduct of critical psychologists. Our article is a sketch of the problems with the Parker-complex using his extended condemnation of relativism as the main diagnostic tool.

We will highlight the way Parker's philosophical posture of critical realism acts as a three-layer safety curtain. The first layer helps prevent the highly combustible mix of assertions, theories and empirical claims coming into contact with substantive work in sociology, history, political science, and history of science from outside of psychology. The second layer helps insulate his work from evidence, which can be dismissed as low-level empiricism. The third layer helps insulate it from participants – people, *the* people – and their constructions and orientations. Without critical realism the whole Parker-complex could burn. That is why relativism is so dangerous. We do not have space to substantiate the existence of all these layers in the safety curtain here – but we hope that our identification of themes in his critique of relativism can support this general argument and highlight tensions in the Parker-complex.

Most of the descriptions of relativism in Parker's article are wrong. Let us take them in three clusters. First, he repeats the claim that relativism takes the view that 'anything goes', that it is a refusal to take a position, which calls for a permanent suspension of judgements about things that lie outside the text and, indeed, an abandonment of all assumptions about the world. Given the explicit repudiation of this mistaken view in Edwards *et al.* (1995), which is a main target of his paper; and also in Potter (1998), which is in a book Parker edited, and, at length, in Smith (1988, 1997) which we have cited and will cite again, we are not sure what to make of its unqualified repetition here.

The response to this claim is the same as before: 'anything goes' is a variant of realism, suggesting merely a different arrangement of cogs in the underlying generative mechanism; relativists make judgements (such as the judgements that relativism makes sense, that this article's account of relativism is wrong, and that the article is confused); relativists make assumptions about the world, but they also hold those assumptions to be permanently open to examination and critique.

The second cluster of points in the article revolves around the idea that relativism embodies a collection of polarities. For example, academic knowledge is separate from the world; the individual is separate from the social; facts are separate from values. The emphasis in Edwards *et al.* (1995) on relativism as an academic position highlights the need for scholars and philosophers to take these ideas seriously; it is certainly not claiming that they do not have relevance in 'the world'. The individual/social polarity is a mystery, given the relativist emphasis on 'truth', 'certainty' and 'evidence' as situated practices, more Durkheim than Descartes, but certainly not endorsing that polarity. Again, the suggestion that we employ a facts/values polarity is particularly odd given that it should be obvious, and it is repeated often enough, that a relativist, anti-objectivist position treats facts as inseparable from judgements.

We will not spend long on the third cluster of claims, which include the following: relativism is a celebration of Western culture; it is *no more than* a turn in a conversation; it tolerates anything; and it is a programme of balance like the BBC. Given space constraints, we will just note them as wrong and encourage readers to read the original Edwards *et al.* (1995) and compare it with Parker's glosses.

One final point is worthy of note, however. Parker treats relativism as a full-scale perspective, involving procedures for analysis and theories of society. This generates substantial confusion in a number of ways; most crucially, it confuses theorizing and analysis with philosophical argument. Relativism is not a position, equal and opposite to critical realism, let alone a large-scale perspective. For example, Barbara Herrnstein Smith helpfully glosses relativism as a 'more or less extensively theorized questioning – analysis, problematizing, critique – of the key elements of traditional objectivist thought and its attendant axiological machinery' (1988: 151); that is, not a theory at all, let alone a theory of society.

Rather than emphasize this confused view of relativism, however, the point that is of interest is in how it paves the way for presenting critical realism as, equivalently but oppositely, a full-scale perspective.

That is, critical realism becomes more than a conceptual account of what kind of thing justifiable knowledge can be, and is turned into an entire perspective on society, social change, analysis and morality, which purports, for example, to be capable of allowing us to 'comprehend the historical, institutional context within which the human sciences operate, the ideological apparatus which provides the conditions of possibility for psychology and the moral-political interests that are served by those who pursue only relativism'. Parker needs to distort relativism in this way so he can make critical realism seem to be able to do the important work it is needed for.

Rhetorical troubles

One of the most interesting features of Parker's article is the trouble it has with rhetoric. Parker develops a traditional contrast between 'rhetoric' as a set of persuasive tricks, which can be tediously analysed, and a proper appreciation and evaluation of 'argument'. Three observations are worth making about this. First, as will be readily apparent to anyone who reads it, quite a lot of his own article is an attempt to document persuasive tricks, deft sleights of hand, and so on in relativist work. So his complaint about rhetorical analysis applies to his own article as much as to anyone else's work.

The second observation is also about consistency, but of a more general kind. Take Derrida's work, for example. Parker has used Derrida's writing for a decade – 'deconstructing' *The Archers*, psychopathology, social psychology and various other things in the course of it. However, one of the central features of Derrida's critique of philosophy has been his resistance to a rationalist distinction between 'the argument' and the 'style of its presentation'. The radical nature of the work for philosophy comes from resisting the abstraction of argument and considering truth as the outcome of the figurative organization of philosophical texts. Parker may try to argue/rhetorically persuade that his emphasis on the importance and unimportance of rhetoric is a kind of 'balance' – but it looks like confusion to us (cf. Hepburn, 1999).

Third, and more generally, Parker's intellectual career has involved regularly promoting (as well as criticizing) discourse analysis and more recently discursive psychology (Parker, 1997b). If discourse and its rhetorical organization turn out now to be so tedious and unimportant, how does this fit with this continuing concern with it (e.g. Parker and the Bolton Discourse Network, 1999)? Put another way, what can this programme of work now be offering? We will return to that.

Recruiting the tortured, oppressed and murdered

Parker recruits the tortured, oppressed and murdered people of the world to his philosophical position (critical realism), as if their suffering and death bore testimony to his vision, and sided with his (ambivalent and occasioned) dislike of non-Foucauldian discourse analysis, conversation analysis, ethnomethodology, and epistemic relativism. Conversely he links our arguments to notorious Holocaust-deniers such as Faurisson who, he claims, would 'delight' in our arguments. This is extraordinary and distasteful. Faurisson should have no more truck with our arguments than Parker. Indeed, a more telling comparison is between Faurisson and Parker in their philosophy, we hasten to add, not in their politics which are poles apart. They are both realists; their disagreement is about precisely what is real. Both prioritize politics over epistemics, preserving a favoured version of how the world works while using relativistic critique against opposing positions. Both see the opposition as serving entrenched ideological and economic interests, whose 'real' nature underlies a veil of appearances, the removal of which is the analytic, polemical task each of them embraces. Faurisson is Parker's analytical mirror-image, preserved in form but inverted in content. He is surely no relativist.

The use of Geras to claim that relativism will be no help in the solution to war crimes is particularly odd given that earlier Parker had celebrated the use of relativism as an important feature of his own rhetorical (yet non-rhetorical) armoury against the (realist?) orthodoxies of psychology. The quote from Geras suggests that focusing our analysis on 'discourses or language games or social practices' deprives victims of oppression or injustice 'of their last and often best weapon, that of telling what really happened'. It does not deprive them of anything of the sort. We have often suggested that realist, experiential claims and narratives are among the most effective rhetorical weapons that anyone can use (Edwards, 1997; Potter, 1996).

Further, how is it to be claimed that 'telling what really happened' *is* such an effective 'weapon'? How do people get it accepted, that that is what they are doing? How *are* reality-claims made, contested, undermined, bolstered against refutation? Is that not the very thing we are studying? Of course, the Geras/Parker line depends on there being something else going on, that might serve as a 'weapon' – that 'telling what really happened' is precisely and merely that, telling what really happened. It is difficult to know where to begin with such a notion. It begs all the questions. How is it so effective, not only for victims to do it, but for Geras to write about it, and for Parker to quote it, given its self-contradictory weakness: that such a 'telling' is somehow an effective weapon beyond the analysis of discourse and social practices? This is a view of telling apparently untouched by Wittgenstein, Derrida and Sacks.

The Geras example works, first, by ontological gerrymandering (authoring-in a reality beyond the text), which is how vignettes of this kind generally work, in circular fashion. Second, it uses a 'death trope' (who would deny victims of oppression their claims to truth?). We find it distasteful to recruit the oppressed and dying into arguments for philosophical positions on textual analysis and realism in this way.

A final point is worth underlining. The Holocaust was not brought into this debate by us to support relativism. It was introduced by realists in their criticisms of relativism, and continues here to be introduced by realists in a rhetorical case against relativism.

Critical realist psychology and critical realism in and against psychology

In one of the most telling sections of Parker's paper he frets over the relation of critical realism to psychology. His solution to a perceived dilemma, over psychologists starting to use critical realism to further psychology's reactionary ends, is to emphasize the importance of taking a position of 'critical realism in and against psychology'. This seems to be a useful distinction. However, it raises two questions.

First, should we now consider Parker's output (including the varied writings on method, the new *Annual Review of Critical Psychology*, his contribution to an introductory book on critical psychology, and so on) as not part *of* psychology but *about* it?

Second, if this output is not part of psychology, where is it coming from? An obvious answer might be that it comes from taking a sociological stance, or a historical, or a political science perspective. After all Nik Rose, inventor of the concept 'psy-complex', has conducted his scholarly Foucauldian critiques of psychology from a base in sociology for some time. The problem for Parker is that if he took this route he would have to address the grounding and coherence of his disparate collection of theoretical and analytic concepts.

Ironically, and despite the conservative implications for interdisciplinary work, Parker favours having 'our allies in other disciplines' each keep to their own patch, and take their understanding of psychology from him and his colleagues. That would indeed prevent those 'allies' making embarrassing appeals to the very notions that Parker is seeking to undermine. Meanwhile, however, his own importation of concepts from philosophy, politics, Marxist sociology, post-structuralism, etc., shows no sign of struggle, no sign of their being wrested from agonistic debates and crises of their own. When taken and applied to psychology's problems, they merely shine forth and clarify what is Real.

Although we have, for the most part, followed Parker's request that we abstain from tediously tracing rhetorical devices, there is something particularly striking about the paragraph in which he introduces the distinction between critical realist psychology and critical realism in and against psychology. What intrigues us is the *non sequitur* at the centre of the paragraph. We quote:

> [critical realism in and against psychology] challenges each and every claim to truth that is deployed to make it more efficient. It is not surprising, *in this light* [!], that the depoliticizing effects of relativism have been an unwelcome ally for feminists.
>
> (emphasis and exclamation added)

Parker started his article by saying that he is happy to use relativism as a locally useful strategy precisely for undermining psychology's truth-claims. So it is notable that it is *now*, and just *here*, described as depoliticizing. Moreover, the construction textually mobilizes feminists on his side and as a general category, as if feminists in general and as a whole found relativism unwelcome. Of course, there is a wide range of feminist positions, some critical realist (e.g. Gill, 1995), some relativist (e.g. Hepburn, 2000), many rather uninterested in what could easily be seen as an arcane epistemological cul-de-sac removed from practical concerns about exploitation and visions of emancipation. Indeed, critical points supporting relativist positions from a feminist perspective have recently been made from an explicitly feminist perspective by Bronwyn Davies (1998) in a book edited by Parker himself.

Our general point, then, is that this *non sequitur* appears here, because it draws attention away from one of the most important tensions within Parker's work. Let us end with this tension.

Trouble in the Parker-complex

We started with the suggestion that critical realism serves as a safety curtain, or firewall, to prevent the incendiary mix of theories, positions and claims that make up the Parker-complex from bursting into flame. We have noted how Parker turns and misdescribes relativism into a full-scale perspective to facilitate turning the much more important (for him) construction of critical realism as an equal and opposite perspective. Making critical realism this big means it can then do the theoretical work that would have to be done by history, sociology and political science. In other words, these important questions that have engaged large numbers of researchers and theorists across the social sciences seem to be answered by *a priori* philosophizing.

Critical realism is built up in this way to provide the space for criticizing psychology without having to be troubled with interdisciplinary scholarship. Parker does not have to engage with Stuart Hall's attempts to reformulate notions of ideology in relation to new social formations, for example. Nor does he need to take seriously (nor, indeed, take in any way at all) Barry Barnes's work, say, on the role of social interests in scientific development. He can make assertions about ideology and the political role of science as if they were straightforward issues that have long been sorted out. The paradoxical consequence of this is that, for all his criticisms of psychology, Parker needs a strong psychology to work in and against. It is psychology and its obfuscating legacy of secure theoretical walls that allows these limitations in interdisciplinary scholarship to remain hidden. The danger is that the legacy of the Parker-complex will not be radical critique of the very existence of an independent discipline of psychology but merely a reassertion of its power and sovereignty.

Let us end by noting that there is, and always has been, a space for a lively and critical Marxist position in (and against) psychology. However, the critical realist enterprise developed in this article raises a number of questions. What is its stance on science, evidence and academic scholarship? How does the critique of empiricism square with the production of methods textbooks? How does the critique of rhetoric mesh with championing of deconstruction? How precisely should we understand ideology in the arguments developed? For example, does the support of Foucauldian over conversation analytic notions of discourse not extend to supporting the Foucauldian critique of Marxist notions of ideology? What kind of thing is the 'bourgeois polity', and how does it relate to class and nationhood in a world after Gordon Gekko and George Soros? Parker could valuably bring the Marxist passion about exploitation and inequality to bear on psychological issues, but we think there is some work to be done first.

Acknowledgement

We would like to thank Alexa Hepburn, David Middleton and Sue Speer for comments on an earlier version of this chapter.

3b
The Quintessentially Academic Position

Potter *et al.*'s response to my 'Against Relativism in Psychology, on Balance' neatly summarises what they take a 'critical realist' position to be and how 'relativists' should defend themselves. Their response also illustrates why the version of critical realism I elaborated is more thoroughly critically relativist than Potter *et al.* assume and how their version of relativism actually rests on a rather uncritical subscription to realism.

If the world, and academic debate within it, divided neatly into fixed, consistent and self-evident positions then this 'relativism–realism' debate would be clear-cut and quickly decided. This is exactly what Potter *et al.*'s response seem to assume, and, paradoxically, they betray motifs in studies of discourse which do attend to flexibility, contradiction and (particularly in Foucauldian work) meaning produced in relations of power. I took these motifs seriously in my 'Against Relativism in Psychology, on Balance' and have shown how dialectical critique can take them further in relation to relativism, linguistic idealism and 'postmodern' theory (Parker, this volume, Chapters 2 and 4). What Potter *et al.* are up to is not mere paradox, however, for it reveals how they shift under pressure, by virtue of their own subscription to a particular academic–political location, from their version of relativism into uncritical realism.

Uncritical realism of the type exemplified by Potter *et al.* thinks it is able to tell us what relativism really is as something fixed and what a 'mistaken view' of it would be. So if Gergen (1991: 7), for example, celebrates relativism in contemporary culture as a world in which 'anything goes' this, I suppose, would be ruled out of court. There is a curious assumption that there are real 'correct' representations and people like me who 'distort relativism'. The paradox here is that it is the 'relativists' who characterise what they are doing as if it were a thing and in the process they turn realist to defend it.

Uncritical realism must then set itself against those who are inconsistent or, rather, those these relativists assume *must* be inconsistent for their caricature to work. Since we are dealing here with writers who are concerned with attributions of intentions in argument as interested 'stakes', it is pertinent to ask what the stakes are for them when they assume that I will 'worry more about inconsistencies' and when they puzzle about whether the different things I do are really part *of* psychology or *about* it. With respect to my work on discourse and my critique of discourse analysis they pose the question 'how does this fit?', as if it should. Here the paradox is that my inconsistency becomes problematic for those who are by now in this turn of the conversation only ostensibly relativists.

Uncritical realism in discursive psychology – the kind of psychology that has spawned relativism as a credo rather than as a practical–tactical guide to action – all too often manifests itself in crass textual empiricism, and its English variants carry the marks of a philosophical position as an ideological 'empiricist discourse' (Easthope, 1999). This is a world divided between what is self-evident in a text or in an argument (and its correlative 'basic errors') on the one hand and 'rhetorical weapons' on the other, and the paradox here also exposes Potter *et al.*'s claim to transcend a fact/value polarity or a distinction between the social and the individual. They themselves tell us how things really are as but the background for a subjective evaluation of what is right and wrong. Why, for example, is the 'recruitment of the oppressed' 'problematic'? It turns out, twice-stated in their response, to be because they find it 'distasteful'.

To understand how relativists so easily fold into uncritical realism we do need the kind of sensitivity to language that the thorough-going epistemic relativism espoused by critical realism provides us, and we need to embed our understanding of the paradoxes displayed by Potter *et al.* in a dialectical critique of where their argument comes from and the functions it serves.

The relativism–realism debate is often rather tedious. Why? Potter *et al.* seem to imagine that the only way of escaping this 'arcane epistemological cul-de-sac' is to 'recruit' the oppressed *et al.* into an academic argument. This is 'distasteful' to them, but this is the only way it could be because, after all, 'relativism is the quintessentially academic position' (Edwards *et al.*, 1995: 37). So they avoid questions of theory and ideology and press all the more firmly down the 'safety curtain' that divides academic argument from everyday life. Critical realism, however, *relativises* the relationship between this debate and practical concerns so that we are able to see how academic positions in general and (in this case) psychology in particular function in certain appara-tuses of power which (most of the time) reproduce exploitation and inequality. Marxists (among others) address exactly these issues, but they are not 'psychological issues' at all, and an effective challenge to them precisely means that we should not 'each keep to our own patch' either in disciplinary or academic terms.

Once again, when uncritical relativists defend themselves they take certain realities for granted, and while they are all too 'realistic' about what (they assume) defines 'empirical work', 'scholarly critique' and an 'academic position', a thorough-going critical relativism is necessary to disturb these realities, and the part the psy-complex plays in enforcing them.

4
Against Wittgenstein
Materialist Reflections on Language in Psychology

Wittgenstein's writing offers to psychologists a series of critical perspectives on concepts regularly employed by the discipline, and it assists in the deconstruction of facile appeals to notions of 'cognition', 'drive' or 'self' in which traditional psychology trades. However, academic and popular representations of the Wittgensteinian focus on language, and on the discursive setting for all varieties of mental and cultural phenomena also threaten to obscure the material structuring of contemporary institutional power, power that both inhibits and incites speech. Selected aphorisms from Wittgenstein that have been used to warrant radical linguistic reflections on psychology are examined in this chapter, and it is argued that these theoretical points need to be contextualised and reworked to accommodate an historical materialist account.

Critical theoretical work has an acknowledged place within psychology now in large part because of the 'turn to language' that occurred in the late 1960s and early 1970s (Harré and Secord, 1972; Gauld and Shotter, 1977). This turn to language, and then to discourse, has provided a helpful climate for people who wanted to explore the way subjectivity is *socially constructed*, and that social constructionist impulse underpins much critical work which operates with post-structuralist, feminist or even Marxist agendas. However, there is also something worrying about social constructionism when it is taken too seriously as a full-blown world-view, particularly when the social construction of phenomena is reduced to the work of language alone. It then scorns the possibility of any other agenda, because the only agenda it can tolerate is the 'social construction' of reality. In many popular interpretations of this position in critical psychology this is also taken to be equivalent to *relativism*, a world-view in which it seems as if everything goes. This is a world in which a multiplicity of realities jostle alongside one another, and none must be permitted to have a claim to a better account.

One writer who has been especially influential within relativis varieties of social constructionism, one who has provided many of the language games that its advocates play, is Wittgenstein. It is worth stepping back from his work, then, and asking whether we can both take it seriously as a social constructionist account that is helpful to critical discursive work *and* contextualise it more thoroughly to bring in phenomena of power and history. We need both to acknowledge its value *and* to provide a better account.

One of the advantages of social constructionism in psychology, and it is a tendency that is strengthened by Wittgenstein's writing, is that everything is put into question, it is for 'a pluralism in which *nothing goes*' (Curt, 1994; Sawacki, 1991). What we need to do now is to step back and say that Wittgenstein himself should not be exempt from that critical scrutiny, and we can develop an historically grounded account which looks to the material effects of what has gone before, what made Wittgenstein tick, and what we often forget when we get caught in Wittgensteinian language games. The trouble is that Wittgenstein also smuggles some presuppositions into critical psychology that are less helpful than his work first appears. These presuppositions fuel relativism, and I will deal with those by examining some of the statements that Wittgenstein makes, statements that are picked up by social constructionists in the discipline.

In order to do this we have first of all to emphasise the difference between a starting point on the one hand and presuppositions on the other. One of the tricks that relativism often plays upon its enemies is to elide the difference between these two things. In order to develop a critical argument it is necessary to have a theoretical starting point. That starting point is always the socially, historically constructed ground from which we develop an argument, not at all a pre-given fixed point of truth, as social constructionists sometimes seem to fear and relativists always presume. Presuppositions, on the other hand, are the notions we slip in to catch the reader in a way of thinking, a way of speaking. Presuppositions are concealed accounting devices that produce and sustain, what we would call in Foucauldian terminology, 'truth effects' (Foucault, 1980). In Marxist terms, they would be seen as supports for particular ideological forms (Eagleton, 1991). This chapter attempts to avoid presuppositions, no doubt unsuccessfully, and I will argue that we can find in Wittgenstein's work a valuable critique of presuppositions that govern psychology, both as discipline and popular knowledge.

The starting point for this chapter, then, is an engagement with, and continuation of, the history of a particular practice of critical reflection on ideology and psychology, that of historical materialism. As a theoretical position it draws upon analyses of structures of class, gender and culture. These analyses trace the emergence of particular forms of economic organization in contemporary Western culture and their mental cognates. As a research position it draws upon a history of Marxist and Foucauldian perspectives on language and social structure.

I share with many Wittgensteinian writers the Marxist (and Foucauldian) view that psychological phenomena are culturally and historically determined. However, I use Marxist notions of dialectics and class structure as devices to illustrate shortcomings in Wittgenstein's work. These devices, insofar as they operate as rhetorical devices, lead the reader into a particular way of seeing the world (indeed, much as a Wittgensteinian 'language game' would), but their function in the chapter is to 'show' something of the nature of Wittgenstein's argument. Wittgenstein, like Marx and Foucault, draws attention to the cultural and historical specificity of psychological verities, but he misses issues of power. It would not be satisfactory to 'solve' this problem by simply adding to Wittgenstein's descriptions the point that social actors enjoy certain rights to speak and that these are given by institutional and discursive structures. Rather, we need to draw upon the historical materialist view of structures of power being tied to economic class interests and riven by contradiction, and once those notions of historical sedimentation and resistance are included in the picture we necessarily break from the Wittgensteinian frame. We need to attend to the contradictory progressive and stultifying impulse of Wittgenstein's work which 'returns language to social practice at the same time as too complacently endorsing existing practices' (Eagleton, 1981: 153). When I deploy Marxist notions to show the incompleteness of Wittgenstein's picture, I shall also, in the course of the argument, draw attention to the way post-structuralist (Derridean and Foucauldian) notions could also accomplish much of the same critical conceptual work. There is, incidentally, a telling paradox in the development of French philosophy whereby its retreat from radical political engagement in the work of Sartre, Foucault and Derrida has been accompanied by a renewed interest in 'ordinary language' and Wittgensteinian accounts (Descombes, 1980; Montefiore, 1983). In the process of developing this critique of Wittgenstein, I hope to avoid a simple assertion of Marxism as a set of presuppositions that should 'replace' Wittgensteinian ones.

It is necessary to start, then, with due acknowledgment of the value of Wittgenstein's writing to critical psychology, to the ways in which his work has been deployed to 'deconstruct' the discipline. I will describe the Wittgensteinian challenge to psychological models before moving on to consider problems in his account of logic and usage in language, and then to his own disturbing and paradoxical appeal to 'anchors' to meaning which are imagined to lie inside and outside language, and thence to the cultural context for the reception of his account of language.

Wittgenstein and psychology

The Wittgensteinian critique of psychologism, of the essentialising of certain mental activities and the projection of these into the heads of individuals, has a remit far wider than the discipline of psychology itself. This is significant, for it both indicates something of the cultural appeal of Wittgenstein's writing in academic and wider cultural life and the ways in which psychologists using his work are dependent upon *representations* of Wittgenstein as well as the particular texts that bear his name as author. Wittgenstein's work has been of interest to sociologists of science, for example, who have been keen to unravel the truth claims of those who claim to have privileged access to 'reality' (Phillips, 1977). Scientific practice, for these writers, can be seen as a form of life into which members are inducted, and their observations are made possible by the interplay of persuasive strategies that interpret reality in different ways. Wittgenstein (1953) says, for example:

> We feel as if we had to penetrate phenomena: our investigation, however, is directed not towards phenomena, but, as one might say: towards the '*possibilities*' of phenomena.
>
> (no. 90)

Wittgenstein thus draws our attention away from discrete mechanisms in the mind or the sense that a particular individual might make of the world to the way the world is structured such that it constitutes certain phenomena (such as mechanisms or individual experiences). The Wittgensteinian question, one which animates much critical work in psychology, is 'what linguistic, cultural and historical circumstances have made these phenomena, that psychology takes as given, come to be?' It is in Wittgensteinian spirit, then, that we should also consider the ways in which representations of Wittgenstein's arguments structure the understanding that psychologists, including critical psychologists, have of his work. Wittgenstein could not write as an independent monad, separated from the circumstances in which he lived, and the cultural *'possibilities'* of the Wittgensteinian phenomenon include writings in literature and cinema. A thorough-going scepticism about the nature of 'reality' and of human 'nature' has also made Wittgenstein's work appealing to activists in sexual politics because it appears to offer, in its popular form, a different vision of relationships than simply determined by a fixed 'human nature'.

The Derek Jarman (1993) film *Wittgenstein*, which was initially scripted by Terry Eagleton, is an example of a progressive politically motivated reading and representation of Wittgenstein's ideas, and also an example of how different 'readings' of Wittgenstein can be generated for different contexts. The Jarman film presented Wittgenstein as if he were an English eccentric disconnected from wider modernist debates, and itself is an eccentric reading, to the extent that it broke from the more critical published script (Eagleton, 1993). Nevertheless, the film provides a setting for the elaboration of Wittgenstein's arguments in context, and thus allows us to explore how issues of context may throw some of the more abstract pronouncements of the writer into question. The wider cultural reception of Wittgenstein's work, which includes cartoon introductions (Heaton and Groves, 1994), is an important context for the way his arguments have persuaded some critics working in psychology.

Wittgenstein's anti-psychology

Wittgenstein's main target in psychology is the cognitivist fallacy that it is possible to understand activities by conceptualising them as formal processes or structures operating inside the head. It has been argued, for example, that:

> Wittgenstein rejects the possibility of a scientific psychology; that is, any theory that purports to explain behavior in terms of inner mental causes.
>
> (Williams, 1985: 205)

This is a definition of 'scientific psychology' that some critical psychologists would reject (e.g., Tolman, 1994), and Wittgenstein's writing could be seen as supportive of attempts to reformulate the ways in which the objects and procedures of a properly scientific psychology could be understood (Harré and Secord, 1972). Nevertheless, it does draw attention to the ways in which Wittgenstein's work has been used to challenge the way in which the discipline has characterised itself as a 'scientific' enterprise.

This is useful for those of us who want to emphasise the discursive nature of human action, and its cultural historical context. Wittgenstein argues along a number of lines that cause trouble for traditional psychology. Williams (1985) identifies four. First, causal explanations are inappropriate for understanding what we take to be mental phenomena. Second, practices of recognition or memory are not mental phenomena at all. Third, an appeal to inner processes provides pseudo-explanations. Fourth, the practice of introspection does not penetrate to some hidden interior realm. It should be noted that ambiguities and contradictions in Wittgenstein's writing open his work to different interpretations, some of which, for example, would rescue causal accounts of mental phenomena from his work (Gustafson, 1984). However, some writers have gone so far as to argue that the first two arguments, having to do with causal notions and the necessity for mental explanations, have forced a retrenchment by cognitive theorists such that the realm of 'scientific psychology' has virtually been abandoned (Williams, 1985).

Although Fodor (1975, 1983) attacks Wittgenstein for being a behaviourist and mistaking the goals and methods of psychology, some Wittgensteinians interpret Fodor's (1975) shift of emphasis from the explanation of intentional activities, perception and learning to an account of discrete 'modules' which, he believes, would be free of contextual and linguistic matters (Fodor, 1983), as a retreat which is a result of the Wittgensteinian assault (Williams, 1985). In this view, Fodor's shift of emphasis from 'cognitive' phenomena to strictly neurophysiologically-based processes represents a failure to account for the role of linguistic context in thought, and so a triumph for Wittgensteinian arguments. Although this could be seen as an over-optimistic view of the impact of Wittgenstein's work in psychology, it does indicate the way in which Wittgenstein can be helpful to critics of cognitivism.

Williams argues that both Fodor and Stich (1983) propose supposedly 'autonomous' descriptions that are closely tied to the domain of *neurophysiology*, and they have thus retreated to such an extent that they have virtually abandoned attempts to provide psychological explanations. Stich (1983) is more optimistic about the distinct contribution of psychology to providing a 'descriptive language' which would be sufficiently 'opaque' and thus superior to 'folk psychology', but the scope of the description he proposes is very limited. One of the consequences is that we are forced to recognise that 'psychological theory simply won't explain what we thought it was going to explain, namely why we engage in the actions we do, what motivates us; the nature of memory, recognition; how we learn' (Williams, 1985: 216).

Even if cognitive psychology has not given up its domain of study to Wittgenstein, a space is opened up for linguistic, contextual and social accounts of human practice. The rooting of psychological description in 'ordinary language' encourages us to treat the discipline of psychology too as a social construction and provides, if nothing else, another legitimating discourse for radical critique in the discipline. And the relativist dynamic to Wittgenstein's writing is also corrosive of other varieties of psychology as well as cognitivism. This relativism dissolves the truth claims of the discipline. Despite attempts by psychologists arguing against the cognitivist tradition – those working within behaviourism, for example – to draw Wittgenstein into alliance with them (e.g. Begelman, 1975), the sustained ground-clearing that his perspective on language invites makes his work as opposed to a strict Skinnerian approach as much as it does to Skinner's critics such as Chomsky (cf. Waller, 1977). Wittgenstein (1973) also argues, against Freud's assertion that the unconscious must be understand causally, that 'the fact that there *aren't* actually any such laws seems important' (ibid.: 77). Again, the attempt of a psychological account to fix human subjectivity in a particular pattern of causal explanation, one which would individualise and reproduce present-day images of experience, is challenged. The claim that psychology provides a distinct knowledge and expertise is thus thrown into question.

There is a problem: at the same time as Wittgenstein's writing can be used to disturb the status quo in psychology, it threatens to reinforce a picture of the world which itself appears undisturbed by the phenomena of ideology and power. What we must do then is to reinterpret some of the assertions and examples that Wittgenstein provides to show that these phenomena *permeate* language. We can then turn to consider how ideology and power conditioned the production and reception of Wittgenstein. There is an alliance and a tension between social constructionism and relativism that we need to be clear about here. Insofar as social constructionism helps to develop an historically materialist account of the development of particular forms of social structure, action and experience in a society at a given point in time, it represents a positive addition to the range of conceptual debate in psychology. Insofar as relativism corrodes each and every critical vantage point on the theories and practices of the discipline of psychology at the very same moment as it bathes psychology in its sceptical light, it represents a danger for radicals who participate in that conceptual debate. Again, the crux of the matter is the way that power should be understood, and I want to argue that it is necessary to pit an acount of power – as something structured through discourse and institutions and riven with conflict – against Wittgenstein. We must use what there is of his work that is social constructionist, and turn that against what there is in him that is relativist.

Words, the world, and power

Wittgenstein is concerned throughout his work with the relationship between language and reality, and with language as a form of reality. Although the 1922 *Tractatus Logico-Philosophicus* (Wittgenstein, 1961) and the 1953 *Philosophical Investigations* (Wittgenstein, 1953) are usually seen as separate systems of thought, it is possible to see a common thread running through his writings (e.g., Pears, 1971). It has been argued that these apparently different systems of thought have:

> ... a unity of purpose far stronger than their surface differences. Conceived as *doctrines*, the work of the two periods looks very different. Conceived as *activities*, as Wittgenstein would have preferred, the work remains on the same path.
>
> (Silverman and Torode, 1980: 44)

These 'activities', as Silverman and Torode (1980) point out, have a slightly different focus in each of the two main periods of writing. The first period, that of the *Tractatus,* is concerned with 'rules of logic', and the second period, that of the *Philosophical Investigations*, with 'rules of usage'. The analysis in the following sections of this chapter revolves around those two different concerns. Let us start with the first of these, the rules of logic.

Rules of logic

Wittgenstein's work carries with it presuppositions that could paralyse a critical perspective. In the case of conceptual interventions in psychology, they could reinforce traditional views of what the aims and limits of the discipline, and those working within it, are and should be. I will focus in this section on the ideological functions such presuppositions serve. Let us take the first and last sentences from the *Tractatus Logico-Philosophicus*, each often quoted, and which together trap the reader in a circle of empiricism and stoicism.

The first sentence of the Tractatus asserts that 'The world is all that is the case' (Wittgenstein, 1961, section 1.1). This statement will make sense, 'work', perhaps, if it is reduced to the level of a conceptual argument, but as soon as it is considered in a practical context, instantiated at any point in the material world, the contradictions within it start to unravel it. By 'material world' here, I mean the wider historical and political context which bears upon immediately apparent forms of life, and I will be turning to some arguments within the tradition of Marxist dialectics to look at the way a simple and exclusive attention to the immediately apparent world obscures what has rendered that world possible. I have chosen arguments from Trotsky's (1973) writing, and, though I do not have space here to go into it in more detail, this seems a politically better source, as part of a sustained struggle against power, than, say, Mao's (1967) writing on similar issues (Parker, 1996a). Dialectics is being used here as a tool to open up insufficiencies in the way Wittgenstein appears to characterise 'the world' here. The text I draw upon, where Trotsky discusses the difference between Aristotelian syllogisms and dialectics was originally published in 1939, when the political consequences of neglecting a theoretical understanding of social processes in favour of pragmatism was a matter of life and death. It was death for the many who perished under Stalin, and for Trotsky himself. I will turn to the Foucauldian question of how the 'conditions of possibility' for forms of logic in society may be understood in the next section of the chapter.

To refer to 'the world' as something that could be 'all that is the case' is immediately to fall foul of one of the core arguments of social constructionism itself, an argument that Marxist discussion of dialectics anticipates. Take, for example, the assertion that 'A' is equal to 'A', a syllogism which has been a starting point of polemics in Marxist philosophy and politics over the dialectical interrelationships between things in the world and their relationship with time. As a conceptual trick, the 'A' that we imagine here can indeed be perfectly mapped upon the 'A' we imagine there. In our mind, or in language as the Wittgensteinian case in point, these two 'A's seem to be able to be in exactly the same place. However, as Trotsky (1973) has pointed out,

> ... in reality 'A' is not equal to 'A'. This is easy to prove if we observe these two letters under a lens – they are quite different from each

other. But, one can object, the question is not of the sise or the form of the letters, since they are only symbols for equal quantities, for instance, a pound of sugar. The objection is beside the point; in reality a pound of sugar is never equal to a pound of sugar – a more delicate scale always discloses a difference.

(1973: 49)

Now, a similar argument could be developed from writers who have been more fashionable in recent social constructionist writing, from Derrida (1981), for example, deconstructing the way a term always 'differs' from itself. A dialectical argument is more apposite in the context of the present chapter because it will more directly link us with an historical materialist view of ideology and power. It forms, we might say, a 'family resemblance' to the arguments developed later in the chapter around the cultural appeal of Wittgenstein. Trotsky (1973) goes on to argue that to presuppose that an object can exist outside time, and therefore be without change, and without differing from a similar object, is to engage in a philosophical fallacy: 'the example "A" is equal to "A" signifies that a thing is equal to itself if it does not change, that is, if it does not exist' (ibid.: 49).

Trotsky's point here is not only a *reductio ad absurdum* of Wittgenstein's world-view, but a critique, like deconstructive critique, of the ways in which Wittgenstein's 'world' becomes conceived as something impossibly self-identical and static. Wittgenstein is presupposing an identity between two sides of an equation, 'the world' and 'all that is the case'. The problem is that if either side of the equation cannot be identical to itself, or to the other, then the proposition collapses. From the moment the proposition is written onward, and through the very moment the writing takes place, the world *changes* and, in various ways, it is always both more and less than 'all that is the case'.

It may be objected, in Wittgenstein's defence, that all that is being offered here is a linguistic representation of the 'world', and that no such claims are being made about the world itself. There is a strong current of Wittgensteinian writing (Shotter, 1993), and one which explores the similarities between Wittgenstein and Marx (Easton, 1983; Rubinstein, 1981), that would eschew such a distinction between 'language' and 'the real world'. We are not concerned with what we imagine Wittgenstein 'meant' though, rather with how his statements function. It is pertinent at this point, then, to move on to consider what Wittgenstein has to say about speech and what may lie outside it.

The famous last sentence of the *Tractatus* opines that 'What we cannot speak about we must pass over in silence' (Wittgenstein, 1961, section 6.5). Here, we are faced with a proposition that seems 'commonsensical', but which compounds the problems that we have explored so far. Again, the issue is how we conceptualise *change*. As the process of change continues apace, we can catch aspects of the world conceptually, to label and compare them, and a degree of dialectical 'tolerance' is needed to hold together objects that cannot really be the same, and which are internally marked by contradictory movements of matter, and textual practice. In this light it is surely logically right to reject Wittgenstein's picture of the world, a picture which appears so far to be quite static, and to work instead with fluidity and contradiction. Despite the argument that Wittgenstein's work is meant to be a challenge to any notion of language as a 'picture' of the world (Shotter, 1993), if we look at how his work actually functions as a kind of account with certain rules of interpretation that govern the community of Wittgensteinian's and other relativists, we see that it does indeed have the character of a 'picture'. This picture provides a particular representation of the world which sits uneasily with other representations, even those representations which also deny their status to be such things. Even the common sense that Wittgenstein celebrates breaks, in ordinary usage, from the formal categories he employs. In a statement that appears to anticipate a Derridean deconstruction of the fixity of taken-for-granted concepts, Trotsky (1973) points out that '"Common sense" is characterised by the fact that it systematically exceeds dialectical "tolerance"' (ibid.: 50).

Again, Wittgenstein treats 'what we cannot speak about' as a state of affairs which renders the search for other ways of speaking a hopeless exercise. It may be objected in Wittgenstein's defence that he is simply pointing out that what is known about the world is known *within* language, and that it is a mistake to imagine an extra-discursive 'reality' lying behind that which is spoken. If this is the case, 'all that is the case', then Wittgenstein's proposition is a tautology, and, furthermore, like other tautologies, it contains the conditions of its impossibility within it. Even if we were to abandon the attempt to comprehend the world through an historical materialist framework, and turn for the moment to Derrida (1981) for help, we would still have to ask what a 'silence' could possibly be like which did not presuppose something which was not, once upon a time, or potentially, 'silent'? Here we are also moving into the realm of Foucault's (1976a) work on the construction of objects through the sustained exercise of 'silence'. At this point, having deconstructed and situated Wittgenstein's own picture of the world, we move from the early Wittgenstein to his later work.

Intermission

The story of the development of Wittgenstein's life and work (Monk, 1990) has it that after the *Tractatus* was finished, just at the end of the First World War, Wittgenstein thought he had solved the problems of philosophy, and so went to work as a village school teacher near Vienna. The break from the rather closed formal system of language in the *Tractatus* came when the Italian Marxist economist Piero Sraffa drew Wittgenstein's attention to the way language can only work in context. Sraffa's example, which was a Neapolitan insult consisting of the fingers being stroked quickly up the neck and flexed out towards the offending party, also makes clear that when one speaks of language, one must also speak more generally of signifying systems, including gesture. This turn to the 'use' of language, which was to be expressed in the *Philosophical Investigations* (Wittgenstein, 1953) still carries with it a silence though, silence about power. So let us turn to look at rules of usage.

Rules of usage

From simple statements about the nature of the world, which may operate in profoundly ideological ways, we now move to an insistence in Wittgenstein's work that such statements must necessarily be true. These statements then operate in ways which cement ideology with power. There is an example of Wittgenstein at work in the recent Jarman (1993) film about him which captures well the way in which the statements that something 'is all that is the case' and that one should 'pass over in silence' the possibility that there may be more or other things, can function as coercive prescriptions.

The film serves an important function in the way Wittgenstein's contribution should be conceptualised and assessed. Among the many productive notions that Wittgenstein provides critical psychology with is the argument that meaning is a function of *use*, and not of the fixed sense that one might be tempted to discover in an original author's text. The film is part of the wider Wittgensteinian canon that makes his work make sense to those wanting to use his writings. It is also significant that although the published script and accompanying introduction to the film are critical of Wittgenstein at points (Eagleton, 1993), the author has used Wittgenstein himself to 'solve' problems of ideology in Marxism (Eagleton, 1991), and the director (Jarman, 1993)

chose to break from that script to provide a more positive representation. Eagleton (1993) points out that Wittgenstein was 'an odd sort
of materialist' who developed a series of arguments which 'provides
an opening for a conservative reading of his works, much in favour in
the pragmatist climate of our times' (ibid.: 8), and complains that the
Jarman film makes it difficult 'to see how *this* man could have generated *these* ideas' (ibid.: 12). The film, however, provides the occasion
for the re-presentation of philosophical arguments in *context*, and the
point at issue here is the way an attention to context can produce an
immanent (dialectical, deconstructive) critique of these arguments.
Note that I am not arguing that this particular context is the 'correct'
one, or that there could ever be a wholly accurate and singular representation of any context, rather that the location of Wittgenstein in
context *per se* is step toward a critique of his arguments. I will be
exploring the specific contours of the context presented in the film to
illustrate how that critique may be developed.

The example in the film is where Wittgenstein is asking his
Cambridge students to attempt to rephrase the sentence 'This is a very
pleasant pineapple' without changing the sense. The point that is
being made in the film, which is a celebration of Wittgenstein's work
and life, reproduces the point Wittgenstein was making, which is that
the proposition holds within it a particular semantic shape that would
be falsified, distorted, were it to be augmented, added to or reworded.
Try and say 'This is a very pleasant pineapple' in a different way, and
you will find that the sense changes, or at least that it changes beyond
the limits that the rules of the example will allow, rules that are supposed, for Wittgenstein, to mirror those that operate in common sense.

The problem with the example, however, lies in the way in which
the rules of the game are set. In order to understand the way common
sense 'systematically exceeds dialectical "tolerance"' (Trotsky, 1973: 50)
we have to look at the way the limits of acceptable 'tolerance' are
constructed and maintained. Let us examine the statement as it
actually operates, as it used within the material world, moving from a
language game to a consideration of it as a discursive practice.
Wittgenstein argues that 'to imagine a language means to imagine a
form of life' (1953, no. 19), and a particular 'form of life', of the school-
room, is represented in this example.

The problem is that although 'This is a very pleasant pineapple'
appears to be the fragment of language that is at issue here, another
form of life contextualises it. We are presented here with a proposition
that functions as part of a pedagogical situation in which the teacher

instructs the pupil in rules of use. Wittgenstein asks the student to carry out a task, but what the student is *not* permitted to do is to produce a metacommentary on the proposition, which may go something like 'this is a teaching example'. As well as being inextricably linked with silence, types of silence we are now at liberty to unravel here, the rules of the particular version of 'common sense' reproduced there are also bound to mental and emotional states. These may be anathema to Wittgensteinians, but they function as a necessary part of what Foucault (1980) terms the 'regime of truth' that is at work. Rather like a 'double-bind' in discourse, there is also an injunction not to name the prohibition that is at work. A second-level metacommentary, which might help the student to understand why the counter–statement 'This is a teaching example' would be treated as an inappropriate response, may look something like 'This is an exercise of power'.

Wittgenstein (1953) defines a 'language game' as a collection of words which bring about effects 'and the actions into which it is woven' (no. 7). In this example, we are presented with words which define certain parameters for appropriate action. The student may struggle, and is puzzled to discover that he cannot break from the precise form of the proposition. In fact we can imagine – and this is certainly the scenario presented in the film and in other second-hand accounts of Wittgenstein's teaching – that the narrative would travel through his puzzlement, realisation at the stupidity and futility of the attempt, and relief at emerging into a new clearing in which he accepts that 'This is a very pleasant pineapple' is 'all that is the case'. Rather like Foucault's (1976a) discussion of confession in Western culture as the desperate and necessary production of a nameless and unknown secret from within the self, the student finds in the limits set by the rules of teaching which condition this proposition some understanding which he was not permitted to discover outside the rules. Once again, it is the very thorough-going contextualism of Wittgenstein's work that helps alert us to the way discourse sets out certain conditions of possiblity for action and experience, defines room for manoeuvre and its limits. And once again we have to look to how power is instantiated in discourse as part of an historically and structurally determined reality above and beyond the intentions of individual actors, rather than being an optional extra, to understand how that context operates and how a failure to picture that power functions as ideological legitimation of present-day 'language games'.

Classroom discursive practices are riven with contradiction and power, and attempts to resist will always participate in forms of language that carry with them institutional sanctions and truth effects (e.g., Walkerdine, 1981). I am not proposing that there is a correct reading of the proposition 'This is a very pleasant pineapple' or that any reading will do. Rather, I am drawing attention to the ways in which the proposition *only* functions insofar as it is embedded in *discursive practices*, practices which frame it so that it may operate as an example, practices which frame it so that it conceals the context in which it operates, practices which subject the student and then the film's audience to power which makes it difficult to say otherwise.

For Foucault (1980) power *produces* forms of action and subjectivity as well as inhibiting them. The subject resists power in discourse, but often becomes all the more thoroughly enmeshed in power as they do so. In this example, then, the subject as Wittgensteinian student is provoked to find 'all that is the case' as the truth of the proposition. At the very moment that they believe they are free of the bewitchment of language, they have fashioned themselves as a subject of power in a particular social world (cf. Foucault, 1984). As we watch the scene reproduced in the film, we too are positioned as Wittgensteinian subjects, held in the limits of a particular regime of truth.

It may be pointed out that it is not beyond the bounds of possibility that students faced with this example, and, more likely, viewers of the film watching the example played out with others captive, *could* refuse to 'play the game'. In this respect, Wittgenstein himself seems to capture the coercive quality of representation and action when he is describing the ways in which we are held in forms of language: 'A picture held us captive. And we could not get outside it, for it lay in our language and seemed to repeat it to us inexorably' (Wittgenstein, 1953, no. 115). Even if one wanted to insist that a student (and viewer) could resist this picture of the world, one would have to allow for the fear of retribution and recrimination for breaking the rules, and the sanctions that are deployed when one is not permitted to warrant one's actions (Eagleton, 1991; Shotter, 1993).

Perhaps it seems so far as if Wittgenstein is under-concerned with the coercive quality of language, and as if he is unconcerned with the way language itself is constrained. Let us move on, then, to look at the surprising way in which Wittgenstein's appeals to the very kind of essentialist anchors to meaning that his social constructionist fans spend so much energy cutting away. One of the paradoxes of relativism as an ideological current is that its proponents often lose their nerve and try to fix the meanings they had succeeded in setting free. One of the ways that it operates ideologically is in fixing meaning

anywhere other than in historically constituted discursive and economic structures of domination. We will see that when Wittgenstein
does turn to consider how language might be conditioned, he does so
in a manner that appeals to varieties of essentialism, and which
conceal how meaning is 'fixed' through a process of dialectical and
historical social construction.

Psychology, again

Even in the later Wittgenstein, the appeal to formal structures of one
kind or another reappears when general statements about the nature of
language and reality are being considered. This happens in two ways,
with the messiness of language being held conceptually in check either
by looking to internal qualities or to external bases.

The real inside language

With regard to the first conceptual checking device, that of internal
qualities, we find an enduring preoccupation with the idea that it is
possible to strip away obfuscation, and then to clearly reveal what
is crystalline and pure in the interior of language. The definition of
'language games' that Wittgenstein (1965) offers at one point, for
example, is of them as 'ways of using signs simpler than those in
which we use the signs of our highly complicated everyday language'
(ibid.: 17). This also holds out the possibility for a version of psychology which looks to simplicity and clarity as the touchstone of
healthy speech and a healthy mind, an invitation that has been
enthusiastically taken up by some writers who want to see
Wittgensteinian work as an essentially therapeutic enterprise (e.g.,
Ferrara, 1994).

Although Wittgenstein is opposed to finding a more wide-ranging
sense to a particular set of observations, is opposed to the development of a meta-language, or, more to the point here, to an account
of the historical material circumstances which give rise to certain
forms of life, regimes of truth, he is happy to look to the *interior* of a
form of life to understand how things really are. He argues, for
example, that:

> When we look at such simple forms of language the mental mist
> which seems to enshroud us disappears. We see activities, reactions,
> which are clear-cut and transparent.
>
> (Wittgenstein, 1965: 17)

Again, the invitation to a therapeutic reading is evident here, but the proposition that were we to look at simple forms, we would then see things clearly also seems to warrant a cognitive-behavioural twist to such an endeavour as one possibility, and so, in the process, even the return of an empirical supposedly 'scientific' psychology.

In the same passage, Wittgenstein smuggles in a series of presuppositions about child development, the possible nature and value of 'simplicity', other language communities as representatives of a simpler past in our more complex present, and, in a restatement of a long-discredited anthropological fallacy, he stresses the relationship between simplicity and the 'primitive':

> Language games are the forms of language with which a child begins to make use of words. The study of language games is the study of primitive forms of language or primitive languages.
>
> (Wittgenstein, 1965: 17)

Here, 'primitive languages' are simpler sets of games which can be studied to throw light upon our more complex forms of life.

The real outside language

This brings us to the second device that Wittgenstein employs to bring a conceptual check to bear on linguistic free play, the appeal to external bases of behaviour. As the quote about development indicates, he has already presupposed 'primitives' and their simpler languages as evolutionary building blocks for present-day ordinary language. Now, when he is considering the phenomenon of 'pain', he starts by disrupting conventional psychologistic appeals to definable internal mental processes. This is all well and good, but he then appeals to a common-sense nostrum that, the reader will 'remember', in order that he may root the response to pain somewhere else:

> Here it is a help to remember that it is a primitive reaction to take care of, to treat, the place that hurts when someone else is in pain ... it is a primitive reaction to attend to the pain-behaviour of another.
>
> (Wittgenstein, 1980, para. 915)

Wittgenstein is here turning attention from the 'pain' in the sufferer to the response of the observer, but he then effectively blocks further consideration of this by asserting that the response is a 'primitive reaction'.

This looks for, and finds very quickly then, a basis *outside* language for the solution to a philosophical problem.

The basis for the 'reaction' to pain is then qualified further by Wittgenstein, and a further presupposition appears in the process. Wittgenstein argues that an appeal to something as 'primitive' means that language is based upon it:

> What, however, is the word 'primitive' meant to say here? Presumably, that the mode of behaviour is *pre-linguistic*: that a language game is based *on it*: that it is the prototype of a mode of thought and not the result of thought.
>
> (Wittgenstein, 1980, para. 916)

You will notice that a presupposition about the nature of development appears again here when the 'prototype' is described as existing before language appears, as 'pre-linguistic'. A biological basis for behaviour reappears in the text, and it does not now appear sufficient to claim that this is progressive simply because it attaches the description to neurophysiology rather than 'scientific' psychology proper (Williams, 1985).

This is not to say that Wittgenstein and his followers would be wrong to theorise what the relationship between the inside and 'outside' of language may be. Far from it, and for two reasons. First, to *abstain* from such theoretical work would be to succumb to empiricism, to the practice of gathering a series of discrete unmediated observations about the world and behaviour, and to refuse to say more about the conditions, internal structural or external contextual conditions, that may have generated them. There is a difference between empirical work and empiricism that is often elided in psychology, because psychologists find it difficult to acknowledge that theory always a part in observation and understanding (Danziger, 1990). Wittgenstein offers a valuable critique of empiricism in psychology, and it would be an irony indeed if an attempt to cleanse his work of unwanted 'speculation' were to lead him to behaviourism. Second, the argument of the present chapter has precisely been that one needs to offer a theoretically informed account of the production of categories of common sense and of what we take to be 'ordinary' language within particular cultural conditions. The question should not be whether we engage in theory in psychology, but where that theoretical work may be usefully developed. A reflection on these matters should also include some account of Wittgenstein's own place in this, and of the appeal of his ideas.

Contexts

At the risk of adopting an *ad hominem* argument, I would like to draw attention to some contextual issues that may help throw light on some of the problems I have explored so far.

Academic work is very often split from everyday life, and one of the attractions of Wittgenstein is his concern with 'ordinary' language, and so with the absurdity and impossibility of much philosophy, and psychology. However, it is important to be aware of the ways in which the academic–everyday split is constituted as much by romanticising what 'ordinary people' do as it is by avoiding them. Structural positions of power and privilege cannot simply be wished away, and to pretend that they could be would operate as ideological mystification. I would suggest that Wittgenstein's failure to acknowledge class as an enduring form of life that conditions language games is a function of his own class position.

Wittgenstein was born into one of the wealthiest families in *fin-de-siècle* Vienna, and this background and easy access to resources facilitated visits to England, where he was first a research student in Manchester, and was then a student at Cambridge. He is sometimes admired for giving away his own money (e.g., Monk, 1990), mainly to his brothers and sisters, but it should be recalled that the transmission of privilege is largely through forms of 'cultural capital' (Bourdieu and Passeron, 1977), something Wittgenstein still enjoyed in abundance. To live an ascetic life in barely furnished rooms at Cambridge, and then to work as a village school master in his sojourn between the *Tractatus* and his later academic career, was an *exercise* of class privilege then, not an absence of it.

From this vantage point the romanticisation of work that one finds him engaging in can be seen as displaying a deep misunderstanding about the nature of power and alienation. Wittgenstein was able to advise one of his younger friends to leave Cambridge University and to get an engineering job (Monk, 1990), but we should read this, perhaps, less as a generous equalising of power in a divided society than as an inability to believe that the adoption of a class position was anything other than a move from one set of language games to another, that could be more than simply stepping across into a different 'form of life'. Wittgenstein's visit to Russia in 1935 and his admiration for the organization of labour there (Moran, 1972), also indicate something of the misplaced sentimentalism among middle-class Soviet 'fellow-travellers', particularly during a period when the political repression under Stalin was at its height, rather than a serious understanding of ideology and power (Foucault, 1976b; Trotsky, 1936).

Similar points could be made about the contradictory cultural positions of marginality and dominance that Wittgenstein suffered and enjoyed. Like many 'overseas students' today who study in North America or Western Europe with financial resources (in the shape of immediate tuition fees or future endowments to the institution) combined with a certain exotic quality that is invested in them (and which attaches both promise and distance to their contribution), Wittgenstein was shown a degree of indulgence and curiosity. His tutor, G. E. Moore, for example, travelled to Vienna to take Wittgenstein's dissertation down by hand, though in the event the degree was not awarded because Wittgenstein refused to supply the references. Despite this, Wittgenstein was awarded a doctorate, again without submitting a dissertation, for the *Tractatus* (which was itself published privately) (Monk, 1990). I suspect that sheer intelligence shining from his speech and writing through 'mental mist' is not the only explanation that could be given for these favours.

This account should be taken, perhaps, alongside a consideration of issues of gender, at a time when women were still largely excluded from the academe, and when rigorous and terrorising teaching styles would be admired as indicative of inner male mental strength. Recent celebrations of Wittgenstein have been overdetermined by the effort to represent him as a gay man (e.g., Jarman, 1993), but in the English cultural climate of the time, the suppression of working-class homosexuality should be contrasted with the toleration that was shown to it, as an eccentric pursuit, among the aristocracy. I should emphasise here that I am not concerned so much with Wittgenstein's personal characteristics but with the way they signified to his various benefactors and audiences at a particular historical moment, and signified alongside a comforting argument that the verities of philosophy and politics were to be found in forms of language, and, by implication, nowhere else.

Connections and conclusions

I have critically examined some of Wittgenstein's aphorisms, and attempted to contextualise these in the light of materialist perspectives on structures of power. Wittgenstein's writing offers to psychologists a series of interesting critical perspectives on concepts which are regularly employed by the discipline, and it assists in the deconstruction of facile appeals to notions of 'cognition', 'drive' or 'self' in which traditional psychology trades. However, the Wittgensteinian focus on language, and on the discursive setting for all varieties of mental and cultural phenomena also threatens to obscure the *material* structuring of contemporary institutional power, power that both inhibits and *incites* speech. Issues of class, gender and culture are obscured, and a number of presuppositions about the nature of social organization are relayed to the reader, concealed in a seductive appeal to the linguistic determination of experience and activity. Foucauldian views of power as both constraining action and producing it allow us to see how Wittgenstein's work operates in a particular social context, and Marxist accounts can contextualise that work still further to help us to understand the historical functions of certain key Wittgensteinian elisions and evasions.

It would, perhaps, be possible to combine a Wittgensteinian approach with a Foucauldian one (e.g., Aron, 1978), and to bring that ground-clearing activity and conceptual apparatus to bear upon psychology. Wittgenstein taken alongside Foucault would help us problematise psychology's attempts to individualise distress when it locates it in faulty 'cognitions' about the social world, in the vicissitudes of the 'drives' as they work their way toward inappropriate objects, or in the relationship the true 'self' has formed with 'reality'. An understanding of the fiction of the internal 'core', which is sometimes seen by psychologists as the source of disorder and sometimes of clarity, but which is neatly dissolved by Wittgenstein into varieties of language game, can be usefully augmented by a Foucauldian attention to the apparatus of confession and compulsory care of the self that pervades Western culture (Foucault, 1976a, 1984). It is important to remember here, however, that this apparatus, for Foucault, is locked together in practices and discursive practices, not only in language.

It would also be possible to link Wittgenstein's work with a Marxist view of the social construction of individuality and collectivity in specific forms of culture (e.g., Zimmermann, 1978). The language of a society carries with it prescriptions for compliance and agency that 'bewitch' even the most culturally competent members into forms of language that are self-defeating and alienating. The constitution of 'facts' about the nature of the social totality, 'society' or 'the economy', re-presents social order to the individual subject as if it were always necessarily out of their control, rather than as a form of life that they *produce*. What Wittgenstein saw as the 'sickness' of the present historical period can be interpreted as a critical commentary on Western culture, and the 'cure' can be seen as an engagement with language and a different collective practice (von Wright, 1982). There is a humanist impulse in Wittgenstein's work that has been picked by some writers who have wanted to connect the concern with creativity and the yearning for unalienated labour with that to be found in some of Marx's writings (Easton, 1983; Rubinstein, 1981).

My use of arguments from dialectical materialism, and my more general adherence to a Marxist theoretical framework, is not designed to imply that the task of analysis in psychology should be to search for a 'transcendental' reality (cf. Stenner and Eccleston, 1994), and such an endeavour would not be Marxist. Marxism is concerned with the *social construction* of relatively enduring, but quite intransigent forms of power tied to varieties of economic organization. To understand these, for a Marxist, must also be able to assess, and, when appropriate, to struggle with and to *change* them (Marx, 1845), to permit the pace of transformation of social categories to proceed. One problem a Marxist analysis of ideology homes in on is exactly the way social construc-tions are presented as if they were everlasting verities, and here it is helpful to consider the way language is part of a form of life. It is worth noting, for example, the way in which every reference to Wittgenstein in Eagleton's (1991) exploration of ideology is sympathetic, and how an appeal to Wittgensteinian argument is used to conceptualise ideo-logy as 'a network of overlapping features rather than some constant "essence"' (ibid.: 193).

In a sense, Marxists are social constructionists, and it is entirely understandable that Foucault (1980) declared his work to be situated within the broader project of Marxism. Marxists are concerned with the way social relationships and conceptual categories are constituted through an historical process, a process that also contains within it the possibility for forms of resistance and transformation. What also needs to be included in the account, however, is a reflection on how that resistance and transformation are prevented, by the networks of power that existing social relationships entail and by the legitimation work that existing conceptual categories perform. Even Derrida (1994) clearly and explicitly situates his work in that tradition (though see Ahmad, 1994). What Foucault's attention to the organization of dis-course allows us to do is to show how questions of logic, which operate ideologically, are tied to questions of usage, and reproduce power. Many Marxists and Foucauldians would be happy to agree with the notion of 'language-*game*' when it 'is meant to bring into prominence the fact that the *speaking* of language is part of an activity, or a form of life' (Wittgenstein, 1953, no. 23). The analysis of structures of power and economic organisation has much to learn from the Wittgensteinian insistence that little is accomplished by a 'prior' analysis which then pretends to settle questions of debate. The critical reading of Wittgenstein's role in psychology, of the problems in some of the formulations in his writing, and the context for the reception of his work, has been as a form of analysis which discloses insufficiences *in* his texts, not the simple assertion of truth against which his mistakes may be measured. The uses of Marxism and Foucault in this chapter have been in the spirit of constructive encounter and critique.

These alliances between different theoretical positions would assist the Wittgensteinian imperative to reflect on language as a collection of practices which constitute who we are, and how we may remake ourselves. This reflection is a therapeutic enterprise, but like all therapy it is a culturally and historically specific form of life. How we make something of Wittgenstein must be located, then, in a materialist account of how we and he have been *made*. In this sense, in a deconstructive and dialectical reading, we must also be against Wittgenstein.

4a

The Practical Turn in Psychology

Marx and Wittgenstein as Social Materialists

John T. Jost and Curtis D. Hardin

Parker alleges that Wittgensteinian presuppositions of essentialism and relativism obscure the role of social power in linguistic discourse. Not only is this claim self-contradictory, it is wrong in each of its component counts. Strands of essentialism in Wittgenstein's early writings were skewered effectively in his own later philosophy. Although Parker is not alone in charging Wittgenstein with relativism, we argue that a careful reading of Wittgenstein's work belies such a claim. This is because the meaning of a given language-game is fixed by patterns of ongoing social interaction among people who share a particular 'form of life'. Against Parker, we show that Wittgenstein's (anti-)philosophy is in fact largely congenial to Marx's (anti-)philosophy, with both writers allied against the doctrines of individualism, subjectivism, mentalism, idealism and metaphysicalism. Although it may be true that Wittgenstein the person was relatively silent about issues of social and political power, Parker has failed to establish that Wittgensteinian metatheory is incompatible with the analysis of power in social discourse. In sum, we argue that Wittgenstein, like Marx, was a social materialist (rather than a social constructionist) whose writings articulate the foundations of mind and meaning in terms of concrete social practice.

The practical turn

While for centuries most theories of mind and behavior did more to mystify than to enlighten social and psychological functioning, Marx and Wittgenstein were committed to understanding human psychology and behavior in terms of their actual social and material circumstances. Although Marx was concerned largely with exercises of power that develop within specific 'modes of production' and Wittgenstein was concerned largely with 'language-games' that develop within particular 'forms of life', both may be regarded as 'social materialists' who strove to de-mystify social and psychological explanation (Jost and Hardin, 1994). The unity of their approaches is evident in numerous passages such as the following:

(1) Where speculation ends – in real life – there real, positive science begins: the representation of the practical activity, of the practical process of development of men. Empty talk about consciousness ceases, and real knowledge has to take its place.

(Marx and Engels, 1846/1970: 48)

(2) One of the most dangerous ideas for a philosopher is, oddly enough, that we think with or in our heads ... The idea of thinking as a process in the head in a completely enclosed space, gives him something occult.

(Wittgenstein, 1967, §§605-606)

(3) The production of ideas, of conceptions, of consciousness, is at first directly interwoven with the material activity and the material intercourse of men, the language of real life. Conceiving, thinking, the mental intercourse of men, appear at this stage as the direct efflux of their material behaviour.

(Marx and Engels, 1846/1970: 47)

(4) Only in the stream of thought and life do words have meaning.

(Wittgenstein, 1967, §173)

(5) ... the human essence is no abstraction inherent in each single individual. In its reality it is the ensemble of the social relations.

(Marx, 1845/1975, Thesis VI)

(6) How could human behaviour be described? Surely only by sketching the actions of a variety of humans, as they are all mixed up together. What determines our judgment, our concepts and reactions is not what *one* man is doing *now*, an individual action, but the whole hurlyburly of human actions, the background against which we see any action.

(Wittgenstein, 1967, §567)

(7) All social life is essentially *practical*. All mysteries which lead theory to mysticism find their rational solutions in human practice and in the comprehension of this practice.

(Marx, 1846/1970, Thesis VIII)

Theoretical commitments such as these led both Marx and Wittgenstein to reject a number of interrelated doctrines that have long dominated philosophy and social science (see Jost, 1995), including all of the following: (a) *individualism,* which posits that human behavior is to be explained ultimately in terms of properties of individual persons, as opposed to social groups or collectivities (see [2] [3], [5] and [6]); (b) *subjectivism,* according to which human action is interpretable only in terms of social actors' intentions, motivations and subjective understandings of their own action, and not in terms of objectively specified categories of interpretation (see [1], [3] and [6]); (c) *mentalism,* which assumes that meaning is defined by internal mental states of thinkers or language-speakers, rather than by a system of communal practices that are external and observable (see [2], [4] and [5]); (d) *idealism,* which regards reality to be indistinguishable from the human perception of reality, having no material existence independent of human perception (see [1], [3], [4] and [7]); and (e) *metaphysicalism,* in which philosophy is viewed as an exercise in abstract thought, rather than a practical attempt to resolve problems inherent in specific social contexts (see [1], [2], [3], [4], [5] and [7]). The joint perspective that emerges from the work of Marx and Wittgenstein, therefore, may be characterized as objective, social, externalist, practical and materialist (see Rubinstein, 1981).

Ian Parker opens his 'dialectical materialist' critique of Wittgenstein by making reference to the 'linguistic turn' in 20th-century philosophy, to which Wittgenstein undoubtedly contributed. But passages such as the above make clear that Wittgenstein joined Marx in an equally important metatheoretical movement, and that is the 'practical turn' away from metaphysical conceptions of human behavior and toward an account in terms of actual social interaction. It is our contention that Wittgenstein's accomplishments in the philosophy of mind and language largely parallel Marx's accomplishments in the philosophy of history and politics. Thus, while Parker is correct about some of the differences between Marx and Wittgenstein, his paper misses the profound similarities, perhaps because he relies on misleading second-hand representations of Wittgenstein's philosophy.

We regard Parker's failure to appreciate the social, practical and anti-metaphysical bases that unite Marxian and Wittgensteinian philosophies to be his primary error of omission. Unfortunately, however, his errors of commission are even greater, accusing Wittgenstein of philosophical crimes that he did not commit. First, Parker complains that Wittgenstein's presuppositions 'fuel relativism'. Second, risking logical contradiction with the first charge, Parker claims that Wittgenstein subscribes to an essentialist theory of meaning. Our view of Wittgenstein, which emphasizes his compatibility with Marx (see Jost, 1995; Jost and Hardin, 1994), renders Wittgenstein innocent on both counts.

Wittgenstein was not a relativist

For much of the paper, Parker compliments Wittgenstein for his alleged 'relativist dynamic', insofar as it 'can be used to disturb the status quo in "psychology"' by undermining scientists' smug assumptions that they have 'privileged access to "reality"'. He also approves of the feminist use of Wittgenstein to critique the notion of a universal human nature and the anti-cognitivist use of Wittgenstein to reject the concept of internal mental states. Ultimately, however, Parker turns on Wittgenstein for being relativistic, implying that his philosophy suggests 'a world in which a multiplicity of realities jostle alongside one another, and none must be permitted to have a claim to a better account'.

We argue that the criticism of Wittgenstein as a relativist is based upon a misreading of his work. Unfortunately, it is a common misreading among psychologists who draw on Wittgensteinian themes. Gergen (1988), for example, attempts to use Wittgenstein to buttress explicitly relativistic claims such as the following: 'Any given action may be subject to multiple interpretations, no one of which is objectively superior' (ibid.: 35). Wittgenstein never says that no interpretation may be considered superior to any other (Conway, 1989), nor does he say that valid interpretation of human action is impossible (Gustafson, 1984), as Gergen (1988) suggests. At one point, Wittgenstein (1969) notes explicitly that it is possible to 'compare our system of knowledge' to someone else's and to conclude that 'theirs is evidently the poorer one by far' (§286).

In passage (2) quoted above, Wittgenstein criticizes one type of interpretation, namely mentalistic forms of interpretation, for being inferior, on largely the same grounds that Marx in (1) criticizes idealist interpretations of history – for taking something concrete and using philosophy to mystify it. In passage (6), Wittgenstein, like Marx in (3) and (5), proposes a superior form of interpretation, namely a social or anti-individualistic form, establishing that he, like Marx, believes meaningful analysis of social behavior to be possible (see Jost, 1995). Wittgenstein's analysis of language-games avoids relativism because it ties the use of certain concepts to particular forms of life, that is, to specific material social practices, just as Marx ties individual consciousness and behavior to particular modes of production. According to both theorists, 'concepts of the world … emerge from a dialectical interaction between the social subject and the object' (Rubinstein, 1981: 177).

As Charles Taylor (1988) points out, Gergen and others take an unwarranted leap when they spin Wittgenstein's theory of meaning as use into an epistemological view that is relativistic and skeptical of the possibility of objective interpretation. The fact that, according to Wittgenstein, genuine descriptions of human behavior must make reference to the broader context of language and society (see Jost, 1995) does not mean that all descriptions are equally valid. Rubinstein (1981) has argued, on the contrary, that one of the most important contributions of both Marx and Wittgenstein was to 'show that meaning is not a feature of subjective experience but of systems of social praxis … [and] that the "subjective" meaning of an action cannot be determined apart from the "objective" system of action within which it occurs' (ibid.: 23–24). Wittgenstein therefore joins Marx, Dewey, Mead, Bakhtin, Vygotsky and many others in underscoring the objective social basis of mind and behavior.

Although few if any commentators have come right out and claimed that Wittgenstein *is* a 'social constructionist', many have implied very close connections between Wittgenstein and social constructionism (e.g. Bloor, 1983; Coulter, 1979; Gergen, 1988, 1994b; Harré, 1989a; Shotter, 1991). Gergen (1994b), for example, writes that 'social constructionism is a congenial companion to Wittgenstein's (1953) conception of meaning as derivative of social use' (1994: 52), an assumption that is made also by Parker.

If social constructionism is considered to be a theory of the person as a product of ongoing social relations (e.g. Kruglanski, 1992), then perhaps Marx and Wittgenstein may be regarded as social constructionists in this sense. More often than not, however, the term 'social constructionism' is used to describe an epistemological position that is relativistic and skeptical about the possibility of objective knowledge (e.g. Gergen, 1994b). Whether some versions of social constructionism manage to escape imputations of relativism is a crucial and exciting question for psychological metatheory of (see Greenwood, 1989; Osbeck, 1993; Stam, 1990), but it is beyond the scope of the present commentary. With regard to Wittgenstein, it seems that issues about his relation to social constructionism come very close to debates about whether his philosophy is in any way idealistic (Malcolm, 1982) and whether it tends toward relativism (Conway, 1989). Our own position is that none of these labels apply well to Wittgenstein's later philosophy.

We believe that the term 'social materialist' is a better characterization of the views of Marx and Wittgenstein, because they do not make the epistemological assumption that social reality more than physical reality adheres to a mere 'construction' of the human mind (e.g. Gergen, 1994b), an assumption that may be identified as idealist in the sense outlined above. As should be clear from the quotations reproduced at the outset, for Marx and Wittgenstein the social is as real as anything; it is the primary substance of human life, the principal foundation of ideas and action. This is different from saying that social factors are reducible to economic conditions alone, as Harré (1979: 26–33) takes the 'socio-materialist' position to imply. Rather, we are arguing that according to Marx and Wittgenstein social life *is* one of the most important material bases of human experience.

(The later) Wittgenstein was not an essentialist

If Parker's first major complaint is that relativism keeps Wittgenstein's analysis from going 'beyond language' to a critique of ideology and power, his second major complaint is that essentialism leads Wittgenstein to adopt concepts that are abstract, universal and insensitive to historical context. While the charge of relativism implies that Wittgenstein is incapable of close speaking about matters of truth and falsity, the charge of essentialism is that Wittgenstein takes 'simple statements about the nature of the world' and insists that they 'must necessarily be true'. Although most of Parker's paper addresses the later philosophy, he must resort to an attack on Wittgenstein's early work, the *Tractatus Logico-Philosophicus*, in order to claim that Wittgenstein makes a 'disturbing and paradoxical appeal to "anchors" to meaning which are imagined to lie inside and outside language'.

Parker tries to use Trotsky to criticize Wittgenstein's early 'picture theory of meaning', but Wittgenstein himself did a far more thorough job of skewering it in his later writing. That the later Wittgenstein eschewed linguistic essentialism is demonstrated not only in passage (4) quoted above, but also in several remarks such as these:

> the *speaking* of language is part of an activity, or of a form of life.
>
> (1953, §23)

> it is our *acting* which lies at the bottom of the language-game.
>
> (1969, §204)

In fact, Wittgenstein explicitly criticizes the essentialist view for being metaphysical and for obscuring the meanings of words:

> This finds expression in questions as to the *essence* of language, of propositions, of thought. – For if we too in these investigations are trying to understand the essence of language – its function, its structure, – yet *this* is not what those questions have in view. For they see in the essence, not something that already lies open to view and that becomes surveyable by a rearrangement, but something that lies *beneath* the surface.
>
> (1953, §92)

> When philosophers use a word – 'knowledge', 'being', 'object', 'I', 'proposition', 'name' – and try to grasp the *essence* of the thing, one must always ask oneself: is the word ever actually used in this way in the language-game which is its original home? – What *we* do is to bring words back from their metaphysical to their everyday use.
>
> (1953, §116)

Wittgenstein's famous doctrine of 'meaning as use' is clearly at odds with the essentialist theory that Parker mistakenly ascribes to him.

The politics of Wittgenstein

Parker is on strongest ground when he critiques the personal politics of Wittgenstein. It may be correct that Wittgenstein himself was politically conservative, holding many of the values consonant with upper-class Viennese society. Politically speaking, it is probably true that he was no Marxist. As Parker concedes, however, this is an *ad hominem* argument, and it may overlook the fact that Wittgenstein's philosophical method was in fact largely Marxian (Kitching, 1988; Rubinstein, 1981), even though Wittgenstein the person was not.

Parker is also correct that Wittgenstein's remarks about language and forms of life are unduly conservative at times, 'leaving everything as it is' (1953, §124), as the phrase goes. It is not the case, however, that Wittgenstein's perspective depends in any crucial respect upon the notion that language-games and social practices are not to be revised; he does not render 'the search for other ways of speaking a hopeless exercise', as Parker claims (see Conway, 1989: 101). Wittgenstein admits that 'a reform for particular practical purposes, an improvement in our terminology designed to prevent misunderstandings in practice, is perfectly possible' (1953, §132). Even Eagleton (1986), on whom Parker relies heavily for his allegations about Wittgenstein's conservatism, notes that Wittgenstein's work on language-games and forms of life

... is not an expression of political conservatism: there is no reason why what has to be accepted are *these particular* forms of life, and indeed little reason to believe that Wittgenstein himself was in the least content with his own society. It is just that even if existing forms of life were to be revolutionized, those transformed practices and institutions would still in the end provide the only justification for why people spoke and thought as they did.

(ibid.: 107)

In other words, the Wittgensteinian point is that thought and action derive their meaning from the material social context (see Jost, 1995).

Whether social or linguistic practices are in need of change is indeed a political question, and Parker may be right that it goes beyond the conceptual analyses provided by Wittgenstein, which, it is true, seldom if ever lead to an analysis of social power, in the way that Foucault's analyses do. However, Parker has not shown that Wittgenstein's own philosophical purposes necessitated a discussion of power, nor has he shown that Wittgenstein's analysis excludes a discussion of power. Indeed, Foucault and Derrida are cited approvingly by Parker for their application of Wittgensteinian methods to the subject of power. There are at least two ironies here: (1) Derrida and Foucault were influenced tremendously by Wittgenstein and may never have accomplished 'much of the same critical conceptual work' had there been no Wittgenstein; and (2) Derrida and Foucault are far more explicit in their affinities for social constructionism and relativism than Wittgenstein ever was, although it is the alleged social constructionism and relativism of Wittgenstein that Parker finds objectionable.

Synthesizing Marx and Wittgenstein

We believe that Marxists have too long ignored Wittgenstein and that Wittgensteinians have too long dismissed Marx. Unfortunately, Parker's piece encourages more of the same. What is needed is a constructive synthesis of the two (anti-)philosophers and a fuller embrace of the practical turn they envisioned for social and psychological theory. Wittgenstein should be regarded as neither a relativist nor an essentialist. Like Marx, Wittgenstein was a 'social materialist' (rather than a social constructionist), who believed that 'if fleas developed a rite, it would be based on the dog' (1979: 73).

Acknowledgements

We thank Lawrence Jost, Lisa Osbeck, Russell Spears and Hank Stam for helpful advice concerning this commentary.

4b
Reference Points for Critical Theoretical Work in Psychology

Jost and Hardin's defence of Wittgenstein fails to address the ways in which that writer's texts function in different discursive contexts to warrant essentialist and relativist positions. The strategy of assembling bits of text from Wittgenstein and Marx to illustrate similarities of perspective is unconvincing, for it neglects the mobilization of theoretical arguments in the context of institutionally situated language games or forms of life. There are deep problems with Wittgenstein's work as the underpinning for a critical position in psychology, as I argued in my chapter, but we can still, paradoxically, understand why that may be so by taking seriously some of the insights in Wittgenstein's own writing.

John Jost and Curtis Hardin provide a spirited defence of Wittgenstein against my critical appraisal of his contribution. They argue, quite rightly, that he *can* be recruited to the cause of critical theory in psychology, but they are unfortunately a little too anxious to support the radical credentials of Wittgensteinian work in the discipline. We must, as I pointed out in my chapter, take care not to assume that Wittgenstein's writings will necessarily be helpful to those of us who wish to challenge conservative positions, and if we wish to use what is of value we *also* have to be against Wittgenstein.

Let me trace through this dialectical proposition in a slightly different way. This will help us to see how Jost and Hardin fall, by a curious paradox, into a most un-Wittgensteinian line of argument to defend him.

Wittgenstein and Marx

Jost and Hardin start with a helpful review of some points of agreement between Wittgenstein and Marx. The seven passages they juxtapose certainly illustrate some common philosophical threads in the work of the two writers, but to assert that my chapter 'misses profound similarities' is really to miss the point. Gergen (1994b) is dragged into their argument with me, perhaps through some guilt by association, for I took care not to mention Gergen in my chapter. Perhaps this is because I am more sympathetic to his social constructionist unravelling of psychology then they are, and I feel that a debate within a common cause against psychology is more helpful than labelling certain mis-readers or false Wittgensteinians as the problem, as if that were the difficulty. It is not, for the problem lies in Wittgenstein's own writings. To gather quotes to demonstrate 'profound similarities' is a dodgy strategy, for it often obscures more than it reveals. It would be possi-ble to find statements supporting a social standpoint, thorough anti-subjectivism, non-mentalist descriptions of 'psychological' phenomena, an attention to philosophical reasoning as a form of practice and a concern with the materiality of meaning in the writings of a host of intellectuals influenced by European thought, ranging from Jacques Derrida to Ken Gergen. There are, for instance, 'profound similarities' between dialectics and deconstruction (Ryan, 1982), but Jost and Hardin would be wary of conflating the two, and rightly so. Surely there are different views of language, community and class at stake and different political consequences that follow from the adoption of arguments from Dewey, Mead, Bakhtin or Vygotsky. To incant this list of names, as Jost and Hardin do, is to blend together disparate theoretical positions, and to wilfully ignore the various ways in which some of them have been enrolled to conservative politics in the human sciences (cf. Novack, 1975).

Jost and Hardin seem to take the position that it would be possible to clear up confusions about what Wittgenstein 'really' meant by finding a term that would capture the essence of his approach to meaning and practice. To this end we are taken through a discussion of Gergen's (mis)reading of Wittgenstein in the service of social constructionism, a consideration of the possibility that Marx and Wittgenstein might both be regarded as social constructionists, and then to the argument that we should view them as 'social materialists'. I am not sure what either Marx or Wittgenstein would have made of this new category. I guess that they would want to explore what it meant, how it func-tioned and, in Marx's case no doubt, what contradictions it contained by virtue of its production and use in certain ideological and practical settings. Here we find the category employed in an academic setting to resolve some ambiguities of interpretation. Unfortunately the ambiguities are located in sets of contradictions that are more powerful than Jost and Hardin seem to allow for.

Contradictions

From their vantage point it is evidently inconceivable that the corpus of writings signed by Wittgenstein could be 'self-contradictory'. Let me pick apart a little further what a reading of Wittgenstein, or any other writer, offers that is able to risk an attention to what Jost and Hardin term, when they notice it in my text, 'logical contradiction'. Texts, signed or not, do not carry a pure and original meaning from their authors to all their different readers. Followers of Derrida and Foucault, for example, were later attracted, in the early 1980s, to Wittgenstein's writing precisely because post-structuralist debates had alerted them to the ways in which meaning in language operates by virtue of its *relation* to surrounding context and practice (Montefiore, 1983). This argument informed the development of Foucauldian varieties of discourse analysis in psychology (Parker, 1992). Here, by the way, the two ironies Jost and Hardin note dissolve, for they assert, quite erroneously, that Derrida and Foucault were 'influenced tremendously' by Wittgenstein, and they are apparently unaware of the *critical* appropriation of their arguments in discourse analysis (e.g., Parker and Burman, 1993).

Despite what Jost and Hardin think they are able to divine about Wittgenstein's real thoughts on the matter, his writing fragments into many contradictory patterns of meaning that make different sense in different contexts as they are enrolled and read as part of different practices and institutions. Wittgenstein, is, then, at points, essentialist. Or rather, there is a warrant for essentialist arguments in his writing, and there is a 'Wittgenstein' available for those who would like to find a way to discover underlying 'primitive reactions', perhaps in 'primitive forms of language'. The quotes Jost and Hardin marshall would then slip into the background and reference could be made to other bits of Wittgenstein's work (1965, 1980). Wittgenstein is *also*, at times, relativist, and Gergen (1994b) is not hallucinating when he reads his Wittgenstein (1953) as warranting the study of social worlds as wholly defined by the contours of language games as forms of life. Once could then even imagine Gergen writing about Wittgenstein with someone who is a Marxist, and indeed such an unlikely thing has happened, when Gergen recently gave a paper with Fred Newman (Newman and Gergen, 1995). The deep problem in Jost and Hardin's approach to this issue of reading theoretical texts is that they could only account for such strange alliances by discovering 'misreadings' (traceable to misunderstanding or 'logical contradiction' in thought perhaps) and, as the other side of the coin, defending what Wittgenstein really meant. A more productive way of 'reading' such conjunctions of different theoretical traditions would be by tracing the material context for the development of 'thought' in political institutions, which in that particular case also means subjecting the 'Marxist' in the pack to critical scrutiny (Parker, 1995b).

Synthesis

The 'constructive synthesis' between Wittgenstein and Marx that Jost and Hardin hope for is not something that can be brought about through the kind of generous reading of Wittgenstein as a 'social materialist' that they propose. Their collection and juggling of quotes which seem to be saying the 'same' thing are surely an exercise in abstract thought, they treat the ideas as if they had no material existence in different institutional settings, they assume that if we knew what Wittgenstein really meant we could save him from those who misread him, they assure us that although he was not actually a political radical, his method was 'Marxian', and that we can grasp the trajectory of his thinking toward his later writing as if that revealed what he actually thought as an individual abstracted from social context. And we should also be aware what their line of argument would do to Marxism. It would reduce a practical political tradition of critique and resistance to what we think the individual Marx might have thought.

Although Jost and Hardin may wish to bring Wittgenstein into line with Marxism, they do so in such a way that they lose sight of what is most radical in Marxist theory, its attention to contradiction and dialectical reversals in the battle of ideas and everyday practice. The Wittgenstein they end up defending is a writer who must function, if we are to follow their argument, in static final state form. The Wittgenstein I felt it important to attack is a writer riven by ambiguity of meaning, someone who says different things and is able to operate as a radical or a conservative in different language games. It is crucial that we be aware of how the integrity of the most radical theorist dissolves in the practical forms of life that constitute and re-constitute them around different agendas of resistance or legitimation of power. In that sense we could say that to acknowledge and understand the *problems* with his work in a deconstructive and dialectical reading, we must also be for Wittgenstein.

Part II

The Turn to Discourse as a Critical Theoretical Resource

This second Part of the book moves into a more positive constructive mode of argument, and the task in these chapters is to explore what can be progressive about theoretical frameworks when they are put into practice as a critical form of discourse analysis. Chapter 5, which was originally published in an amended shortened simplified form as a chapter in an introduction to critical psychology (Fox and Prilleltensky, 1997), sets out five axes of debate which structure how discourse analysis is conceptualized in psychology at present. It is published here in this original form for the first time. There is a discussion of the process of cultural translation from the version published here to the chapter published by Fox and Prilleltensky in Parker (in press). Themes that have been introduced in Part I are now specifically directed to discursive psychology in a review of the way reductionism, essentialism, quantification, relativism and theory itself operate there for good or ill. Chapter 6 sets out methodological steps for the analysis of discourse, a version of which was subsequently published as a chapter in *Discourse Dynamics* (Parker, 1992), and there are responses to these proposals (by Potter, Wetherell, Gill and Edwards from a discourse analytic perspective, and by Abrams and Hogg from a more mainstream social psychological vantage point). My reply situates these concerns in the context of debates about 'reality' and the critical context for theoretical and practical work in discursive psychology.

5
Discursive Psychology Uncut

The terms 'discourse' and 'discourse analysis' often present problems for researchers from a psychology background coming across them for the first time. This is because the terms do not have an easily understood everyday meaning in the way that 'personality' or 'development' do. This is both a strength and a weakness for critical psychologists, as we shall see. The terms also present problems because many 'introductions to discourse analysis' describe discourse from a linguistic or sociological point of view. We can then lose sight of the distinctive critical contribution of a discursive approach to this discipline. There are, in addition, strong disagreements amongst discourse analysts as to what it is they are actually studying and how they should study it.

I will start with one set of definitions to guide us through this chapter, and look at other approaches to discourse along the way. In the following sections I will run through these definitions of key terms before briefly reviewing the recent historical background to two different strands in discursive research. I will then discuss five 'axes of debate' that have implications for a critical perspective, and conclude with some remaining questions for those who would like to do work in this area.

Defining 'discourse'

Discourse analysts study the way texts are constructed, the functions language serves and the contradictions that run through it. The term 'discourse' is used because our conception of language is much wider than a simple psycholinguistic or sociolinguistic one. 'Discourse' comprises the many ways that meaning is relayed through culture, and so it includes speech and writing, non-verbal and pictorial communication, and artistic and poetic imagery. The linguist Ferdinand de Saussure (1974) once imagined that there could be a new science called 'semiology' which would study the life of signs in society, and the exploration of semiological patterns of meaning has sometimes been carried out under that heading, sometimes under the heading of 'semiotics' (Hawkes, 1977).

Although discourse analysts in psychology have tended to focus on spoken and written texts, a critical 'reading' of psychology as part of culture should encompass the study of all the kinds of symbolic material that we use to represent ourselves to each other. All of this symbolic material is *organized*, and it is that organization that makes it possible for it to produce for us, its users, a sense of human community and identity. Semiology in general, and discourse analysis in particular leads us to question the way subjectivity (the experience of being and feeling in particular discursive contexts) is constituted inside and outside psychology.

The organization of discourse through patterns and structures in different texts fixes the meaning of symbolic material, and this makes it possible for discourse analysts to take those texts, unpick them and show how they work. The process of focusing on specific texts might lead us to treat these as abstracted from culture when we carry out our analysis, and so we have to be aware of the ways in which the meanings we study are produced in their relationship to other texts, the way they are 'intertextual'. Nevertheless, when we take a ready-made text or select some material to create a text, we are able to trace connections between signs and regularities which produce certain circumscribed positions for readers. We can then study the ideological force of language by displaying the patterns and structures of meaning. That is, we can identify distinct 'discourses' that define entities that we see in the world and in relationships, and as things we feel are real in ourselves.

This is where we can connect with a wider critical approach to the discipline, for we treat the variety of things that psychologists tell us they have 'discovered' inside us and among us as *forms of discourse*. We study accounts of action and experience as discourses, and as part of powerful discursive practices in Western culture that define certain kinds of activity and thinking as normal and other kinds as abnormal (Parker *et al.*, 1995). There are two aspects to our critical activity here. First, traditional psychology is treated with suspicion, for it presents its stories about the mind and behaviour as if they were factual accounts. Our analysis can unravel the ways in which those stories work, why they seem so plausible, and which institutions and forms of power they reproduce. Second, traditional psychology is seen as consistently misleading us about the place of mental phenomena, which it invariably locates inside individual heads. Discourse analysis explores the way these phenomena operate between people, in language. The stuff of mental life, then, lies in discourse, and it then makes sense to say that we are elaborating an alternative 'discursive psychology'.

Historical resources: two traditions

Discursive approaches in psychology draw on debates outside the discipline, and we can identify two approaches now that have emerged from quite different theoretical traditions. This is not to say that there is no overlap, and we often find writers borrowing ideas and moving between theoretical frameworks.

Foucauldian approaches to discourse

The first strand is still the most radical, and this develops the work of the French historian and philosopher Michel Foucault (Parker, 1995a). This work was introduced, along with 'post-structuralist' philosophy and psychoanalysis into Anglo-American psychology in the late 1970s in the UK-based journal *Ideology & Consciousness* (Adlam *et al.*, 1977), and then in the book *Changing the Subject* (Henriques *et al.*, 1984). Foucault's detailed description and reflection on modern notions of madness (1961), punishment (1975a), confession (1976a) and the self (1984) focused on the 'rules of discourse' that allow our present-day talk about these things to make sense. Foucault's task was to lay bare the 'conditions of possibility' for modern experience, and he engaged in an 'archaeology' of culture and a 'genealogy' of knowledge which uncovers the ways the phenomena psychology takes for granted came into being.

Many psychological and social phenomena can seem trivial if they are studied on their own, separated from culture. One of the main problems with traditional laboratory-experimental psychology is that it focuses on one issue, such as 'memory' or 'prejudice', at a time, and it then carries out thousands of studies exploring its different permutations in different contexts. There is an illusion in this type of research that the psychologist will be able to reveal the 'essence' of the phenomenon, to discover what 'memory' or 'prejudice' really are. A discourse researcher asks instead 'how has this phenomenon come to be like this?' The most innocent bits of consumer culture can help us understand the workings of power, ideology and forms of subjectivity in a society if we ask what discursive conditions made them possible (Parker, 1994). Foucauldians would then look at how the organization of language in a culture provided places for the phenomenon to make sense, and at the 'surfaces of emergence' for certain representations and practices of the self. We would then study the kinds of representation, or 'orders of discourse' that comment on the phenomenon, elaborating it, making it natural and encouraging us to take it for granted.

Some of the original editors and authors of *Ideology & Consciousness* and *Changing the Subject* have continued this Foucauldian research into psychology as part of a wider perspective on the 'psy-complex' (Rose, 1985, 1989), or have combined an analysis of discourse with psychoanalysis to look at gender, sexuality and class (Hollway, 1989; Walkerdine, 1990). Psychoanalysis has to be handled very carefully and sceptically in this work, and Foucault (1976a) provides a powerful argument against treating psychoanalytic notions as underlying truths about the human mind.

The next generation of researchers were influenced by these ideas, and have worked on subjectivity and race (Mama, 1995) and on links between psychology, culture and political practice (Burman *et al.*, 1996; Parker, 1992). A particularly useful idea that runs through this work is the notion of the 'psy-complex'. The psy-complex is the network of theories and practices that comprise academic, professional and popular psychology, and it covers the different ways in which people in modern Western culture are categorized, observed and regulated by psychology, as well as the ways in which they live out psychological models in their own talk and experience.

The psy-complex is part of a particular 'regime of truth' which makes our talk and experience about 'the self', 'personality' and 'attitudes' make sense. While academic psychologists tell stories about people and so participate in certain discourses about the individual, professional psychologists make those stories come true and help police discursive practices. At the same time there is always room for manoeuvre, for resistance, and our study of the ways in which certain discourses reproduce power relations can also, in the most critical variants of discourse analysis, be an occasion for the elaboration of 'counter-discourses' (Foucault, 1977).

'Interpretative repertoires'

A second strand of discourse analysis developed in the 1980s in social psychology and was first presented as an alternative to traditional attitude research (Potter and Wetherell, 1987). The main theoretical resource for this strand was work on the 'sociology of scientific knowledge' which treated scientists' activities as procedures to be explained rather than as merely discovering and representing reality. For example, scientists talk about what they do in contradictory ways, and a close analysis of their discourse identified contrasting 'interpretative repertoires'; an 'empiricist' repertoire which included reference to close observation and testing, and a 'contingent' repertoire in which they acknowledge the role of intuition and personal rivalries (Gilbert and Mulkay, 1984).

The term 'interpretative repertoire' is still used in the later work from this tradition, even in research which moves closer to a critical approach to ideology and to some Foucauldian concepts (Wetherell and Potter, 1992; Edley and Wetherell, 1995). The term 'discursive psychology' was first coined in an extension of this work which looked at the way memory, attribution and 'facts' were constructed in people's talk (Edwards and Potter, 1992).

This second strand of discursive work has proved more acceptable to social psychology and, to an extent, to psychology generally. This has been partly because of the promise of an alternative 'Discursive Action Model' for the discipline (Edwards and Potter, 1993) which (i) contains the work of discourse analysis within traditional psychological categories; (ii) evades reference to politics or power; (iii) functions to relativize categories that psychology likes to see as essential and unchanging; but (iv) restricts its analysis to a particular text rather than locating it in wider discursive practices which regulate and police people's understanding of themselves. As a consequence, much of the research in this tradition is rather descriptive, and a range of techniques from micro-sociology are used to make the description look more objective.

This style of discourse analysis has, however, provided a pole of attraction for writers from 1970s' 'new paradigm' social psychology (Harré and Secord, 1972), and has helped legitimate qualitative research in psychology departments in the last decade. This has then led to the argument that it is possible to yoke the 'turn-to-discourse' to a 'second cognitive revolution' in which most of the mental machinery will now be seen to have been out in the public sphere all along (Harré and Gillett, 1994). Some critical writers in social psychology who had been tempted to turn to the study of rhetoric as an alternative to laboratory-experimentation (Billig, 1987) and to the study of the way that people handle dilemmas in everyday talk (Billig *et al.*, 1988) would now see their work as 'discursive', and would also make claims based on that research that they now know more about the nature of human thinking (Billig, 1991). For a critical appraisal of Billig's turn to rhetoric, see Reicher (1988).

Discourse analysis in psychology

The second strand of discourse analysis is more comfortable with the term 'discursive psychology' than critical Foucauldian writers. There are certainly advantages in this strand, for it makes some key aspects of discourse analysis accessible to a psychology audience. Potter and Wetherell (1987), for example, helpfully draw attention to three characteristics of discourse and, in the process, lead the researcher away from their dependence on traditional psychological notions.

Three characteristics of discourse, power and practice

Some ideas from philosophy and sociology have been useful here to look at language, and I will briefly describe how these have found their way into discursive psychology, and then connect each to some more critical perspectives on discourse which attend to the same issues. An attention to 'variability', 'construction' and 'function' takes the researcher several steps away from mainstream psychology, but we still need something more to help them leap over to a critical standpoint. Each of these three characteristics of discourse had already been described in Foucault's (1969) reflections on method and in the writings of other French 'post-structuralist' writers, and there is now a strong alternative tradition of research which draws out the consequences for critical analyses of language, institutions, practices, and psychology's place in the world.

From variability to contradiction. The first characteristic is 'variability'. Psychologists tend to search for an underlying consistency of response, or for a set of items on a questionnaire or test that cohere, or for parsimony of explanation. Psychological explanation looks for tools that will predict consistently, and interpretation in traditional work – positivist or phenomenological – looks for pure undivided meaning, whether in observation statements or in reports of experience. In contrast, discourse analysts will always attend to inconsistency, and to the variation in accounts. This is not to catch people out, but to lead us to the diverse fragments of meaning that come together in any particular text.

For example, Wetherell and Potter (1992) studied the accounts of Pākehā (white) New Zealanders focusing on racial and cultural categories, and their views of the Māori people. Within these accounts there were competing and overlapping descriptions of culture. On the one hand, culture would be talked about as 'heritage' with the Māori positioned as if they were a protected species. At other points in the conversation culture would be represented as 'therapy' with worries that young Māori might behave badly because they were disconnected from their cultural group. These different 'interpretative repertoires' or 'discourses' could be found in the interview transcript of the same person, and the different contradictory notions of culture would have different consequences for how the minority community could be understood.

Foucault's historical research focused on *contradictions* between discourses and the ways in which the self is torn in different directions by discourse. The unified image of the 'self' in contemporary psychology and society is no more than that, an image, and so discursive psychology has to take care not to assume something undivided in the person underneath discourse. The term 'deconstruction' is sometimes used in this context to describe the way in which a text can be unravelled and the contradictions in it displayed so that it becomes clear what ideas are being privileged and what the costs are of that. A critical discursive reading is always, in some sense, a deconstruction of dominant forms of knowledge, and the reader constructs a different account as they deconstruct a text (Derrida, 1981; Eagleton, 1983). While the notion of variability tends to celebrate diversity of meaning in pluralist spirit, the notion of contradiction links more directly with struggle, power and the deconstruction of discourse in practice.

From construction to constitution. The second characteristic of discourse is 'construction'. This refers to the way in which every symbolic activity must make use of cultural resources to make sense to others. Traditional psychology treats each individual as if they could, in principle, be separated from culture, and it treats each individual mental process as if it were disconnected from the rest of the life-world of the 'subject'. Discourse analysis sees the meanings of terms, words, turns of phrase, arguments or other seemingly discrete aspects of language as intimately connected to other meanings and activities, and as re-created by speakers in the context of those meanings and activities. An important resource here has been 'ethnomethodology' (Garfinkel, 1967) which sees meaning as always 'indexical', defined by context, and 'conversation analysis' which looks at the mechanics of turn-taking and the way order is maintained in speech (Atkinson and

Heritage, 1984). People cannot make up the meaning of symbols as they go along, but they participate in already existing meanings. Meanings are not transmitted from one head to another, but are produced in discourse as people construct new texts. Discourses then construct ways in which people are able to relate to one another.

For example, Hollway (1989) analyzed the accounts of heterosexual couples, and the ways in which notions of intimacy and sexuality were described. She highlighted three contradictory discourses which had powerful consequences for how the partners could experience themselves as men or women in a relationship. The 'male sexual drive' discourse positions the man as impelled by forces out of his control and the woman only as object and recipient of his needs; the 'have/hold' discourse positions the man and woman as bound together for life with moral responsibilities to maintain the relationship having priority; the 'permissive' discourse celebrates the possibility of other relationships and the freedom of each partner to find fulfilment as they wish. These discourses not only prescribe certain behaviours, they produce 'masculinity' and 'femininity' as objects to be understood and positions to be lived out in ways that might be liberating or oppressive for those subject to them.

Foucault's (1966) study of different 'epistemes' in Western culture, and the emergence of the modern episteme in the nineteenth century which governs the way we talk and think about science, progress and personal meaning, was a structuralist enterprise. That is, he described structures of knowledge. His 'archaeology' of the human sciences showed how the concepts we take for granted in psychology and in our daily lives have a long history which is marked by rapid shifts and mutations in knowledge. Our ideas are *constituted* within patterns of discourse that we cannot control. Foucault's later work, and post-structuralism generally, emphasized the instability and struggles over meaning that mark human activity, and he came to prefer the term 'genealogy' to refer to the messy and sometimes bloody way in which meanings emerge. Structures were now seen as always contested, and the power they hold is always met by resistance. A Foucauldian account of the psy-complex, for example, focuses on the way that differences of perspective in language are policed and individuals are made to tell one coherent story about themselves to the authorities, to each other, and to themselves.

From function to power. The third characteristic is 'function'. Discourse does not provide a transparent window onto the mind of the individual or onto the world outside, as many psychologists would seem to believe. Rather, language organized through discourse always does things. When we seem to be merely describing a state of affairs, our commentary always has other effects; it plays its part in legitimizing or challenging, supporting or ironizing, endorsing or subverting what it describes. In both everyday language and in psychological description, our utterances are what are termed in British analytic philosophy – which is one of the theoretical resources for this version of discourse analysis – 'speech acts' (Austin, 1962). Discourse analysts will focus, then, on what these acts are doing. Speech act theory saw everyday talk as an alternative to mentalistic explanations of individual activities, and the work of Wittgenstein and other writers in this tradition see psychological phenomena as products of 'ordinary' language (Wittgenstein, 1953; Parker, this volume Chapter 4).

The attention to functions of discourse is also radicalized through Foucault's (1980) account of *power*. Power is bound up with knowledge, and those who are subject to power continually remake it and their subjection to it as they participate in discourse and regulative practices. A Foucauldian view of power differs from many standard social – scientific accounts which reduce it to a kind of potential that an individual possesses and wields when they wish (Ng, 1980).

For example, Walkerdine (1981, 1990) analyzed the interaction between a female teacher and a little boy in class. In the brief piece of transcript, the teacher was able to control the boy until he responded with a stream of sexist abuse. She withdrew, and was then unable to reassert her authority. Walkerdine explored the way that competing discourses of devalued female sexuality and liberal education theory were framing the way the participants could relate to one another. The boy was able to position the teacher as a woman, and so silence her, and the woman who had been trained to value the free expression of children positioned herself as a good teacher, and was unable to silence the boy. These discourses could only work here, of course, because of the wider systems of power in male – female relationships and systems of ideology in education. Power was played out in this classroom in such a way that the woman participated in, and reproduced her own oppression.

Discourse sets out a range of 'subject positions', places in the discourse which carry certain rights to speak and specifications for what may be spoken, places which people must assume for it to work (Davies and Harré, 1990). Discourse also recruits readers into subject positions by 'interpellating' them, calling out to them and constructing forms of identity that they must experience for the discourse to make sense (Althusser, 1971). When the notion of 'subject position' is linked with developments in Foucauldian and post-structuralist theory, we have a valuable tool for cutting through to a better understanding of abuses of power and ideological mystification in psychology and its wider culture. This means that theory is very important in critical work on discourse. I will return to this point towards the end of the chapter.

Theory and ideology

A theory of language – Saussure's (1974) 'structural linguistics' – underpinned the development of structuralism and post-structuralism. Saussure made a useful distinction between individual 'speech acts' on the one hand and the 'language system' which determined how they may be produced and what sense they would be able to have on the other. Barthes' (1973) extended this analysis to look at the way terms in language do not only seem to refer directly to things outside language, through 'denotation', but also link in with a network of associations, through 'connotation', and operate as part of an ideological 'second-order sign system' which he called 'myth'.

Myth naturalizes cultural meanings and makes it seem as if language not only refers to the world, but also reflects an unchanging and universal order of things. Because it does not make a direct claim to represent the way the world should be, but insinuates itself into taken-for-granted frames of reference, myth is one of the effective ways that ideology works. Foucault (1980) was very suspicious of the term 'ideology' because it may prompt people to find an essential underlying 'truth' that could be counterposed to it, but Foucauldian discourse analysis in psychology now is more sympathetic to the ways in which radical literary theorists have struggled with the term and have tried to save it for a reading of texts (Eagleton, 1991). If we connect our work with the Foucauldian tradition in this way, the approach can function as a bridge to a critical understanding of contradiction, the constitution of the modern psychological subject and its place in regimes of knowledge and power. It is then possible for the researcher to break completely from mainstream psychology and to view it as a series of practices that can be 'de-constructed'.

Axes of difference in discursive research

As with any other approach in psychology, there is much disagreement about what discursive psychology is, and some doubt as to whether it could be seen as an 'off the shelf' alternative to the mainstream discipline. It is certainly not consistently reliable as a critical tool for examining psychology when we get it home and try to use it. There are some important fault-lines in discursive approaches which bear serious attention. In this second half of the chapter I will draw attention to some of the key debates and divisions in discursive research and their consequences for critical psychologists by laying out five 'axes' around which differences revolve at the moment.

Micro–macro

Reduction in explanation to the individual has long been a problem for critical approaches in psychology (Billig, 1976). Psychology is founded on the study of the person abstracted from social context, and *micro*-reduction which sees the individual as the source of all psychological processes is usually a conservative mode of explanation. In contrast, critical psychologists have insisted that it is necessary to focus on patterns of social relationships and structures of the wider culture to explain how psychological phenomena come about. Only then is it possible to connect psychology with questions of ideology and power.

In discourse analysis there is a good deal of work on the interpersonal level, and upon texts of conversations and interviews, and there is a progressive movement away from the individual to the contexts in which they make and remake relationships with others. Micro-sociological perspectives such as 'conversation analysis' and 'ethnomethodology' have been imported here to describe, for example, how a person attributes and gains identity as part of a group through their use of 'membership categorization devices' (Sacks, 1974), or how a deviant career is constructed for others through the redescription and 'cutting out' of what is made to seem unusual behaviour (Smith, 1978). This focus does help us to understand how identities and institutions are co-created as 'accomplishments' rather than as simply being pre-given settings for activity. Researchers are urged to treat aspects of the social world as a 'topic' here rather than simply as a 'resource', and so there is a critical reflexive impulse in this work. Some important issues of gender and power in language can also be picked up using conversation-analytic accounts of language (Crawford, 1995).

However, while the shift of focus up from the individual is necessary and some conversation-analytic and ethnomethodological work is useful, this micro-sociological view is often quite stubborn in resisting a shift further up to higher-level social and cultural analysis. Critical psychologists will need at some point to refer to the character of a particular society, economic structures, classes and systems of oppression based, for example, on gender or race. The micro-sociological perspective prevents them from doing this, and will encourage them to treat terms for collections of individuals as no more than abstractions that 'reify' (make into things) the sense that people make of the world as an ongoing process. There is, then, little place in this micro-sociology for an analysis of the weight of history, for people are seen as freely creating a version of the world in their talk as text and in their own interpretations of other texts (Garfinkel, 1967). There is a danger, then, that 'discursive psychology' could be restricted in its focus and refuse to take account of the role of ideology and power.

At the other side of the micro–macro axis lie various approaches that explore the historical and cultural background to this small-scale activity of sense-making. It is certainly necessary for critical discourse researchers to pay due attention to the micro level, rather than simply insisting that an analysis of historical forces and social structures is sufficient. The feminist argument that the 'personal is political' (Rowbotham *et al.*, 1979) is one that critical psychologists need to take to heart, and an account of discourse should be able to identify the ways in which processes of ideology and power find their way into the little stories of everyday life. Some writers who combine feminism with ethnomethodology have attempted to show how the accomplishments of individuals in social interaction often become reified, and how an analysis of broader rules of discourse can reveal what purposes that reification serves (Smith, 1974).

A discursive psychology which is to reflect critically on the accomplishments of actors must explore the rules they have followed and the material they have worked upon. But to do that it must take seriously the way wider structures of power set the scene for the way we make sense of things in discourse and the way those structures themselves limit our understanding of how they function. This is where their ideological aspect comes to the fore. We need, as some realist writers have pointed out, to attend to unintended consequences, unacknowledged conditions, unconscious motivations and tacit skills that prevent the world from being a fully open and transparent place (Bhaskar, 1989; Parker, 1992).

Inside–outside

As well as reducing explanation to the level of the individual, the conservative goal of most psychologists is to produce an account of what is happening *inside* the head. Psychology here reproduces the deeply felt experience of most people in Western culture, that their thinking first takes place in an interior private realm and is only then 'expressed' and communicated to others. The danger with explanations which try to look inside the subject is that all too often they smuggle essentialism back into our picture of social action. Essentialism is a mode of explanation that looks to underlying fixed qualities that operate independently of social relations. Essentialism can be found in contemporary discursive accounts in at least four ways: where the discourse user is seen as deliberately manipulating rhetorical devices (e.g., Edwards, 1985); where there is a temptation bring in some notion of the 'self' to explain identity in discourse (e.g., Burr, 1995); where certain characteristics of thought are assumed to underpin what people are doing in discourse (e.g., Billig, 1991); or where there is an attempt to justify a discourse perspective by appealing to cognitive models or neurophysiology (e.g., Harré and Gillett, 1994).

However, there is also a danger with an alternative 'critical' account which simply insists that everything is in language, and that all of our cognitive skills, decisions, experiences of selfhood and intentionality can be dissolved in discourse as it washes through us. The discursive argument against the existence of cognitive machinery inside the head can appear uncomfortably similar to traditional behaviourist accounts, and to their refusal to speculate about what is going on inside the mind as if it were a kind of closed box. It is true that a thorough-going discursive psychology is strongly 'anti-humanist', and there is suspicion of the notion of a unified 'self' that lies underneath discourse. The worry here, though, is about the individualist essentialism that underpins much humanist rhetoric rather than its moral claims, and the most hard-line discourse analysts will still often nurture the possibility of transforming language so that it may better serve human agency.

A critical discursive account reframes questions about the inside and the outside of the individual subject to turn the activity of speakers and listeners, writers and readers into places in discourse. When a sense of self is constituted by a subject in discourse, certain reflexive 'powers' are produced which are now necessary for those living in a human community, and these powers make subjectivity a resource as well as a topic of inquiry. Discourse researchers prefer the term 'subjectivity' to 'experience'. This is because while the category of experience presupposes an individual self that enjoys or suffers it, subjectivity refers simultaneously to the sense of selfhood and to the production of that sense of self at a place in relation to others in language.

Humanist psychotherapy, for example, tries to uncover experience of the self as if it were always there under the surface guaranteeing the integrity of the subject independent of social relations. Discursive psychotherapy which draws upon the work of Foucault and Derrida, in contrast, is concerned with tracing distress to networks of social relations and to patterns of language. A turn to discourse in therapy has helped therapists who want to link their work to wider issues of social justice to de-construct the client's problem by, first of all, locating that problem in discourse, by 'externalizing' it (White and Epston, 1990). This innovative therapeutic work which is part of the 'anti-humanist' trend of much critical discourse research leads, then, to a more challenging and empowering social humanist practice.

Quantitative–qualitative

The third axis runs from the quantification of discourse-analytic accounts to the more hermeneutic qualitative styles of explanation. Most traditional psychology operates on the conservative premise that the only things worth studying are those that can be measured. Quantification of psychological and interpersonal processes is seen as one of the guarantees that research is scientific. Critical psychology has challenged this scientific status in a number of ways. One strategy has been to refuse to adopt the term 'science' altogether and to argue, in ethnomethodological style, that scientific explanation is a particular way of making sense of the world, one which revels in its own reification of social accomplishments (Woolgar, 1988). Another strategy has been to demonstrate that scientific inquiry need not resort to quantification, and that it is often a sign of bad science that practitioners should want to quantify phenomena before a careful description of singular cases (Harré and Secord, 1972).

The difference between these qualitative and quantitative tendencies in discourse analysis is played out in the debate between those who look to the skill of a theoretically informed critical 'reading'and those who would like to take short-cuts with computer software to code the material. The problem is that this sort of coding must always operate as a form of content analysis, of course. It saves time in skimming a large corpus of textual material, but all too often it leads to a view of language as a set of discrete packages of meaning that always carry the same value regardless of context and which are each neatly labelled ready to be picked up.

Barthes (1977) described the development of structuralist and post-structuralist analysis of literary texts as entailing the 'death of the author', as assuming that we could not understand the meaning of a text by tracing it back to the person who 'wrote' it. The other side of this argument, however, and just as important, is that the kinds of reading he was proposing required the 'birth of the reader' as an active participant in the text. The discourse analyst is an active reader who encourages those who are positioned by discourse to read the texts they live within and so to assume a position of understanding and greater control over their lives, the positions they would want to adopt.

This does not mean that discourse analysts would want to take up the position of 'reader reception theorists' in literary theory, however (Iser, 1974). The notion of 'reader reception' also invites us back into a cognitivist notion of the individual as having some sort of inter-pretative paraphernalia inside their heads that helps them to decode what was happening around them. It presupposes that there could be a position for a reader that was free of discourse, and that this indepen-dent reader would be able to analyse what was going on in the text from an objective standpoint (Eagleton, 1983). Discourse analysts looking to literary theory are more impressed with some of the other descriptions in Barthes's work of 'readerly' and 'writerly' texts, of different kinds of discourse that either seem closed and only able to be read or seem open to be written as well as read, open to be changed (Barthes, 1977). Readerly texts only allow the reader to reproduce them. Writerly texts are open to the reader to participate and transform the meanings that are offered. There are problems of reading and interpretation here that cannot be addressed by quantitative approaches.

Quantitative approaches are made for readerly texts, and do not take us any further than description, than reading. Computers help us in doing this, but they also restrict us to this. Qualitative approaches, however, that are also sensitive to what Barthes (1975) called 'the pleasure of the text', will be able to read writerly texts, to engage with them to change them, to engage in something close to what in other traditions of social science would be called 'action research'.

The first three axes of difference sometimes find the more conservative varieties of discursive psychology in broad agreement with some of the key assumptions made by traditional psychology; they like reductionism, essentialism and quantification. The fourth and fifth axes are a little more complicated, and find critical psychologists having to make some difficult choices, and having to risk some strange alliances.

Relativism–realism

There is a powerful tendency in discourse-analytic work toward a relativist position, and an understandable refusal to take on good coin the
'findings' that psychology claims to have made so far about what goes
on inside human beings. There are, however, also serious risks in this
social constructionist view of psychological concepts. The theoretical
resources that critical and discursive researchers have drawn upon are
part of a wider discursive turn in the human sciences that carry conservative as well as progressive prescriptions for social activity.

At the same time as deconstruction and discourse theory cuts away
the positivist ground from beneath traditional psychology and rela-
tivizes their claims about the nature of human nature, these theoretical
currents also relativize the truth claims of the critics, and so sabotage
principled resistance to the discipline. Deconstruction was mentioned
earlier as a useful source of work for discourse analysts, but there is also
a conservative variant of deconstruction which reduces the reading of a
text to a free-play of meaning in which no critical position can be
taken toward it.

Now the stakes are higher as some defences of relativism in discourse
research would seem to have the effect of throwing into question any
position from which a critique could be developed. In one particularly
pernicious example, 'discursive psychologists' have resorted to
analysing the way in which references to the Holocaust function as
part of a 'bottom-line argument' against relativism (Edwards *et al.*,
1995). They wish to make the case for relativism in research, but they
also, in the process, undermine the truth claims of those who may
refer to the Holocaust as a real historical event. Apart from these more
gross and dangerous manifestations of relativism, a relativist position
in social constructionism or discourse analysis makes it difficult for us
to sustain the project of a critical psychology, and it is not surprising
that feminist psychologists have been alert to this danger (Burman,
1990; Gill, 1995).

Critical realism would appear to provide an answer to this problem,
for it both exposes positivist psychology's pretensions to model itself
on what it imagines the natural sciences to be like, and it grounds
discursive accounts of mentation in social practices whose underlying
logic and structure can, in principle, be discovered (Bhaskar, 1989;
Parker, 1992). Critical realism runs alongside the social constructionist
attacks on the discipline while preventing a wholesale collapse into
discourse idealism, the position that there is nothing but discourse.
This solution is not as clear-cut as it seems, however, and 'realism' of

different varieties could always be mobilized by those sympathetic to mainstream psychology to warrant it as a science and to rebut social constructionist critiques (Greenwood, 1994). It would seem, in this light, that even 'critical' realists could end up falling into the arms of science as they look for certainties in this confusing landscape, and only relativists who go all the way can really resist the truth claims of psychology.

There is a way out of this problem. A critical engagement with relativism and realism needs to address (i) how psychological facts are socially constructed and (ii) how subjectivity is discursively reproduced within present social arrangements *and* (iii) how the underlying historical conditions emerged that gave rise to the 'psy-complex'. Only by understanding how the discipline of psychology reproduces notions of individuality and human nature – a realist endeavour – will it be possible to transform it, and to socially construct it as something different, something better.

Common sense–theory

This final axis of difference within the discursive tradition maps onto the previous one, for all the worst errors of relativism are compounded when they are combined with a celebration of commonsense. There are a number of paradoxes here, for both conservative and critical psychology are part of everyday knowledge outside universities and clinics. It is easier to grasp how this paradox is played out if we focus on the notion of contradiction in discourse, and the way contradictory meanings constitute objects that reinforce or challenge power.

The problem is that although traditional psychology does not usually value the common-sense understanding that people have of their activities and the accounts they offer about psychological states, it does still rest upon common-sense assumptions about the mind and behaviour. There is a two-way traffic of ideas here. On the one hand, psychologists base their theories upon hunches and intuitions about people that they gather from common sense. On the other hand, psychological 'facts' and theories find their way out from the discipline into the real world and become part of common sense. Psychology itself operates as a kind of 'myth' in common sense, and it runs alongside a range of exclusionary and pathologizing practices that common sense justifies as being natural and unquestionable. Common sense in general, of course, consists of cultural and historical discourses which reproduce the very oppressive social relations psychology essentializes and ratifies.

This is why an analysis of psychological phenomena needs to be undertaken alongside an analysis of practices of psychology in Western culture, and then that analysis has to extend its scope to the way in which psychology relays images of the 'others' of Western culture through its own practices. It is difficult, then, to appeal to common sense as an always trustworthy resource to attack psychology when, for example, both common sense and psychology are saturated by racist imagery and are rooted in colonial imagery (Howitt and Owusu-Bempah, 1994). On the other hand, critical perspectives in psychology often develop through researchers looking to their own experience to challenge the lies that the discipline peddles about them. The development of feminist psychology, for example, would be inconceivable without a challenge based on women's 'common sense', their experience of their position, and this is something that has also had an impact on discourse research (Wilkinson and Kitzinger, 1995).

The tension between common sense and expertise draws attention to two vital prerequisites for critical research. The first is an awareness of context, and the second is the use of theoretical resources. With respect to the first, an awareness of context, it is not surprising, perhaps, that some of the most radical discourse-analytic studies have been carried out in contexts where it has been impossible to feel comfortable with common sense. The development of discourse analysis in South Africa, for example, was in a setting where the society and the academic world was politicized, where there were continual questions and struggles over identity, and where conflicts over culture and 'race' had a knock-on effect on the ways in which researchers understood power and ideology (Levett *et al.*, 1996). In the liberal democracies, on the other hand, especially where the student population is skewed to the more comfortable middle-class side of the general population, there is little impetus to question what may be wrong with social arrangements and ways of speaking. It is more difficult to politicize language, but discourse analysis does at least help us to keep those questions around in psychology.

With respect to the second prerequisite for critical research, theory, it is necessary to draw upon frameworks which separate us from the language which makes the world seem 'just so'. Structuralism, semiology, post-structuralism and deconstruction have been laboured in this chapter because they enable us to step back from language and to understand the way it is organized to lead us to see the world in certain ways and to obscure other ways of seeing that may be more empowering. What is at stake here is the space for a critical standpoint to develop from which to view the ideological functions of the discipline of psychology. That standpoint is not given to us by common sense. Rather, we have to construct it, and we need good theory to do that. Critical psychology requires a critical distance from its object of study, and our task is to maintain that critical distance without devaluing the understanding that people have of their own lives.

Remaining questions

Discursive psychology has been presented here as a radical alternative to most research in the discipline. There are, nevertheless, problems that cannot be solved within this framework, and there are problems that it creates for researchers. Some critical psychologists will find elements of a discursive approach difficult to agree with. There will be occasions, for example, when good quantitative research into the impact of exploitation, over-crowding and poverty on people's lives will be better than reams of textual analysis. Aspects of a discursive approach, such as its relativism and celebration of common-sense categories of experience, have already made it something of a liability for critical researchers.

Worse than this, there is no simple line that we could trace through discourse analysis using, for example, the work of Foucault, which would ensure that we would assemble a reliable critical perspective. The different axes of debate in discourse theory in psychology constitute a field of theoretical and political struggle. One of the paradoxes in discourse research is that those who are critical will already, almost spontaneously, do 'discourse analysis' on the texts they read and live, for they read and live at a distance from language, experiencing its ideological character and the effects of power.

Those who are comfortable with the positions language offers them in culture, or who are not confident about mobilizing their critical awareness of power to focus on what psychology does to them, on the other hand, will trail through handbooks of discourse analysis, and be unable to see the point; for language does no more than represent the world as it is and as they think it should be. These arguments have been rehearsed before, along with a number of other problems in discourse analysis (Parker and Burman, 1993). What these issues come down to is that there is no place *in* psychology, or even in 'discursive psychology' for critical work to start. A critical psychology has to be constructed from theoretical resources, life experience and political identities *outside* the discipline. Only then does it make sense to deconstruct what the discipline does to us and to its other subjects.

6
Discourse
Definitions and Contradictions

With the question 'What is "discourse"?' as the starting point, this chapter addresses ways of identifing particular discourses, and attends to how these discourses should be distinguished from texts. The emergence of discourse analysis within psychology, and the continuing influence of linguistic and post-structuralist ideas on practitioners, provide the basis on which discourse-analytic research can be developed fruitfully. This chapter discusses the descriptive, analytic and educative functions of discourse analysis, and addresses the cultural and political questions which arise when discourse analysts reflect on their activity. Suggestions for an adequate definition of discourse are proposed and supported by seven criteria which should be adopted to identify discourses, and which attend to contradictions between and within them. Three additional criteria are then suggested to relate discourse analysis to wider political issues.

Introduction

What is 'discourse'? The term is becoming increasingly important in social psychology, and the development of discourse analysis there has implications for the rest of psychology. The definition which Potter and Wetherell (1987) provide in their useful introductory guide *Discourse and Social Psychology,* has succeeded in engaging the interest of a number of groups of researchers. The definition is wide enough to encompass much of the material that social psychologists would want to study: discourse includes, they say, 'all forms of spoken interaction, formal and informal, and written texts of all kinds' (Potter and Wetherell, 1987: 7). When a researcher is faced with a mass of discourse, and wants to pick out particular *discourses,* however, the definition becomes less helpful. It is difficult to use. This chapter is concerned with the task of defining discourse. I will draw attention to some of the descriptions of discourse outside psychology, and then set out some criteria for identifying discourses. My main focus will be on the practical problems which confront a researcher attempting to carry out a discourse analysis. However, each practical problem raises broader philosophical issues about the nature of language, discourse and texts. I will also argue, towards the end of the chapter that discourse analytic research should go beyond the seven necessary criteria for the identification of discourses, and consider other issues which relate to ideology and power.

The turn to language

There are many aspects to the 'turn to language' in psychology in recent years. One of the influential forces inside the discipline has been the group of writers who participated in, and exacerbated, the 'crisis' in the late 1960s and early 1970s. The self-styled 'new paradigm' psychologists – a group which includes Harré (1979, 1983) and Shotter (1975, 1984) – drew attention to the importance of meaning and the accounts people gave of their actions. These writers selectively imported ideas from microsociology – ethomethodology, for example (Garfinkel, 1967) – and analytic philosophy – such as speech act theory (Austin, 1962). The new paradigm critiques of traditional laboratory-experimental social psychology are still relevant to contemporary debates about the role of (spoken or written) accounts as well as appropriate methods to study language, and they provide the context for the recent interest in discourse analysis. (It is still useful, for example, to employ Harré's distinction between the 'practical' and the 'expressive' orders of society, as will be seen below.) Potter and Wetherell (1987) repeat the story that microsociology and analytic philosophy (along with semiology) were the main driving forces in the turn to language, and discourse analysis is social psychology today is placed by them in that tradition. It is true that Potter and Wetherell acknowledge the role of 'post-structuralist' work on discourse outside psychology, but the emphasis on this tradition (evident in the references to semiology) is much reduced, unfortunately, in comparison with their earlier work (Potter *et al.*, 1984).

However, the crisis inside social psychology which has produced discourse analysis was a pale reflection of debates over structures of meaning outside, debates which were to give issue to post-structuralism

(Parker, 1989). By post-structuralism I mean the set of writings on language, discourse and texts produced by a number of French philosophers and historians in the 1970s and 1980s, a group which includes Foucault (1969, 1980), Barthes (1973, 1977), Derrida (1976) and Lyotard (1984). It is not possible in this chapter to describe these debates in detail (cf. Dews, 1987 for a critical review of post-structuralist philosophy). However, as will become increasingly apparent as this chapter progresses, my only understanding of discourse is informed by post-structuralist work.

Discourse analysis strikes a critical distance from language, and one useful aspect of the approach is the reflexivity urged upon a researcher (and reader). I want to argue, however, that this reflexivity needs to be grounded if it is to have progressive effects, and that work in the post-structuralist tradition can locate discourse and reflection historically. In addition, the study of discourses carried out by Foucault, his co-workers and followers has implications for how we describe the emergence of academic psychology and the 'psy-complex' in Western culture, and for how we understand the discipline and its objects today (Rose, 1985). Foucault (1961), for example, described how a discourse which was about 'madness' as a medical category came into being, and the ways in which medical discourse involved the categorization of a section of the population. Debates over rationality and responsibility in the 19th century were informed by such discourses. In another study, Foucault (1975b) then collected legal chapters and accounts given of a murder at that time, and showed how these discourses framed the possible explanations that could be given of that event. Foucault (1975a, 1976a) connects the development of discourses which describe (and prescribe) forms of individual reason, responsibility and pathology with discipline, surveillance and power. These discourses informed legal practice, and they helped constitute contemporary psychology. Discourses about rationality and individual responsibility that we still employ today, then, have a history.

It is also possible for discourses to fall into disuse. Only a few centuries ago dogs and pigs could be tried for murder and flies excommunicated, and a French defence counsel could have made his legal reputation by securing the acquittal of a ferret on a technicality (Evans, 1906). The attribution of responsibility then was framed by discourses pertaining to animals as moral beings, legally liable. In contrast, the dominant psychology we have today is informed by particular conceptions of rationality, discourses in which one attributes internal mental states to individuals which, we suppose, direct behaviour (Costall and Still, 1987).

A number of points arise from the history of discourse. Discourses do not simply describe the social world, but categorize it, they bring phenomena into sight. A strong form of the argument would be that discourses allow us to focus on things that are not 'really' there, and that once an object has been circumscribed by discourses it is difficult *not* to refer to it as if it were real. They provide frameworks for debating the value of one way of talking about reality over other ways. Types of person are also being referred to as the objects of the discourses. The final point for the moment is that when we look at discourses in their historical context, it becomes clear that they are quite coherent, and that as they are elaborated they become more carefully systematized.

I suggest, then, that a working definition of a discourse should be that it is *a system of statements which constructs an object*. However, this definition needs to be supported by a number of conditions. In the next section of this chapter, then, I will set out seven criteria, the system of statements, that should be used to identify *our* object, to enable us to engage with, and in, discourse analysis. One reason for laying out these conditions for recognizing discourses is to fill a gap in Potter and Wetherell's (1987) account of the method, their 'ten stages in the analysis of discourse' which bewilder new researchers as it dawns on them that each step rests on a bedrock of 'intuition' and 'presentation'. At points the reader is told that discourse analysis is like riding a bike, is warned that the stages are not sequential, and advised that 'there is no analytic method' (Potter and Wetherell, 1987: 169). I do not want to suggest that the criteria presented here should be employed sequentially (or that they are scientific), but that they do help to clear up some of the confusions that have attended the incorporation of discourse analytic ideas into psychology.

Criteria

These seven criteria deal with different levels of discourse analysis. There is a degree of conceptual work that needs to go into the analysis before the material is touched, and then, as the analysis proceeds, it is necessary to step back a number of times to make sense of the statements that have been picked out. Each criterion raises questions about the theoretical framework the researcher is using.

(1) A discourse is a coherent system of meanings

The metaphors, analogies and pictures discourses paint of a reality can be distilled into statements about that reality. It is only then that it becomes possible to say that a discourse is 'any regulated system of statements' (Henriques *et al.*, 1984: 105). This definition of discourse explicitly draws on Foucault's work. The statements in a discourse can be grouped, and given a certain coherence, insofar as they refer to the same topic (employing culturally available understandings as to what constitudes a topic). This is not to say that the set is ever watertight. (I will return to the role of contradictions within particular discourses below.)

There is a similarity here between this aspect of a definition of discourses and the way 'interpretive repertoires' are defined in *Discourse and Social Psychology*. It is worth building on the idea that we are indeed looking for 'recurrently used systems of terms used for characterizing and evaluating actions, events and other phenomena ... a limited range of terms used in particular stylistic and grammatical constructions ... [often] ... organized around specific metaphors and figures of speech' (Potter and Wetherell, 1987: 149). We should be cautious, though, about three aspects of this characterization of an 'interpretive repertoire': (1) to talk about 'grammatical constructions' is inaccurate and risks getting bogged down in formalism at the expense of content; (2) the assertion that there is a 'limited range of terms' feeds a corresponding hope for an ultimate closed picture of a particular system; and (3) the term 'repertoire' has uncomfortable resonances with behaviourism (especially when we are invited to look for systems of terms which are 'recurrently used'). It is surely more accurate to label sets of metaphor and statements we find as '*discourses*'.

To return to the problem of how to recognize one discourse when faced with a mass of text, how do we employ this notion of coherence? Take a simple example; Dan Quayle, American vice-president, is speaking at a Thanksgiving festival:

> I suppose three important things certainly come to my mind that we want to say thank you. The first would be our family. Your family, my family – which is composed of an immediate family of a wife and three children, a larger family with grandparents and aunts and uncles. We all have our family, whichever that may be ... The family ... which goes back to the nucleus of civilisation. And the very beginnings of civilisation, the very beginnings of this country, goes back to the family. And the time and time again, I'm often reminded, especially in this presidential campaign of the importance of the family, and what a family means to this country.

And so when you pay thanks I suppose the first thing that would come to mind would be to thank the Lord for the family.

(*The Guardian,* 8 November 1988)

Quayle attempts to define the 'family' here, but what I what to draw attention to is the way we have to bring our own sense of what 'the family' is to this text in order to make it coherent. In this case we are able to do this because there is such a strong 'familialist discourse' in our culture: 'society has been familiarized' (Barrett and McIntosh, 1982: 31). We have to bring a knowledge of discourses from outside onto any example or fragment of discourse for it to become part of a coherent system in our analysis.

(2) A discourse is realized in texts

Where do we find discourses? It would be misleading to say that we ever find discourse as such. We actually find pieces of discourse. I want to open up the field of meanings to which discourse analysis could be applied beyond 'spoken interaction ... and written texts' (Potter and Wetherell, 1987: 7) by saying that we find discourses at work in *texts*. Texts are delimited tissues of meaning reproduced in any form that can be given an interpretive gloss.

I was given a small Liquid Crystal Display electronic game for Christmas. The buttons on the left and right move a male figure at the bottom of the screen from side to side. The figure is waving a crucifix at the ghosts descending from the top of the screen to their graves. As each ghost is prevented from landing and is despatched to the flames at the right-hand side I get awarded 10 points (and the penalty for letting each spirit through is a lost life). This is a text. A Christian discourse inhabits this text, and it is the translation of this text into a written and spoken form that renders that discourse 'visible' or, more accurately, in which the category 'discourse' becomes appropriate.

It is useful, as a first step, to consider all tissues of meaning as texts and to specify which texts will be studied. All of the world, as a world understood by us and so given meaning by us, can be described as being textual, and it is in this sense that, once this process of interpretation and reflection has been started, we can adopt the post-structuralist maxim '*There is nothing outside of the text*' (Derrida, 1976: 158). This does not necessarily commit us to a particular position on the nature of reality, textual or otherwise. I am merely drawing attention to the effects of describing, for research purposes, the world in this way. Speech, writing, nonverbal behaviour, Braille,

Morse code, semaphore, runes, advertisements, fashion systems, stained glass, architecture, tarot cards and bus tickets are forms of text. In some cases we could imagine an 'author' lying behind the text as source and arbiter of a true meaning. But the lessons to draw from this list are first, that, as Barthes (1977) argued, there need not be an author, and second, that once we start to describe what texts mean, we are elaborating discourses that go beyond individual intentions. The second step in a discourse analysis, then, should be a process of exploring the connotations, allusions, implications which the texts evoke. A helpful guide to this exercise in cultural anthropology is Barthes's (1973) work on modern 'myth'.

Sometimes different discourses are available to different audiences. The distinction between the inside and outside of psychology is a good case example. On the one hand, the ψ sign gives a text a meaning for those of us inside psychology. The discourses which inhabit a text containing that sign will often be discourses coherent to psychologist. On the other hand, an image of Freud's face gives a text a meaning for those outside the discipline. The discourses which give that sign meaning (and it often means 'psychology' for outsiders) would not be accepted by many psychologists.

Discourse analysis, then, involves two preliminary steps (turning our objects into texts, and locating those texts in discourses) in which material is interpreted and thus put into a linguistic form. It is right, then, to adopt the formulation that discourses are 'linguistic sets of a higher order than the sentence (while often reducible to a sentence) and *carried out* or *actualized* in or by means of texts' (Marin, 1983: 162).

(3) A discourse reflects on its own way of speaking

Not every text contains a reflection on the terms chosen, and not every speaker is self-conscious about the language they use. However, a condition which applies to each discourse taken as a whole is that it is possible to find instances where the terms chosen are commented upon. At these points, the discourse itself is folding around and reflecting on its own way of speaking. The devices employed to bring about this reflection range from the uneasy phrase 'for the want of a better word' through disingenuous denials of a position being advocated ('don't get me wrong') to full-blown analyses of the implications of a world-view.

This raises the issue of 'intuition' in the research, for the analyst needs to relate the questions raised by the first two criteria to the way the discourse is able to take itself as an object. How are the contradictions in the discourse referred to, and how would another person (or text) employing this discourse refer to the contradictions within the discourse? When these questions are answered, other instances of a discourse have been identified. It is important here to articulate instances of a discourse into a coherent pattern, and to take it back to the speaker or to relate it to other texts.

A related point has been made recently by the authors of *Ideological Dilemmas* (a product of the research group which now includes Jonathan Potter) that it is necessary to attend to different layers of meaning. Working on the assumption that assertions in a discourse also pose an opposing position, they argue that we should attend to 'hidden meanings': 'discourse can contain its own negations, and these are part of its implicit, rather than explicit meanings' (Billig *et al.*, 1988: 23). They suggest that we should engage in hermeneutics to recover these meanings. Now, it is true that a hermeneutic style of inquiry is being used at points in discourse analysis, but it is a type of hermeneutics which does not attempt to trace the meanings to an author. There are such varieties (e.g. Ricoeur, 1971), but I am not sure whether this stretches the term too far beyond its own original meaning for us to continue using it here. One definition of discourse from contemporary literary theory argues that it is 'language grasped as *utterance*, as involving speakers and writing subjects and therefore, at least potentially, readers or listeners' (Eagleton, 1983: 210). What we should take from this is that analysis can bring in other readers and listeners, and should use their understanding of a discourse to bring it out.

For the discourse analyst, the reflexivity of a discourse is useful not only as a marker that the discourse analyst is actually picking up a discrete discourse. We can also think of this part of the research as proceeding in three steps in which: (1) it enables us to reflect on the terminology being used; (2) it then allows us to treat the discourse itself as object; and (3) it encourages a reflection on the term used to describe the discourse. This third step will involve moral evaluation and political choices on the part of the analyst: Potter and Wetherell (1988a) for example, quite rightly refer to the themes they describe in their New Zealand research not as 'race' discourses, but as 'racist' discourses.

(4) A discourse refers to other discourses

Post-structuralists contend that thought is bound up with language, and that reflexivity is continually captured, and distorted, by language (cf. Dews, 1987). If they are right, then reflexivity should be understood to be the employment of other discourses. At the very least, to take a weaker line on this, the *articulation* of our reflections on discourse must require the use of other discourses. The criterion that a discourse refers to other discourses, then, is a necessary correlate of the point that a discourse reflects on its own way of speaking. Discourses embed, entail and presuppose other discourses to the extent that the contradictions *within* a discourse open up questions about what other discourses are at work.

It is in this sense that it is right to argue that '[t]he systematic character of a discourse includes its systematic articulation with other discourses. In practice, discourses delimit what can be said, whilst providing the spaces – the concepts, metaphors, models, analogies – for making new statements within any specific discourse' (Henriques *et al.*, 1984: 105–106). This point raises, in turn, two further issues. First, metaphors and analogies are always available from other discourses, and the space this gives a speaker to find a voice from another discourse, and even within a discourse they oppose, is theoretically limitless. (It is not limitless in practice, and this point will be taken up when the role of institutions, power and ideology is discussed below.)

Secondly, analysis is facilitated by identifying contradictions between different ways of describing something. The examples I have referred to so far include familialist discourse, Christian discourse, and racist discourse. It is possible to imagine ways in which each of these can contradict the others. The metaphors of family used to describe the human race used alongside the currently popular liberal–humanist discourse could characterize Christian doctrine and racism as coterminous and equally dangerous. Alternatively, some versions of liberation theology include conceptions of community which are suspicuos of the nuclear family and are committed to anti-racism. Then again, racist discourses which appeal to mysticism take forms hostile to the modern family and liberal Christianity. Now, I am *not* intending to imply that each of these discourses is discrete in practice. You may have to stretch your imagination to accept some of combinations I suggested. At the moment, it could be argued that the discourses draw metaphors and institutional support from each other, and the process of distinguishing them is purely conceptual. Well, this is precisely the point, for we need to understand the *inter-relationship*, the interrelationship between *different* discourses in an analysis.

(5) A discourse is about objects

'Analysis' necessarily entails some degree of objectification, and in discourse there are at least two layers of objectification. The first is the layer of 'reality' that the discourse refers to. It is a commonplace in the sociology of knowledge (e.g. Berger and Luckmann, 1971) that language brings into being phenomena, and that the reference to an object, the simple use of a noun, comes to give that object a reality. Discourses are the sets of meanings which constitute objects, and a discourse, then, is indeed a 'representational practice' (Woolgar, 1988: 93) in that the representation of the object occurs as previous uses of the discourse and other related discourses are alluded to, and the object *as defined in the discourses* is referred to. Discourses are, according to one post-structuralist writer, 'practices that systematically form the objects of which they speak' (Foucault, 1969: 49).

I want at this point to attempt to close off some routes to linguistic idealism that have attracted discourse theorists in post-structuralism (Anderson, 1983). Discourse constructs 'representations' of the world which have a reality almost as coercive as gravity, and, like gravity, we know of the objects only through their effects. Take, for example, descriptions of medieval Anglo-Saxon sorcery in which the world is full of spirits and physical illness is attributed to the shots fired by elves (Bates, 1983). What we now can describe as discourses created and reproduced spirits and elves. Then, they were real in the way that atoms and electrons are real today. Many of the objects that discourse refers to do not exist in a realm outside discourse. However, we know when we kick our foot against a stone that there is more to the world than discourse. There are fuzzy borders between the set of things we know exist outside discourse and the things which may only have a reality within it. The only rule to guide us through this, perhaps, when we sit on a chair, lean on a table, and see print on chapter is to say 'there isn't any less than this, but there may be more'.

It is also sometimes insulting (and sometimes politically dangerous) to apply the phrase 'social construction of ...' to a particular object, when we are looking at the way in which discourse reproduces the social world (cf. Seidel, 1986a). One example which raises this problem, also serves to draw attention to the second layer of reality that a discourse refers to. The example is a badge given away at the Commonwealth Institute in London in 1988 with 'Dialogue on Diarrhoea' printed around the top. It says 'international newsletter' around the bottom, and these phrases frame a picture of a woman feeding an infant with a spoon. There were also huge posters around the cafeteria with the same message blazoned across them. At the first level of meaning, we have the object 'diarrhoea', and the badge is a text which reproduces the object in particular ways: (1) we know that 'diarrhoea' is, among other things, a medical description, and so we identify a medical discourse; (2) we assume that the woman feeding the infant is the mother, and so a familialist discourse also touches the text; and (3) we understand the image and message as located in an appeal, located in a discourse of charity. The second layer of reality is that of the 'dialogue', and here there is a reflection in the text on a discourse, and the text says that there is another 'object' which is the set of statements about diarrhoea. A discourse, then, is about objects, and discourse analysis is about discourses as objects.

(6) A discourse contains subjects

The object that a discourse refers to may have an independent reality outside discourse, but is given *another* reality by discourse. An example of such an object is the subject who speaks, writes, hears or reads the texts where discourses live. I will stick with this rather abstract and dehumanizing terminology a moment longer, and say that a subject is a location constructed within the expressive sphere which finds its voice through the cluster of attributes and responsibilities assigned to it as a variety of object. (Here I am adopting Harré's (1979) distinction between the 'expressive' sphere in which meanings and selves are presented and contested and the 'practical' order of society in which the physical world is organized and worked to sustain life.) A discourse makes available a space, and it addresses us in a particular way. When we discourse analyse a text, we need to ask in what ways, as Althusser (1971) put it when referring to the appeal of ideology, the discourse is hailing us, shouting 'hey you there' and making us listen.

It has been said that discourses are 'ways of perceiving and articulating relationships' (Banton *et al.*, 1985: 16). This is right, but it is more than that; we cannot avoid the perceptions of ourselves and others that discourses invite. There are a number of ways in which this works, and discourse analysis both attends to and intensifies each of these. First, there is the relation between the addressor (which we should think of here as being the text rather than the author who may have originated it) and the addressee. When a badge says 'Dialogue on Diarrhoea', who is it addressing? To put it crudely (and to employ an old social–psychological discourse), what 'role' are we having to adopt to hear this message? (1) a medical discourse could draw us in as a carer, but merely to supplement the work of those who are medically qualified; (2) the familialist discourse draws us in as protector (with different subject effects depending on the gender position we have in other discourses); and (3) the charity discourse draws us in as benefactor, and the 'dialogue' is about listening, understanding and giving. The second way in which we are positioned as a subject in discourse flows from that last point about what we are expected to do when addressed. What rights do we have to speak in a discourse? The medical discourse, for example, is one in which we adopt the position of nonmedic, and while we may use a medical vocabulary in some situations, there are others in which it is inappropriate. At the doctor's surgery the translation of the deliberately prosaic and everyday language we use into medical terminology is their task. We know we are the patient in this discourse. The third way in which we are positioned is where we are placed in relation to the discourse itself. A scientific discourse is one in which rights and powers to speak are clearly signalled by the amount of knowledge held, and the desire to be a scientist may be provoked when we hear or use that discourse. We may also resist it, but we have to take a position.

(7) A discourse is historically located

Discourses are not static. I have already pointed to the relationship between different discourses, and the ways in which discourses change and develop different layers and connections to other discourses through the process of reflection. When we think about discourses as consisting of a system of statements, it could appear as if an appeal is being made to the 'synchronic' dimension of language which inspired structural linguistics (Saussure, 1974). However, just as post-structuralism moved beyond the distinction between a system (the 'synchronic') and the development of terms (the 'diachronic'), so discourse analysis cannot take place without locating its object in time in a particular way. Discourses are located in time, and are about history, for the objects they refer to are objects constituted in the past by the discourse or related discourses. A discourse refers to past references to those objects.

For discourse analysts, the structure and force of particular discourses can only be described by showing other instances of that discourse, and explaining how it arose. The familialist discourse, for example, is about the history of the family, the way that history is reinterpreted to legitimate the Western nuclear family form, and the way the metaphors of family are used not only to describe other forms of life, but also to reinforce the notion of the family as natural, as going back to the beginnings of civilization. When we analyse the discourse of the family, we are disconnecting ourselves from that history. Similarly, discourse analysis of religion and racism switches back and forward from the elaboration of coherent systems of statements out of the text it studies to look at what those discourses meant as they emerged, and so what the present allusions actually 'refer' to.

It then becomes possible to use our knowledge of the historical weight of racist and religious discourses, say, to understand occasions when they combine. A reflection on the importance of language comes together with these themes in a statement made in 1986 by a supporter of a campaign in Southern California against the use of Spanish as a second language in the county. It runs: 'If English was good enough for Jesus Christ, its good enough for me'. Of course, a reading of this phrase needs not only an understanding of what discourses there are, and how they arose. It also calls for a study of the types of texts within which those discourses became dominant in the last 50 years or so. My guess in this case would be that Hollywood films would be powerful texts in which these discourses fuse and alter each other.

Auxiliary criteria

Although the seven criteria I have outlined are necessary and sufficient for marking our particular discourses, I want to draw attention to three more aspects of discourse that research should focus upon. The three further aspects of discourse are concerned with institutions, power and ideology, I will go through each in turn, and indicate why each is important and why these final three should be conceptually distinguished from discourse as such.

(1) Discourses support institutions

The most interesting discourses are those which are implicated in some way with the structure of institutions. The medical discourse, for example, exists in a variety of texts. Medical journals and books, research reports, lectures, General Medical Council decisions and popular medicine programmes, as well as the speech in every consultation with a doctor. In cases such as these, the employment of a discourse is also often a practice which reproduces the material basis of the institution. Feeling an abdomen, giving an injection or cutting a body are discursive practices. For Foucault (1969), discourses and practices should be treated as if they were the same thing, it is true both that material practices are always invested with meaning (they have the status of a text) and that speaking or writing is a 'practice'. Foucault's (1975a) work on discipline and power is concerned with the ways in which the physical organization of space and bodies developed. It is possible to identify a distinction between physical order and meanings in his work, and it is more helpful to hold onto a conceptual distinction between meanings, the expressive, and physical changes, the practical order (Harré, 1979). 'Discursive practices', then, would be those that reproduce institutions (among other things).

(2) Discourses reproduce power relations

We should talk about discourse and power in the same breath. Institutions, for example, are structured around, and reproduce power relations. The giving and taking away of rights to speak in medical discourse, and the powerlessness patients feel when in the grips of medical technology point to an intimate link between power and knowledge (Turner, 1987). A prediction that a discourse analysis which employed my three auxiliary criteria as well as the first seven outlined above may back up is that psychology upon Chartering too will both be able to popularize the discourses which constitute it objects ('behaviours', 'cognitions' and the such like), *and* be able to police the boundaries between its regime of truth and the other outside, the 'charlatans'. Psychology's increasing institutionalization will, in this way, increase its *power* both over those outside and those inside it. Foucault (1980) produced the couplet 'power/knowledge', but the two terms are not the same thing. It is important to distinguish discourse from power.

Discourses often do reproduce power relations, but this is a different claim from one which proposes that a criterion for recognizing a discourse is that there is power. If this criterion were to be adopted, we would fall into the trap of saying that 'power is everywhere' and that if power is everywhere, it would be both pointless to refer to it, and politically disarming (Poulantzas, 1978). There are three good reasons why we should not talk about discourse and power as necessarily entailing one another: (1) we would lose a sense of the relationship between power and resistance, with both power as coercive, and resistance as a refusal of dominant meanings being emptied of content; (2) we would lose sight of the ways in which discourses that challenge power are often tangled in oppressive discourses, but are no less valuable to our understanding of relationships and possible future relationships for that; and (3) it would be difficult, as researchers, to support the empowerment of those at the sharp end of dominant discourses and discursive practices. Lying behind each of these objections to confusing discourse and power, of course, is a political position. This has to be even more explicitly marked when we talk about ideology.

(3) Discourses have ideological effects

One deleterious effect of the rise of discourse analysis has been that the category of ideology virtually disappeared. In part, this has been a result of Foucault's (1980) insistence that the term ideology presupposes truth, a dubious truth which is no more valid than any other. It is right, I think, to say that discourse analysis need not necessarily be concerned with ideology, but it would be wrong to avoid it altogether. The category of ideology has progressive political effects, and it is not necessary to buy the whole package of 'mystification' and 'false consciousness' that Foucauldians caricature (e.g. Henriques *et al.*, 1984). However, if we are to hold onto the term 'ideology', there are two theoretical traps we do need to avoid.

The first trap is to say that all discourses are ideological, and thus to follow in the steps of sociologists who claim that 'ideology' is equivalent to a belief system (e.g. Bell, 1965). As with the category of power, this position makes the term ideology redundant. It neatly folds in with the discourse which claims that the ideas of those who resist existing power relations are as ideological as those who support them, and it has similar political effects: this relativism either evacuates politics of any meaning (other than leaving things as they are) or confines politics to the sphere of individual moral choice. Both these positions are ideological positions. The second danger is that we try and distinguish between discourses which are ideological and those which tell the truth. For those who want to defend the use of the category of ideology, this is the simpler and more attractive trap.

The mistake being made in both these cases is that ideology is being treated as a thing, or is being evaluated according to its content. Ideology is a description of *relationships* and *effects,* and should be employed to describe relationships at a particular place and historical period. It could be, for example, that Christian discourse functions in an ideological way when it buttresses racism as a dominant world-view. But it is also *possible* that such a discourse can be empowering, and that even claims that it is a 'subjugated knowledge' (in Foucauldian jargon) could be well founded (Mudge, 1987). If discourse analysis is to be informed by descriptions of institutions, power and ideology, then the history of discourses becomes even more important.

Reflections and conclusions

The three auxiliary criteria I have proposed, and in particular the final one concerned with ideology, prompt a question which is implicit in much of the discourse analysis literature, and which occurs routinely in discussions with those new to the area; 'how do we escape discourse?' If it is true that discourses frame the way we think about the objects they construct, and the way we are positioned as subjects, is there any way out? One way out is to address the question instead of attempting to answer it. In this respect, four points can be made to support the tactic of *not* answering the question.

First of all, attempts to escape discourse invite us to regress to exactly those conceptions of individual culpability for social practices that discourse analysis attempts to avoid. When we choose words that have connotations we think we did not intend, and which effectively reproduce a discourse we know is oppressive, this does not mean we have failed. Discourse analysis draws attention to language, and can help us reflect on what we do when we speak (or write), but the *reflexivity* advocated by some discourse analysts (e.g. Potter and Wetherell, 1987) is not a solution. Reflexivity is necessary and has been employed to good effect in discourse analytic work (Potter, 1988a), but it does not dissolve discourse.

A second related point is that we need to be cautious about what discourse analysis can accomplish. If we take the first seven criteria, then we shift the balance of the discipline from being, in Rorty's (1980) terms, a systematizing approach to an edifying type of inquiry. We cannot escape systematizing when we research into discourse. However, discourse analysis should bring about an understanding of the way things *were*, not the way things are. If we adopt the three auxiliary criteria, we describe, educate and change the way discourse is used (and so, what discourses can be). Discourse analysis should become a variety of action research, in which the internal system of any discourse and its relation to others are challenged. It alters, and thus permits different spaces for manoeuvre and resistance.

A third point connected with the previous two is that both reflexivity and discourse analysis are historically and culturally bound. This is not to say that people in other cultures do not reflect on what they do, but that reflexivity seen as a solution is specific to our time and place in Western culture. Similarly, this should not be taken to mean that it would be impossible to go and pick out discourses in other cultures. We now have specified an object which is discourse, and we could see it everywhere in the world where there is meaning (that is, everywhere). We have not 'discovered' it, but it is available for us as a topic, and we have to intervene in the contradictions it contains. Discourse analysis is both a symptom and part of the cure: the pre-occupation with language in contemporary psychology is a symptom of an evasion of the material basis of oppression (in the practical order) on the part of academics, but an attention to language can also facilitate a process of progressively politicizing everyday life (in the expressive sphere). Linked to the positive side of this process is the feminist claim that the personal is political (Rowbotham *et al.*, 1979).

A fourth and final point relates to the politics of discourse and to the importance of contradiction. Politics here is bound up with history; both in the sense that we have discourse now at this point in history (here we feel the weight of the past), and in the sense that politics and power are about the ability to push history in particular ways (there we construct a hope for the future). The difference between discourses is aggravated as one discourse is employed is supersede the other. When progress and change are notions built into contemporary political discourse, and things are changing so fast, it is hardly surprising that this dynamic should be reflected in our everyday experience of language. In political debate, the dynamics of resistance are of this discursive kind, and we have to have a sense of where discourses are coming from and where they are going to understand which are the progressive and which the reactionary ideas at different times and places.

Now there is a discourse discourse, and this may be an aspect of the postmodern world (Lyotard, 1984) and its study of itself is social psychology (Parker, 1989), but this is an open question. Other discourses, and the powerful practices which psychology supports, may turn discourse analysis into yet another useless, or even oppressive, part of the discipline. Alternatively, we could intervene to make it serve a progressive purpose. Insofar as a reflection on the presupposition and practices of psychology is possible, that reflection has traditionally taken place in the discourses which constitute the rational individual – in post-struturalist terminology, the 'unitary subject' – as an object about which psychology attempts to discover 'the truth'. One criticism of discourse analysis is precisely that the unitary subject is left intact (Bowers, 1988). On the other hand, discourse analysis has succeeded in provoking a reflection on psychological practice, and the philosophical assumptions which underpin it, by examining psychologists' discourse (Potter 1988b).

At the beginning of this chapter I briefly described histories of 'psychology' in which attention was drawn to the ways rationality and responsibility have been located in the minds of individuals. Inside the discipline these burdens have been supplemented by a variety of cognitive paraphernalia, and this has been supported by, and in some cases necessitated, the operation of a variety of dubious discursive practices (Shotter, 1987). The advantage of discourse analysis is that it reframes the object – individual psychology – and allows us to treat it not as truth, but as on 'truth' held in place by language and power. Now the old question about whether our discipline is helpful or harmful comes to depend on our place in a contradiction between two views of truth, whether one takes the side of psychology or the side of discourse.

6a
Discourse
Noun, Verb or Social Practice?

Jonathan Potter, Margaret Wetherell, Ros Gill and Derek Edwards

This chapter comments on some of the different senses of the notion of discourse in the various relevant literatures and then overviews the basic features of a coherent discourse analytic programme in Psychology. Parker's approach is criticized for (a) its tendency to reify discourses as objects; (b) its undeveloped notion of analytic practice; (c) its vulnerability to common sense assumptions. It ends by exploring the virtues of 'interpretative repertoires' over 'discourses' as an analytic/ theoretical notion.

Introduction

In the last few years the analysis of discourse and rhetoric has become increasingly established as a major alternative perspective on issues of psychological concern. For example, it has offered critical reassessments of such basic psychological notions as attitudes (Billig, 1987, 1988a, 1989a; Condor, 1987; Potter and Wetherell, 1987, 1988a; Smith, 1987), gender (Billig *et al.*, 1988; Frazer, 1988; Hollway, 1989; Marshall and Wetherell, 1989; Potter *et al.*, 1984; Walkerdine, 1988; Wetherell, 1986; Wetherell *et al.*, 1987) and memory (Billig, 1990a; Bogen and Lynch, 1989; Coulter, 1985; Drew, 1989; Edwards and Middleton, 1986, 1988; Edwards and Potter, 1992a; Wooffitt, 1989) as well as a reworking of major social psychological notions: categories (Billig, 1985, 1987; Condor, 1988; Potter, 1988a; Potter and Wetherell, 1987; Widdicombe and Wooffitt, 1990), social representations (Billig, 1988b, 1990b; Litton and Potter, 1985; McKinlay *et al.*, 1990; Potter and Litton, 1985; Potter and Wetherell, 1987), and racism (Billig, 1988; Condor, 1988; van Dijk, 1984, 1987; Essed, 1988; Potter and Wetherell, 1988b; Reeves, 1983; Sykes, 1985; Wetherell and Potter, 1986, 1992).

It is worth commenting on the term discourse analysis and its history as it provides a context for our later discussion of the very interesting paper by Parker and, at the same time, illustrates some of the basic issues that are at stake. In the early 1980s at least four distinct strands of work laid claim to the title discourse analysis. The most psychologically orientated of these had close links with cognitive science and often characterized its concern as with discourse processes, for example, the way the pattern of discourse effects the recall and understanding of events (e.g. van Dijk and Kintch, 1983). A second strand was strongly influenced by speech act theory and aimed at providing a systematic account of the organisation of verbal interaction, for example in classrooms (Coulthard and Montgomery, 1981; Sinclair and Coulthard, 1975). The third strand was centred in the entirely different tradition of continental social philosophy and cultural analysis. While most proponents worked with the titles of semiology or post-structuralism, Foucault (1961, 1973) is notable for characterizing his 'archeology' of madness and medicine as discourse analysis. This strand of work is closest to that outlined by Parker. Finally, within the sociology of science a distinct position was developed through focusing on scientific discourse which raized important problems for both traditional and radical theories of scientific action (Gilbert and Mulkay, 1984; Mulkay *et al.*, 1983).

If this complication were not enough, discourse analysis is also used in a more encompassing fashion to refer to large bodies of diverse work. For example, it has been used as a summary term for research in speech act, sociolinguistic and social psychological approaches to language areas (e.g. Brown and Yule, 1983; van Dijk, 1985) and in reviews of almost entirely independent developments in structuralism and semiotics (MacDonnell, 1986). This creates it own special complexities. For example, conversation analysis can be one sub-variety of discourse analysis (e.g. in van Dijk, 1985) or conversation analysis can be a competing theoretical position to discourse analysis (e.g. Sharrock and Anderson, 1987). Alternatively, the distinction between discourse analysis and text analysis has been used to mark off the study of actual speech and writing from presumed underlying structures of coherence (Halliday, 1978). Thus quite separate strands of work are called discourse analysis and the term is used with radically varying degrees of specificity and subtle theoretical inflection.

This digression into the variety of discourse analyses illustrates how the terms 'discourse' and 'discourse analysis' can be part of contrasting theoretical and disciplinary debates and can come to mean very different things. Indeed, part of the struggle is exactly over what these terms mean or what they ought to mean. The seemingly innocent definitional question addressed by Parker 'what is discourse?' is thus a particularly charged one, hiding many subtle ramifications behind its apparent simplicity. In this comment, we will address three points. First, we will briefly indicate the rationale for the definition of discourse analysis developed by Potter and Wetherell (1987). Second, we will suggest some difficulties with the way Parker has formulated the problem of identifying discourses. Third, we will document some of the virtues of the alternative theoretical notion of interpretative repertoires.

Discourse analysis: descriptive and constructive

When *Discourse and Social Psychology* was written in 1986 there was very little of what social psychologists now call discourse analysis being published, and so there were choices to make of both a descriptive and constructive nature. For example, should we weigh into the minefield of definitions of discourse and use the established but conflictual term 'discourse' or should we propose an alternative of our own, say 'social text analysis' (as in Potter *et al.*, 1984)? Such a choice would, of course, have implications for whether we wished to present ourselves as doing the 'merely descriptive' work of a textbook or as making an original contribution, a 'new' analytic perspective. We opted for the term 'discourse analysis', not wanting to miss out on the cross-fertilization the use of this term brought to bear, but also tried to suggest three major themes which would distinguish a new social psychological orientation to such research: (1) it would have a concern with functional orientation of language; (2) it would address the constructive processes that are part and parcel of the functional orientation; and (3) it would have an awareness of the variability thrown up by this orientation.

(1) Function

A number of disparate traditions of language research have stressed that it is a medium orientated to action. The most obvious of these are linguistic philosophy and, in particular, speech act theory (Austin, 1962; Ryle, 1949; Searle, 1969; Searle *et al.*, 1979; Wittgenstein, 1953, 1980) as well as ethnomethodology and the conversation analytic perspective which grew out of it (Garfinkel, 1967; Heritage, 1978, 1984, 1988; Atkinson and Heritage, 1984; Sacks *et al.*, 1974; Wieder, 1974). Workers in these traditions stress that discourse is orientated to action; utterances ask questions, make accusations, justify oversights, and so on.

The term function, then, emphasizes the action and outcome-orientated nature of descriptive discourse against views of language as an abstract, essentially referential system which have been prevalent in psychological theory and practice (see Potter and Wetherell, 1987). This must not be understood in a mechanical sense. Just because an account is organized to offer the particular action of blame this does not mean that the blame will be accepted by the recipient or even by the wider community. Indeed, as Billig (1987, 1989b) has emphasized, discourse is organized rhetorically; effective techniques of blaming can be countered by equally effective techniques of mitigation. In part, a study of discourse is an analysis of this rhetorical struggle.

(2) Construction

The metaphor of construction illuminates three facets of this discourse analytic approach. First, discourse is manufactured out of pre-existing linguistic resources. That is, language and linguistic practices offer a sediment of systems of terms, narrative forms, metaphors and commonplaces from which a particular account can be assembled. Secondly, such an assembly will involve choice or selection from possibilities. On the most basic level, philosophers of science such as Kuhn and Popper have stressed that with even the most simple of phenomena it is possible to provide many different kinds of description (see Lynch and Woolgar, 1988). What is picked out in talk depends on the orientation and interests of the speaker. Thirdly, and more generally, the constructivist metaphor reminds us that much of the time we deal with the world in terms of discursive constructions or versions. Our access to world events, the findings of science, or how a particular film should be evaluated are via constructions in texts and talk. In this sense, these texts and talk construct our world, and there are clear parallels here with the constructive emphases of poststructuralism which Parker describes.

(3) Variation

The third central concept, variation, follows from the first two. Given that discourse is constructed and orientated to action, we will expect that with different sorts of activities different sorts of discourse will be produced. If you take an event, say, or a social group or a feature of a person; it will be described in different ways as the functional orientation changes from blaming, for example, to excusing. Stated like this it becomes almost a truism. However, the sorts of variation between descriptive accounts of the same phenomenon can be striking in analytic practice (Gilbert and Mulkay, 1984; Potter and Wetherell, 1987). Again there are fruitful parallels here with the notion of contradiction which dominates ideological analyses and which Parker, rightly, highlights as a central facet of research.

Variability is central for analysis because of its close connection to functional orientation. As this orientation leads to variation, so the presence of variation can be used as an analytic clue to work back to functional orientation. That is, we can predict that certain sorts of functional orientations will lead to certain sorts ol systematic variations and look for the presence of those variations (Gilbert and Mulkay, 1984; Potter and Mulkay, 1985; Wetherell and Potter, 1988).

For us, then, the presence in some form or other of these three theoretical strands provides a rough but principled way of grouping together a body of work as discourse analysis; although within this soft perimeter there are many important theoretical tensions and much that we would take issue with in terms of theoretical claims or simply poorly realized and unscholarly analysis (Billig, 1988c). They are not meant to provide an exclusive definition but rather to mark out an area which would have significant implications for work in social psychology. What we expressly did not do, however, was make an equation of 'discourse analysis' with the 'analysis of *discourses*' as Parker does above. We will elaborate on the reasons for this in the next section.

Reification and intuition

Our dissatisfaction with Parker's argument for an analysis of discourses focuses on three main points: (1) its tendency to reification; (2) its ingenuous version of analytic practice; (3) its permeability to unexplicated common sense.

(1) Reification

The notion of reification is intended to capture the confusion where ideas are thought of or treated as objects. In this case, the problem is not *ideas* being objectified so much as *discourses* in their guize as 'sets of statements'. Parker is endorsing something akin to the geology of plate tectonics – great plates (discourses) on the earth's crust circulate and clash together; some plates grind violently together; others slip quietly over top of one another; volcanoes burst through while massive forces work unseen below. The limitation with this approach is that the discourses in this view become formed as coherent and carefully systematized (Parker, 1989: 5) wholes which take on the status of causal agents for analytic purposes. That is, the processes of interest are seen as those of (abstract) discourse working on another (abstract) discourse. This approach can provide considerable heuristic potency as Foucault's work demonstrates, and the historical twist to analysis associated with this should be welcomed. Nevertheless, it is greatly weakened in Parker's formulation for social psychology by the isolation of the propositional functions of discourse (the statements) from all the rest of the pragmatic work that is done in text and talk.

What is excluded? – the actual working of discourse as a constitutive part of social practices situated in *specific* contexts. Discourses or interpretative repertoires are always versions organized in particular contexts, their study should be based around the performance of procedures or actions; that is, the 'witcraft' analysed in the rhetorical tradition (Billig, 1987) and the interpretative procedures and devices studied in the conversation analytic tradition (Heritage, 1984). A recent study investigating the practices done through meritocratic discourse in the context of race and educational inequality in New Zealand (Potter and Wetherell, 1989) exemplifies this concern. The analysis consists not just of tracing out the socially constitutive role of discourse, in this case through the criticism of programmes attacking inequality, but also (as in other analyses of this type) involved examining in a detailed manner how talk was made effective, and, indeed, self-evident on each specific occasion.

(2) Analytic practice

Parker's more reified version of discourse analysis as analysis of discourses has ramifications for his view of analytic practice. Rejecting Potter and Wetherell's suggestions for ways of approaching discursive materials as bewildering he opts instead for a set of criteria for identifying a discourse. Yet his bewilderment stems, we suggest, from his failure to address the exclusion documented above; the role of discourse in social/interpretative practices and the detailed constructive work needed to mobilize a discourse on any occasion. For Parker, analysis apprehends discourse *directly;* but he can only understand analysis in this way because of his reified view of discourses as independently existing entities. For us, in contrast, interpretative repertoires (as we prefer to call discourses for the reasons outlined below) are *abstractions* from practices in context.

For this reason, then, analysis must be very attentive to what might be called the local geography of contexts and practices and also to the devices through which the discourses are effectively realized. Parker is perplexed by the lengths we go to in this task. However, we are mystified as to how discourse analysis can be done without this; how, as it were, can this Platonic/tectonic realm of discourses be breached without theorizing its entry into the worlds of practical affairs and everyday conversation and sense-making?

For example, it is not clear to us how 'statements' are derived from discourse in the first place; nor how the 'construction of objects' is concretely studied. Is the idea that the words should be compared to the world in some fashion? From our perspective, objects are constructed in talk and text in such a way as to perform actions, and actions can be studied precizely in terms of their context-fittedness and variability, including their uptake – the ways in which phenomena such as next turns, responses and reactions implicate them as actions. The status of 'texts' created by analysts as part of a 'preliminary step' in analysis is equally problematic. There is a danger that a great deal of the interpretative work will be done at this preliminary stage, producing the kind of idealized data that is a feature of much traditional social psychology.

Parker provides several pointers as to how analysts should identify various separate discourses. Partly it is 'purely conceptual'. However, while it is crucial to recognize the role of the analysts' categorizations and intuitions, this is not a good start for a set of criteria that are claimed to be 'necessary and sufficient for marking out particular discourses'. Another part of the identification of discourses relies on the notion of reflexivity. For Parker, a characteristic of 'discourses' is that they refer to themselves and thus this moment of self-naming is proposed as an analytic tool for identification and commentary. However, we would want to ask how these reflexive moments are *themselves* constructed to perform actions. Thus, rather than taking a text's overt claim to belong to a scientific legalistic or medical domain to indicate the character and institutional location of this discourse it can be studied as part of the text's rhetorical organisation. Ultimately, it is not clear to us what role is left for analysis in Parker's framework. There is a real danger that analytic work is simply being replaced by the analyst's common sense.

(3) Common sense

For Parker, discourse analysis starts by 'turning our objects into texts, and locating those texts in discourses'. He seems to be using a sort of correlational view here – the 'objects' of our common-sense experience each have their associated discourse. Indeed, for the analyst to group a set of statements together as a discourse is taken to involve the deployment of 'culturally available understandings as to what constitutes a topic'. This is graphically illustrated when, in the course of his argument, Parker deploys notions of *family* discourse, *scientific* discourse, *racist* discourse, *medical* discourse and *Christian* discourse. That is, the central ideas and institutions of our common sense versions of everyday life each turn out to have their own associated discourse.

But some of the most interesting work, for example, emerges when analysis is more inductive and the role of common sense in producing the social categories for analysis is less inflated. Take, for example, the work of Gilroy (1987) and others on the contemporary meaning of 'race' and the suggestion that traditional racism based on the usual construction of race as a biological object is being superseded by the construction of the English nation and patriotic culture as the new discursive reference point in black/white relations (see also Miles, 1989). As we are sure Parker would agree, sometimes it is crucial to question in detail 'one's culturally available understanding about what constitutes a topic', or to hold them in suspension.

Scientific discourse provides another example. Parker claims a 'scientific discourse is one in which rights and powers to speak are clearly signalled by the amount of knowledge held, and the desire to be a scientist may be provoked when we hear or use that discourse'. Parker works from our common-sense understanding of science and formulates it as having its own distinct discourse. However, numerous analyses have been done which refrain from making this correlational assumption (Gilbert and Mulkay, 1984; McKinlay and Potter, 1987; Mulkay, 1985; Myers, 1990; Potter *et al.*, 1984, 1988a). Put glibly, they suggest that scientific activity (the *institution* of science, if you like) is constituted out of not one single 'discourse of science' but two distinct 'discourses': an empiricist repertoire embodying many of the ideals of story-book science along with nineteenth-century justificationist philosophy, and also a contingent repertoire, which is a fragmentary archipelago of notions about psychology, sociology, social interests and institutional functioning. The crucial point is that it is the *two together,* distributed across scientific arenas, that sustain modern science. A scientific view is warranted by the use of the empiricist repertoire, while the competitors are discounted by the use of the contingent repertoire; this pattern of discourse is endlessly repeated in the face of interpretative problems raized by the generation of 'false knowledge'.

Parker's notion of discourse suffers from the same kind of problem as beset Halliday's (1978) similar notion of register. As registers were simply defined through common-sensically existing social contexts, they became an analytic reification of that common sense (Coulthard, 1977). In this way a critical edge was lost from the analysis which came to merely reproduce its predefined ontology in linguistic form. This circularity is reasonably transparent with Parker's definition of discourse which steers the analyst away from a searching critique of our commonsensical notions. Without going into detail here (see Ashmore, 1989; Mulkay, 1985; Potter, 1988b), this kind of unexplicated building in of assumptions is one of the targets of more recent reflexive developments in discourse analysis (in this role it is certainly not intended to 'dissolve discourse'. The point is not that common sense can somehow be fully purged; it is that Parker's version of analytic practice builds that common sense in at an early stage with little chance of critical explication.

Interpretative repertoires

Having suggested some limitations with Parker's approach to defining discourse it is important to be clear about what we are suggesting instead. In this final section we will suggest some of the advantages of incorporating the concepts of interpretative repertoires as part of a more broadly defined analysis of discourse, and comment on Parker's criticisms of this notion (ignoring his bizarrely empiricist suggestion that discourse is a more 'accurate' word). It is important to emphasize at this point that it is not the term 'discourse' that is at stake – indeed, at times we have been happy to use it as a variant of interpretative repertoires and to signal links to the semiological/post-structural tradition; it is the assumptions that Parker brings to his use of the term.

Using Foucault as backup, Parker defines discourses as regulated systems or sets of statements which construct objects (see also Parker, 1989). We have already noted the potential for reification in this definition where the 'set of statements' is taken to do the 'object construction' in the abstract rather than as part of situated practices. In trying to avoid this, we have deployed the notion of an 'interpretative repertoire' (Gilbert and Mulkay, 1984; Potter and Wetherell, 1987). By interpretative repertoire we mean broadly discernible clusters of terms, descriptions, common-places (Billig, 1988d) and figures of speech often clustered around metaphors or vivid images and often using distinct grammatical constructions and styles.

For example, we have studied the 'community repertoire' in accounts of uprising/riots (Potter and Reicher, 1987; Potter and Halliday, 1990) and of 'community care' of handicapped people (Potter and Collie, 1989). The 'community repertoire' is partly a set of words describing a certain style of cohesive social relationships; 'closeness', 'integration' and 'friendliness'. It is also made up of certain sorts of metaphors involving space ('close-knit'), organism ('growth', 'evolution') and agency (a community 'acts' or 'feels'). Overwhelmingly, 'community' is used as a positive term, as a good thing. Rather than seeing this repertoire as mechanically constructing an object, we have studied the way this repertoire can be deployed in different practices to construct contrasting objects; for example, it can be used to construct versions of uprisings which valorize participants as community members struggling against the police; or it can be used to construct very different versions in which the police are part of the community, the problem is community relations, and the solution is community policing (Potter and Reicher, 1987). The important point here is that the way the object is constructed is dependent on the discursive practice within which the repertoire is invoked.

The idea of a repertoire, analogous to the repertoire of moves of a ballet dancer, say, encompasses the way that different moves (terms, tropes, metaphors) from the repertoire may be invoked according to their suitability to an immediate context. That is, the idea of a repertoire spotlights flexibility of use in practice in way that Parker's organized sets of statements fail to do. However, it is important not to move too far away from Parker's conception here and think of repertoires as infinitely flexible resources that are artfully and knowingly invoked by people. For a particular form of discourse may have consequences which have not been formulated or even understood by the speaker or writer and on any specific occasion there may be powerful constraints on the discourse used. There is a clear tension between seeing people as active users, on the one hand, and seeing discourse as generating, enabling and constraining, on the other. Put simply, discourse analysis studies how people use discourse and how discourse uses people. Parker's point that 'a discourse contains subjects', connected with Althusser's (1971) notion of subject positions, is an important insight here.

Parker expresses specific disquiet over three aspects of our definition of interpretive repertoires: its interest in grammar; its assertion about limits; and its resonance with behaviourism. With respect to the point about grammer it is important to make a clear distinction between topic and resource. We are not suggesting that discourse analysts take over any of the theoretical baggage of grammar as a resource for analysis; rather, we are stressing that in the practice of analysis attention to grammatical forms as a topic may be revealing. A simple example of this appears in the work on science discourse, where it was found that one of the distinctive features separating the empiricist and contingent repertoires was the recurrent use of impersonal grammatical constructions such as 'it was found that ...'

Parker suggests that our talk of a limited range of terms in interpretative repertoires implies an unrealistically closed system. Again, our use of this talk of limits arizes out of our analytic practice; one of the striking things about studying the talk of fifty or so interviewees on a particular topic is the restricted and indeed stereotypic set of terms and tropes which occur again and again. Our use of the idea of a limited range is not meant to place *a priori* boundaries but to highlight this conspicuous lack of variation. Finally, on the point about the resonance of 'repertoire' with the language of behaviourism, we suspect that the prefix 'interpretative' heads off most of this line of connotation at the pass and what little is left is outweighed by the term's usefulness.

It is very important to reiterate that for us the identification and analysis of interpretative repertoires is just one part of a larger analysis of discourse that includes, but is not bound by, analysis of discourses. Moving in one direction, this has involved addressing issues of ideology and the legitimation of exploitation which may involve a study of a whole tract of interpretative repertoires and their interrelations and patterned consequences (Gill, 1990; Wetherell *et al.*, 1987). Moving in the other direction, we are concerned with the 'witcraft' that brings them alive as 'authentically meant' parts of arguments and the more general warranting devices that make them plausible or that fix them as unproblematically factual. Indeed, some discourse studies may be less concerned with organized repertoires than with procedures for warranting, say, or different techniques of accomplishing a variety of actions (cf. Edwards and Potter, 1992b; Potter and Edwards, 1990). There is nothing secondary about this work – each is complementary to the other.

It is here that Parker's polarization between the good/radical post-structuralists and the bad/reactionary ethnomethodologists/conversation analysts is particularly unhelpful (see also Parker, 1989). While the former position is a useful backdrop to the analysis of repertories, providing inspiring analyses such as those of Barthes cited by Parker; the latter is particularly useful for making sense of the implementation of repertoires in practices and the array of interpretative procedures that are on hand to accomplish this. To set them up as alternatives would result in a dangerously stunted enterprize.

To conclude, there is much of value in Parker's argument and much with which we agree. What we have tried to do is sharpen up (at times taking the honing perhaps too far) some of the differences between our position and his. In particular, we have suggested some difficulties which arize when operating with discourse as a noun, when discourse analysis is equated with the analysis of discourses, and when post-structuralist definitions are generalized to the concerns of discourse analysis as a whole.

6b

The Context of Discourse
Let's Not Throw Out the Baby With the Bathwater

Dominic Abrams and Michael A. Hogg

An examination of Ian Parker's definitions of discourse reveals them to be non-distinctive and of limited utility. It is argued that discourse analysis should be integrated with, rather than set against, social psychology. Discourse analysts should attend to the issues of the representativeness and generality of their evidence, should be wary of attributing causality to discourse, and should consider the advantages of systematically investigating, rather than asserting, the social consequences of the use of different discourses.

This commentary is, of course, a discourse. A discourse analysis of it may reveal certain interesting devices, subtexts, statements and contradictions, implicit and explicit boundaries, social categorizations and particularization, mystifications, warrants, justifications and characterizations. However, the more interesting questions are likely to concern the circumstances preceding our writing it, how *we* (rather than someone else) came to be writing it, the issues on which it focuses, to whom it is addressed, what our intentions or motives regarding its impact are, and last, but not least, who will read (interpret) it and what they make of it? That is, the analysis of the text is of only limited value unless it is placed in the context of what people are doing with it. This cannot simply be inferred from the text itself, it requires systematic observation and analysis of social behaviour. In this commentary, we take a social psychological perspective in considering Ian Parker's definitions and criteria for discourse analysis. We argue that if discourse analysis is to be considered a serious alternative to social psychology (cf. Potter and Wetherell, 1987), it is incumbent on its proponents to demonstrate its superiority in dealing with the same phenomena and issues that concern social psychologists. To the extent that discourse analysts simply change the premize of the questions (cf. K. Gergen,

1989a; Harré, 1989b) they deny the possibility of constructive dialogue with social psychology, and it becomes a matter of horses for courses. Our own preference is for integration of theory and method; to enrich discourse analysis and social psychology.

Ian Parker has proposed a set of criteria which may be used to define discourse, and three issues for reflection and analysis. Although there is much with which we agree, there are various assumptions and issues which require pause for thought. One general question must be how far the criteria define discourse as distinct from other facets of human life. Our major concern, however, is that although discourse can be regarded as the social process *par excellence*, it is portrayed by Parker as abstracted, reified and unconnected with individual or social psychological processes.

Parker's definition of discourse as a 'system of statements which constructs an object', attributes agency to the system rather than the users of the system (cf. Harré, 1989b). It is rather like suggesting that computer software produces output whilst ignoring the role of the programmer. Insofar as theoretical stances are a matter of stylistic preference (Zajonc, 1989), we prefer an analysis which focuses on the social processes underlying and flowing from people's use of discourse.

Parker's second criterion, 'discourse is realized in texts', seems to relate more to process than content. That is, anything which undergoes *interpretation* can be regarded as (a) discourse. It is unclear what delimits 'texts', but they would seem to include anything which is potentially interpretable. Once again, the role of the interpreter is obsured. Moreover, the idea that different discourses are 'available' to different audiences is also problematic. Is this something to do with the discourse or with the audiences' ability to interpret it? Presumably, to the extent that something is interpreted, a discourse must have been available to the interpreter. But it seems tautological to say a discourse *only* exists if it is interpretable. An English person may be unable to read, write or speak in Japanese but we are perfectly capable of recognizing that the Japanese text on the back of a hifi system is intended to communicate information.

The third criterion, that, 'a discourse reflects on its own way of speaking', is also rather undistinctive. There is an ambiguity over how explicit the reflexivity must be. Certainly, discourse is used within linguistic and consensual frameworks, wherein 'hot' *implies* the opposite of 'cold', and 'evil' the opposite of 'good'. However, it is unclear whether this is particularly a characteristic of discourse. Objects cannot exist unless they do so in relation to other objects. Similarly, the

subject matter of social psychology is largely based on choices, prefer-
ences, comparisons and so on. Much theorising has explored the
capacity of humans for self-reflection and perspective-taking. In addition, it remains unclear as to whether reflexivity is necessary before a
text can be defined as a discourse, or whether it is an arbitrary and
occasional feature of discourses. Finally, we would argue that
reflexivity is not a property of discourse, but of discourse users (Mead,
1934).

The fourth criterion, 'a discourse refers to other discourses' is open to
the same point. Since all objects can be understood to exist in so far as
they are perceived to be distinct from other objects they must exist in
relation (or with reference) to other objects. Thus, the criterion does
not distinguish discourse from other things.

The fifth criterion, 'a discourse is about objects', and a discourse
analysis is 'about discourses as objects', seems sensible, but also self-
evident. Given that, within Ian Parker's formulation, objects exist only
in a trivial way outside of their construction in discourse, the criterion
might be rephrased as, 'discourse is about the things that are created
through discourse'.

The sixth criterion, 'a discourse contains subjects', is ambiguous.
Does 'containment' refer to active containment or passive inclusion?
On the one hand there is the implication that discourse forces the
addressee into a particular position, while on the other is the idea that
the addressee is merely invited to adopt a position. Tremendous power
is given to the discourse – 'we have to take a position'. We regard this
as too strong a conclusion, as discussed below.

The seventh criterion, 'a discourse is historically located', is completely open-ended. It would be equally true to argue that everything
about human life is historically located, and therefore this criterion
does not help to distinguish discourse from anything else.

These seven criteria are regarded by Ian Parker as 'necessary and
sufficient' for marking out particular discourses. The three 'auxilliary
criteria', concerning institutions, power and ideology are regarded as
important and different from discourse itself. We agree that the role of
language in creation and sustenance of institutions is very important
(but not necessarily involving the '*most* interesting' discourses).
However, the fact that discursive practices may help reproduce institutions does not mean that all reproductive practices are discursive.
Physical repression, for example, as well as physical need, may play a
major role in sustaining various social structures. Moreover, the argument that discourses reproduce power relations seems too strong. It

does seem plausible that power relations are reflected in discourse, but not that *discourse* reproduces these relations. Discourse is not an agent, it is a medium for, and form of; communication.

The power, for example, of Psychology to control its own boundaries depends upon the establishment of its machinery and the operation of legislative power. Moreover, the enshrinement of rules and regulations in verbal form does not embue them with power. Rather, power is the capacity to operate sanctions and contingencies when rules are infringed, as well as the capacity to change the rules and develop consensus regarding the right to power. We shall return to the issue of empowerment and discourse, below.

Parker's distinction between ideology and discourse, while interesting, is not terribly illuminating since the connection between the two is not spelt out. The fact that a religious ideology may (for example), through different discourses, incite donations to charity as easily as murder, neither contradicts the original relevance of the ideology to social order nor the particular purpose served by use of each discourse.

It may be true that, as Parker suggests, the question, 'how do we escape discourse?' is uninteresting. He argues that discourse analysis is necessarily retrospective, but allows the possibility of action research in which the informed analyst challenges an (undesired?) system of discourse (cf. Gergen, 1989b). Parker accuses discourse analysts of evading the 'material basis of oppression' but holds out the hope of politicizing every day life. He hopes discourse analysis can be progressive but concludes by placing it in opposition to psychology.

We have a number of other reservations about the value of discourse analysis, as set out by Parker. Some of these concern the capacity of the approach to answer particular questions, and others concern the accountability of the analyst both to society and to social science. Perhaps the most worrying, from the perspective of social psychology, is that the form of discourse analysis proposed by Parker seems to have no place for psychological processes. This would raize the question, 'what else is there besides discourse?'.

The second issue concerns the methodological rigour and safeguards employed by the analyst. It is very difficult to present all the data on which discourse analyses are based (e.g. Potter, 1988b), and because no objective or formal techniques are employed for classifying texts it is impossible for the reader of a discourse analysis to know what is being represented and what is not (cf. Zajonc, 1989; Crosby and Crosby, 1981). Statistical techniques employed in quantitative research allow some confidence regarding the *representativeness* of evidence. Despite the shortcomings of the manner in which the questions (e.g. in attitude surveys) have been posed, it is possible to describe precizely and in a way that other analysts could replicate exactly, the distribution of responses, behaviours, types or dimensions being assessed. Representativeness of evidence is more important than discourse analysts, such as Potter and Wetherell (1987), seem to suggest. For example, it is important to know not just whether a group of people employs racist discourse but also to what extent such discourse prevails. Prevalence (or 'effect size', see Bond and Titus, 1983 for an example) has implications for action, for the future, and for change. Establishing representativeness requires that the methodology is reliable and valid, at least within its own terms of reference.

Discourse analysis often appears to have considerable face validity because it dwells on issues and arguments with which readers are generally familiar (e.g. Potter and Reicher, 1987). However, we would suggest that the incorporation of already existing methods within social science, such as sampling, content analysis, estimation of reliability and generalizability, even experimentation, would make discourse analysis more persuasive and more informative both to social scientists and to lay people, and the institutions which fund social science research. Indeed, discourse analysis may have more in common with the rest of social psychology than at first appears. The analyst selects a domain of study (independent variables of factors), collects a particular form of evidence, usually linguistic (the data), assembles and condenses the evidence so as to embark on an interpretation (coding the dependent variables), presents typical or representative parts (the analysis/results), in order to make a point (the discussion).

The third issue concerns the assumption of the power of discourse. We frequently come across the idea that particular discourses legitimize or allow certain practices to continue and prevent others from occuring (e.g. Potter and Wetherell, 1987; Reicher and Potter, 1985). Thus, for example, it is assumed, and illustrated, that political discourse is *designed* to have particular effects. This may well be so, but the question remains as to what effects actually arize. We advocate a different emphasis from Ian Parker. In particular, while we accept that discourse involves a process of construction of ideas and meanings, we regard the interesting issue as what people *do* with those ideas. First there are the cognitive elements of perception and memory, accessibility and availability, association and representation of information. A radical Marxist discourse may be powerful in terms of the discourse-analytic implications, but if the reader/listener either cannot understand the terminology, or has already decided that Marxism is not worth attending to, the nature and structure of the discourse has no implications for anything else. Similarly, religious discourses are selective in their effects and consequences.

In addition to the cognitive elements, it would seem critical to embody social and motivational processes in making sense of discourse. Discourse does not just arize, it has to be created. This process involves purpose, objectives, functions and social understanding on the part of the creator. Why *should* a racist discourse be employed? What are people doing with it? These questions are not restricted to discourse, but are broader social psychological questions which discourse analysis may help to answer. Rather than simply imply from an analysis of a discourse that it is racist, the researcher could go back to the source of the discourse and ask whether the interpretation is accurate. It might also be sensible to inquire directly what impression the producer of the discourse was intending to create and on whom. Moreover, behavioural or other measures relevant to construct validation could be employed to see whether discourses which the analyst categorizes as 'racist' have implications for anything else. Another avenue for discourse analytic study would be to examine the impact of different situational factors, different interaction contexts (etc.) on the discourse used in relation to particular topics. For example, is children's discourse about ethnic minorities different in the classroom and the playground?

We are especially concerned about the implication that discourse analysts might consider themselves to be best placed to utilize their work to bring about social change. Embodied in this ambition is the assumption that discourse determines everything else (cf. the Sapir-Whorf strong hypothesis). We very much doubt that, for example, racism can be reduced substantially by changing discourse. The social conditions which give rize to racism will not go away just because the language has been altered (cf. Kinder and Sears's (1981) analysis of symbolic racism). It is also unclear why the mission of discourse analysis should be to 'empower those at the sharp end of dominant discourses and discursive practices' (as Parker claims). In Britain, for example, the fascist National Front is just such a group. Presumably we would not really wish to empower them. What right do discourse analysts have to give *themselves* responsibility for deciding which groups should be empowered? Political action is certainly legitimate, but it is not the case that academics should necessarily take the moral high ground in this way. It is probably true that those who are most likely to be in a position to take advantage of the insights of discourse analysts are those who already hold power. There is no reason to suppose that discourse analysis will be any more liberating than the behaviourist theorizing it echoes (Hogg and McGarty, 1990).

Of greatest concern to us is that many of social psychological processes which sustain particular ideologies or images may simply be ignored by discourse analysts. For example, we know that group discussion tends to lead group members' opinions to polarize in the already favoured direction. The processes by which consensus is arrived at involve classification of the social field, but not necessarily through discourse (cf. Sherif, 1936, Abrams *et al.*, 1990). Indeed the linguistic or informational aspects of a situation may be less important than aspects which provide a context for the discourse. There is no need to discuss in detail the extensive literature on socio-linguistics, speech-accomodation, second language acquisition and social identity here. However, that literature (e.g. Edwards, 1985; Giles and Robinson, 1990; Sachdev and Bourhris, 1990) illustrates how paralinguistic features, and social categorization can dramatically affect reactions to what is being said. Moreover, language is intimately tied up with identity – the experience and sense of who we are. This, like many other essentially social phenomena (e.g., grief, joy, envy, collective effort, personal ambition) is not wholly explicable in terms of discourse. The literature on social influence (Abrams and Hogg, 1990; Hogg and Turner, 1987; Perez and Mugny, 1990; Perry and Cacioppo, 1981) is now replete with illustrations of the relevance of social psychological processes to the way people deal with discourse.

Social psychological theory has tried to address the problem of social change, the prediction of behaviour, the reduction of intergroup prejudice, and so on. Discourse analysis can provide a powerful addition to the battery of methods available, but hardly seems viable as an *alternative*. We prefer to conceive of people as social agents, with a capacity for self-reflection (Abrams, 1990), a desire for self-definition (Abrams and Hogg, 1988), and understanding of the social field (Hogg and McGarty, 1990; Turner *et al.*, 1987) who are often both motivated and deliberate in their actions. People have specific relationships to which they develop commitment, involvement and plans (Abrams, 1989). Discourse is a tool used by individuals, groups, institutions and society. But people are *aware* that it is a tool (cf. Parker's 3rd criterion).

Recent dismissals of the relevance of psychological processes in social phenomena have emphasized the futility of a scientific approach to social practices. Some have argued that since all knowledge is socially constructed it is fruitless to adopt an individual level analysis (M. Gergen, 1989; Harré, 1989b), and that we should instead analyse the discourse of science, and concentrate on a social epistemology (K. Gergen, 1989a). However, these meta-theoretical commentaries may misrepresent both the content and underlying assumptions of much recent social psychological theorizing and research (Stroebe and Kruglanski, 1989). We agree that the theoretical and methodological developments within discourse analysis are valuable for understanding society, but see no reason to jettison the whole of social psychology (or quantitative social science) on that account. This would be to throw the baby out with the bath water. Indeed, we hope that the usefulness of discourse analysis may be enhanced by its incorporation into existing theory and method in social psychology.

6c
Real Things
Discourse, Context and Practice

Discourse (language organized into sets of texts) and discourses (systems of statements within and through those sets) have a power. To say this is not to attribute agency to a system, but simply to acknowledge constraining and productive forces. There are forces of institutional disadvantage and division, for example, which do not flow from individual intentions, and the phenomena of power and ideology need not be traced to conspiratorial machinations. It would be dangerous to attempt to do so, and the unpleasant consequences particularly difficult to challenge if such investigation proceeded under cover of objective science. Discourse analysis unravels the conceptual elisions and confusions by which language enjoys its power. It is implicit ideology-critique But there is more than language, and discourse analysis needs attend to the conditions which make the meanings of texts, and the research project which takes them seriously, possible.

In what sense is discourse 'real', and how real? How does discourse relate to the real world'? These questions provoke, frame and trip up defences and critiques of discourse analysis. There is a 'worried about the real' discourse which operates in different ways, and the objects of such discourse include, with a number of connotations and connections with other discourses, such things as 'practice' (in which discourse analysts attempt to dissolve the object status of discourse through rhetorical distinctions from nouns and verbs) and 'context' (in which critics reinforce its object status through comparisons with bathwater). But to say that such matters are objects of a discourse is not to say that they either only exist in texts (an extreme linguistic-realist position) or that they only exist outside (an extreme brute empiricist argument). It is clear that we need some way of talking about real things to ground discourse analysis.

Object status

It may be useful to conceive of things (in the broadest sense of the word) as being endowed with one of three possible 'object status', in one of three possible categories (but with many things appearing, in different forms, in more than one of the categories). There is, first of all, the realm which Abrams and Hogg seem anxious about their reply to my paper (in which they imagine, for some unknown reason, that 'objects only exist in a trivial way' outside language for me), and in which things have *ontological status*. They are really there, but the status and scope of this realm is over-inflated in much traditional psychology. For a realist, such as Bhaskar (1989), such things belong to an intransitive realm of physical structures endowed with particular powers. Much of the 'practical' sphere that Harré (1979) describes is made up things which have ontological status. A twofold problem arising here is that not only does brute empiricism claim that things with ontological status can be directly known, but it also attributes this type of object status to things that belong to other realms. Abrams and Hogg, for example, write that it is possible to 'describe precisely' and 'replicate exactly' responses, behaviours and responses, and so they are able to declare confidently they that 'know' about group phenomena and the suchlike. This then means that they can seriously argue that discourse analysts should 'demonstrate its superiority in dealing with the same phenomena and issues that concern social psychologists'. We are not, however, dealing with the 'same phenomena'.

There is no simple correspondence between things with ontological status (objects) and the things we have given meaning to, talk about, know about. When Abrams and Hogg say that objects 'cannot exist unless they do so in relation to other objects', they refer to things in a *second* realm. A problem here is that they do seem to believe, mistakenly, that our apprehension of objects as separate things is unproblematic, and they fail to take accounts of the difficulties we have in learning to differentiate objects (compare, for example, Milner, 1950). Such things belong to a realm of things with *epistemological status*. Crudely put, these are the things we have knowledge about. For a realist, it is not possible to obtain knowledge about things with only ontological status (those in the intransitive sphere) without a pre-existing array of knowledge (and techniques) which lie in this second 'transitive' sphere (Bhaskar, 1989).

Harré's (1979) 'expressive' order includes the knowledge we have of things, but I also want to mark out a *third* realm (within the expressive order) in which things have a *moral/political status*. Much talk about psychological phenomena is ideologically loaded to the extent that objects such as 'intelligence', 'race', 'attitudes', etc., can be called into being, and thus given a moral/political status. (The birth of an object into such a realm is not necessarily harmful, a point I will pursue below.) In this third realm of things with a moral/political status, and it is a realm we cannot wish away (it is necessary to human society), we can always remind ourselves that such objects are being advanced for strategic reasons – we can treat them 'as if' they were there. Discourses and texts, having emerged from the third realm, now have epistemological status.

Here, though, there are two related problems. The first is that the (second) epistemological realm contains 'objects' of knowledge which are derived both from research into the ontological realm (with much of the translation in the modern world in this respect conducted by science) *and* from the objects produced in the moral/political sphere (with much of this translation process functioning as the production of fake intransitive material). The epistemological status of things, then, is often contested because such things pretend to represent the real (they derive from objects that really exist) when they actually merely represent items constructed in a political rhetoric (they derive typically from ideological pictures of the real).

The second problem is that the moral/political realm reflects, and reproduces, dominant cultural forms of thought. In higher education and research, for example, there is a dynamic towards individual choice in which a range of forces (companies, local authorities, students, parents) are encouraged to determine how and what is taught (and researched) in the academic institutions. Deliberate policy decisions have changed British Polytechnics into self-governing corporate bodies, but the motivating forces for the transformation of academic issues into matters susceptible to a cost-benefit analysis have been the newly 'empowered' consumers. It is often the case that the nature (and 'powers') of individuals at any time flow not so much from their 'attitudes' or 'motivations' (which they then 'communicate' to others). but from the overall ideological context, we can tease apart that context through analysis of the discourses (of 'choice', individualism', 'efficiency') which set the ground rules for action.

Context

Discourse analysis radicalizes the turn to language in social psychology, but must also attempt to survive in a still powerful traditional

climate of experimentalism in the discipline (Parker, 1989). This tradition has been divided, until the end of the 1980s, between those stub-
bornly clinging to orthodox (mainly trivial) experimental studies (on
verbal behaviour, for example) or ostensibly more radical intergroup
experimental studies (Tajfelian Social Identity Theory). Across this,
orthogonally as it were, the waves of research in attribution theory
(with a massive influence), social cognition (with a sizeable following),
social representations (less so), and discourse analysis (increasingly)
have swept across the discipline. It is discourse analysis, that has
caused most damage to the pretended internal coherence of social
psychology.

On the one hand, the older orthodox experimentalists have reacted
with horror at a qualitative approach which appears non-systematic,
unscientific, and worse even than the new social psychologists (Harré,
1979; Shotter, 1975) that they had to put up with in the 1970s. On the
other hand, the more radical intergroup people (a post-Tajfel generation which has spread from the Bristol and Kent centres) have reacted,
in the main, cautiously or defensively to discourse analysis. The thorough turn to language that discourse analysis provokes has little time
for experimental studies of group identification.

Abrams and Hogg's reply to my paper is useful for it lucidly expresses
a traditional social-psychological response to a discourse approach.
Three points in their argument stand out. First, there is the implication
that the (re)definition of a field of study, in this case as 'texts' and 'discourses' (Abrams and Hogg conflate and confuse the two), should necessarily lead us to being unable to believe that there is anything else
outside language. On the contrary, I am happy to say that when something can be interpreted (and so becomes a text) it does not dissolve
and lose all other object status. When experimental social psychologists define their object of study, they want to see it in all places –
claiming, for example, that 'social behaviour can occur everywhere,
including a crowded subway' (Deaux and Wrightsman, 1984: 5). They
need not wish away everything else as if it did not exist (though it does
sometimes appear that they are tempted by this wish).

A second point arising from Abrams and Hogg's reply is where they
pursue a reductionist account with a fervour that feeds the suspicion
that brute empiricism can really only comfortably operate with
either/or categories. There is a continual appeal to the real, but it is a
fantasized 'real' which owes a lot to individualism (with the 'individual' as an object brought into discourse as a moral/political object). It is
not possible to discover meanings by going to the real 'source', for

'communication' is *not* the transfer of 'intentions' from one individual head to another (cf. Easthope, 1990). To translate terms from discourse analysis into 'dependent variables' and the such-like would simply replace a focus on the organization of language with the traditional attempts to define, predict and control 'behaviours', 'cognitions', etc. (things which are not really there).

The point has been well made that 'everyday human activities do not just *appear* vague and indefinite because we are still as yet ignorant of their true underlying nature, but that they are *really* vague' (Shotter, 1990: 9). Reductionism appeals to the real, but its objects are called into being in the moral/political sphere, and are made to operate 'as if' they were true (as part of the apparatus of regulation which is the psy-complex). This is not to say that we do not need 'models of the person' compatible with a discourse approach (Parker, 1992), but discourse analysis is mainly concerned with the ways in which such 'objects' arose, and the functions they serve in language and social relations.

There is a third point in Abrams and Hogg's reply with which I sympathize. They argue, quite rightly, that different situations will give rize to different meanings. It would be possible to ask questions about differences in discourse in different circumstances. However, such questions can be better framed in terms of the conditions for the employment of different discourses, and their intersection at different subject positions in institutions governed by relations of power and ideology, than in terms of 'situational factors'. To talk about 'situational factors' is to repeat the mistaken assumption that the things a social psychologist studies are discrete entitities which interact with one another in (at least potentially) predictable ways.

Practice

It is true that to talk of discourses intersecting can also lead to an abstraction and reification of theoretical constructs. The risk is worth taking, for it is crucial that we hold to some conception of the *difference* between discourses in order to deal with the real worry that Potter *et al.* voice in their reply to my paper, that commonsense might be reified (and unwittingly celebrated). However, a great deal of the worry here can be traced to projection on Potter *et al.*'s part, for they set up the category 'common-sense experience' as if it was unitary. Just as there are different discourses, there are dominant and dominated cultures, different 'common senses' within the contested domain which is society. To identify a discourse is to take a position, and the ability to step outside a discourse and to label it in a particular way is a function of both the accessing of dominant cultural meanings *and* the marginal (critical) position which the researcher takes (within or alongside another discourse or sub-culture or commonsense).

It is in this context, of practice, that the issue of 'empowerment' which Abrams and Hogg raize could seriously be addressed, for it is only when the wider context is understood (using a Marxist theoretical framework, perhaps) that one gets a sense of how particular discourses reproduce a dominant culture. Just as certain objects are called into being, given a moral/political status which then are researched (given epistemological status) and treated as if they really are there (as if they had ontological status), so certain objects can be studied as objects (solely) perhaps) of a discourse and thereby be deconstructed. The employment of notions of 'intelligence', 'racial character' and the suchlike need to be understood in order to determine in what ways power is exercized by the dominant culture ('race', 'gender', 'class'). The empowerment process in research can then be informed by moral/political choices (not at all a 'moral high ground') to deny or give a 'voice' to participants (Bhavnani, 1990).

Traditional experimental social psychologists appeal to 'real' things that have no ontological status (but which are often attributed with such status), and they attack alternative conceptual frameworks which threaten to deconstruct claims to such a status and which then, it appears (to them), set up objects endowed with the same status. Because the debate between traditional social psychology and discourse analysis (between Abrams and Hogg and myself) is between two frameworks, it is necessary to draw attention to the way that (despite Abrams and Hogg's declared interest in 'context') discourse analysis is precizely concerned with the context within which the 'objects' social psychology takes as 'real' emerge.

Discourse analysts, on the other hand, debate within a common framework. A problem we (Potter *et al.* and myself) have is that language is loaded against us, and much of our energy is spent dealing with objects which we know derive from the moral/political sphere, and which then exist with much power in contemporary discourses in the epistemological realm. We each fear that the other is attributing such objects ontological status. Potter *et al.* are right, for example, to say that there is 'a danger' that discourse analysts will construct 'idealized data' if discourses are continually talked about as if they were things (though I do like their tectonic plates metaphor despite the naughty rhetorical twist later in the reply when the metaphor becomes

'Platonic/tectonic'), and obviously right to catch me claiming that the term 'discourse' is more 'accurate' (when I could have said it was more appropriate or useful).

I attribute to the organization of discourse, to positivist and Cartesian discourses in particular, not to Potter *et al.*'s beliefs, responsibility for some of the bizarrely empiricist claims in their reply: when they argue that they can 'predict' the effects of certain functional orientations (shortly after claiming that what is picked out in talk 'depends on the orientation and interests of the speaker'): when they argue that the notion of a 'limited range' of an interpretative repertoire is supported by a 'conspicous lack of variation' (after rehearing their claim that discourse analysis makes a virtue of variation); and when they employ the trope 'it was found that' to describe one of the recurrent grammatical constructions in scientists' discourse (and Potter *et al.* write that 'it was found that' scientists say this). When they appeal to the claim that aspects of speech are 'alive as "authentically meant" parts of arguments', they would probably acknowledge the typically deconstructive point that such a claim as a quote from a written text, now part of a discourse about rhetoric, could not be 'authentically meant' (perhaps never, in the sense that appears to be meant here).

I do argue that post-structuralism helps us to deconstruct the either/or oppositions which inhabit modern social psychology and the historical conditions which led to its emergence and success. But although I appear to be harder on ethnomethodological positions, I also argue (Parker, 1989) that it is precisely the points of contact between ('bad') ethnomethodology and ('good') post-structuralism which serve to highlight limitations of both (cf. Dews, 1987). It is true that for a moral/political stance, post-structuralism is often unhelpful (e.g. Burman, 1990). The practice of discourse analysis is bound up with the multiplicity of practices that academics, researchers and subjects engage in. It should be part of a greater project (to identify and challenge processes of power and ideology), and the notions of 'discourse' and 'text' employed within that project are both necessarily parts of the problem *and* 'as if devices to help us understand it.

Part III

Critical Discursive Research, Subjectivity and Practice

This third part of the book addresses the role of reflexivity and subjectivity in relation to the practice of discursive research. The purpose of the account in Chapter 7 is to show how existing problematic elements of psychoanalytic reasoning can be transformed theoretically to make them useful for critical work. Just as the chapters in the first two Parts of the book made it clear that we cannot simply take discourse analysis on good coin and assume that it will help us in critical analysis, so Chapter 7 shows that we do have to do some theoretical work to bring out the critical potential of psychoanalysis. Only then will it be possible to go beyond the motifs of 'blank subjectivity' and 'uncomplicated subjectivity' in alternative forms of qualitative research and arrive at something suitably complex, complex enough to do justice to the complexity of human experience. Psychoanalysis here is not used as an interpretive grid that will reveal the true meaning of the text. Rather, it is a framework that informs the reading in order that the researcher may better attend to the forms of subjectivity circulating in the text.

The following two chapters provide concrete examples of how this plays out in research practice. Chapter 8 takes the analysis further with a consideration of the contribution of discourse analysis to our understanding of the way psychotherapeutic discourse operates in contemporary culture. Then Chapter 9 turns this view of therapeutic discourse around to extend the analysis of psychoanalytic subjectivity relayed through discursive complexes to account for the role of behavioural and cognitive motifs in popular culture. We then turn to the surprising ways discursive ideas are used in psychotherapy so that their role as critique – as deconstruction – is augmented by a perspective for progressive constructive change in and against the psy-complex.

7

Reflexive Research and the Grounding of Analysis

Psychology and the Psy-complex

This chapter is concerned with reflexivity in research, and the way research is grounded in the operations of the psy-complex in psychology. A central argument is that qualitative research in general, and a focus on reflexivity in particular, requires theoretical grounding. Distinctions are drawn between 'uncomplicated subjectivity', 'blank subjectivity' and 'complex subjectivity'; and the analytic device of the 'discursive complex' is described. It is argued that such theoretical grounding can usefully draw on developments in discourse analytic, deconstructionist, and psychoanalytic social research. The opposition between objectivity and subjectivity is deconstructed, and psychoanalytic conceptual reference points for an understanding of the discursive construction of complex subjectivity in the context of institutions are explored with particular reference to the location of the researcher in the psy-complex. The chapter discusses the reflexive engagement of the researcher with data, and the construction of the identity of the researcher with reference to professional bodies. An analysis of a document produced by the British Psychological Society is presented to illustrate conceptual issues addressed in the first sections. This illustrative analysis is designed to show how the material is structured by a series of six discursive complexes, and that the institutional structure facilitates, and inhibits, certain forms of action and reflection. It would be a folly, at this stage in our understanding, to seek to restrict psychological science to particular styles of theory or method, (British Psychological Society, 1988: 12).

The issue of reflexivity in social psychological research has become particularly important in the wake of criticisms of laboratory experimentation in the 1970s (Harré and Secord, 1972; Tajfel, 1972; Gauld and Shotter, 1977) and the more recent emergence of discourse analysis

(Potter and Wetherell, 1987; Hollway, 1989; Parker, 1992; Burman and Parker, 1993) The self-image and position of the researcher in the discipline were a preoccupation of early 'new paradigm' writers (Shotter, 1975; Reason and Rowan, 1981), and became the focus of studies reported at the advent of discourse analysis (Potter, 1988b). Feminist researchers have been particularly concerned with the role of reflexivity in psychology (Wilkinson, 1988) and, in this respect, critical reflection on the part of the researcher in social psychological investigation has operated as a bridge between empirical research and a political engagement with social issues. A reflexive analysis of the research process that locates the social psychologist in a clearly specified relationship to her 'subjects' functions in a correlative manner, for example, to claims by feminists outside psychology that 'the personal is political' (Rowbotham *et al.*, 1979).

Reflexive research in qualitative work is also becoming increasingly important for psychologists attempting to comprehend issues of race and class (Phoenix, 1990; Walkerdine, 1990). In qualitative work, where an analysis of reflexivity is encouraged and where new forms of subjectivity are allowed to take shape in the course of the research, there is often a strong personal engagement with the material, a sense of being immersed, overwhelmed, and sometimes of being transformed by the subject matter. This aspect of research is also apparent in settings in which psychology is taught. For students carrying out practical and dissertation research informed by anti-racist and feminist perspectives, for example, what is barely articulated at the beginning of the project often eventually becomes the most difficult and most exciting object of study-themselves (see Burman, 1990). It is then apparent that the task, as well as working with the data, is to develop a political analysis of what it is that the student is immersed in and overwhelmed by. Sometimes that is conceptualized as institutional racism or patriarchy, or capitalism, and sometimes, particularly when past training in positivist methods have hampered research, the problem is seen as closer to home, in the form of the psy-complex (Ingleby, 1985; Rose, 1985).

Although a more detailed history of the growth of the psy-complex as it pertains to psychology, and a review of the role of positivism in social psychological research, are still necessary (Parker, 1989), such work would not, on its own, address and support the experience of researchers, nor would it help a reflection upon the conditions of possibility for research practice. There is also a risk that a purely academic history of the discipline may function merely to alienate further those who feel that something is wrong in psychology, and want to work with their experience. It would not be helpful, in this case, to write off experience as just another social construction, or to reduce the expressed dissatisfaction with positivism as a rhetorical trope, discursive position, or warrant. It is here that the political limitations of social constructionist (Gergen, 1985) and some discursive analytic approaches (Edwards and Potter, 1992a) become apparent. It is necessary to reflect on the structure of the institution of psychology as it operates now. The internal discussions of the British Psychological Society (BPS) on the future of the discipline provide an opportunity for such reflection. In Britain the BPS plays an important role in the representation of psychologists and in overseeing undergraduate and professional courses in psychology. A key BPS document will be analysed in a later section of this chapter.

However, the presentation of empirical material here will be preceded by an argument, one that also affects the structure of the chapter, that qualitative research in general, and a focus on reflexivity in particular, requires theoretical grounding. The theoretical aspect is generated through a conceptual analysis of social psychological research, and the grounding is accomplished through a reading of a BPS text. In the following sections of the chapter the role of objectivity and subjectivity in psychology is deconstructed, and a set of conceptual reference points elaborated. These reference points are then used to illuminate subject positions constructed for researchers within the discipline.

Objectivity

The first difficulty a qualitative researcher attempting to work reflexively faces is an assumption in traditional psychology that objectivity and subjectivity are two separate phenomena, and that they must necessarily be counterposed (Reason and Rowan, 1981; Hollway, 1989). It will be helpful, then, to subject this opposition to a brief deconstruction. Deconstruction, which derives from the work of Jacques Derrida (e.g. 1978), writing in the tradition of French post-structuralist philosophy, can be used to explore assumptions which structure a text, and the approach has been fruitfully employed in psychology (Parker, 1988; Parker and Shotter, 1990). In the present case, the relationship between objectivity and subjectivity, as an opposition that structures social psychological texts, can be subverted so that 'objectivity', which is normally treated as more important – as the privileged term – is seen to be dependent upon 'subjectivity'. A double rhetorical move, which privileges objectivity, organizes much quantitative work in psychology, and that rhetoric and giving of privilege is also used to devalue qualitative research. I will take each of the two aspects of this double rhetorical move in turn.

Zero-sum equation

First, the objective and the subjective are weighed against one another, as if the more there is of one the less there is of the other. In this conceptual version of a zero-sum equation, the attainment of an objective position requires the suppression of subjective interest in the research, for such interest, it is thought, can only prejudice the balance and neutrality of psychology. Double-blind procedures in laboratory experiments to screen out 'experimenter effects' (Rosenthal, 1966) express this concern with bias as a contaminant of pure scientific research. Similarly, it is assumed that if the subjective engagement of the researcher were to run unchecked, it would then be impossible to produce an objective account.

The rhetoric of experimental study reproduces a simultaneously terminological separation between the objective and the subjective, and a confusion as to the nature of their referents. In traditional social psychological research, the objects of study are termed 'subjects' at the very moment that the researcher is encouraged to discard subjective involvement in favour of an objective attitude. In this process the researcher exchanges an affective engagement in the topic (an interest in the research and in a successful outcome) for the object status of the 'subjects'. Criticisms of the role of the experiment in psychology have often focused on the treatment of the 'subjects' and the moral–political importance of according them the status of human beings (Harré and Secord, 1972), but an equivalent process occurs (in reverse as it were) for the experimenter, when she understands her own role only in relation to an objective array of facts and data independent of her, and she suppresses her nature as a human being investigating, and in relation to others. (Needless to say this argument also applies if 'he' is doing research, but is worth noting, as feminists have pointed out, that the male researcher usually finds it much easier to work with facts that are completely separate from his subjective involvement.)

More recently, feminist writers in sociology (Roberts, 1981; Stanley and Wise, 1983) and then psychology (Wilkinson, 1988; Burman, 1990; Walkerdine, 1990) have insisted that we should work with, rather than against, experience to arrive at something closer to an objective account. One of the forms of discourse analysis that brings together feminist, Foucauldian, and psychoanalytic ideas has rehearsed again the argument that to work against subjectivity will only lead social psychologists to produce a bizarre variety of subjectivity, precisely that which positivist social psychologists mistakenly call 'objectivity' (Hollway, 1989). In deconstructionist terms, we see that the 'objective' position of the social psychological researcher, which is normally privileged as scientific, is dependent on subjective qualities. To be separate from the object of study, to be untouched by the emotional aspects of the material, is to enjoy or suffer what we might also now call, in discourse analytic terminology, a distinctive 'subject position' in the research process in relation to our subjects (Davies and Harré, 1990; Stenner, 1993).

Individual and collective action

A second aspect of the rhetoric of psychology that divides objectivity from subjectivity (in order to privilege the former term) concerns the nature of the individual in relation to the collective. An enduring problem in psychology is the way the relationship between the individual and the social is understood, and writers using the post-structuralist variants of discourse theory have argued that the discipline routinely splits the individual from the social (Henriques *et al.*, 1984; Parker, 1989). The problem is compounded when objectivity is treated as a property of the collective, when it is seen as emerging from the consensus of opinion, and when subjectivity is treated as a property of the individual, when it is seen as a set of idiosyncratic beliefs. A paradox, or 'dilemma' (Billig, *et al.*, 1988) here in the rhetoric of psychology is that the culture within which psychology emerged respects the individual as a rational citizen and suspects collective activity to amount to little more than irrational mob-rule (Parker, 1989).

A strategy of discursive policing underpins the dichotomy and guarantees its power. Such discursive policing affects both the activity of the collective when it oversteps the bounds of rational action and the individual when they fail to temper rationality with moral judgement. As critical writers in psychology have pointed out, it is when the collective starts to act as an agent, especially as an agent of protest or change, that it is seen as contaminated by irrational subjective forces. Correlatively, it is when an individual adheres too strongly to an ideologically elaborated, and so a socially shared position, especially when they become a source of protest or change, that they are seen as plagued by rigid, authoritarian ways of thinking (Reicher, 1982; Billig, 1985). Empirical and conceptual work by these writers has been concerned with demonstrating that collective activity is often underpinned by rational and moral considerations (Reicher, 1984), and that individual authoritarian cognitive styles are no less supple or 'dilemmatic' than democratic ones (Billig, 1987).

Different traditions of thought that have a bearing on the principal concerns of this chapter have also emphasized the interrelationship between subjectivity and objectivity in individual and collective action. Writers inspired by the ethogenic tradition, for example, have argued that psychological space includes public and collective aspects, and subjectivity is not confined to the individual or the private sphere (Harré, 1983). The work of accounting is seen here as a property of 'joint action' (Shotter, 1984). More recently, work on collective properties of memory in discourse research has opened up the realm of the subjective beyond the individual (Middleton and Edwards, 1990). The feminist argument that 'the personal is political' (Rowbotham *et al.*, 1979) has also redefined how the boundaries between the individual and the collective may be understood, and how we may value the role of subjectivity in collective activity. In each of these alternative traditions, the individual is seen as dependent on the collective for their memory, reasoning, activity, and identity.

There are far-reaching consequences of such a deconstruction for the ways in which reflexivity and notions of context should be understood in research. Reflexivity must now be seen as embedded in a collective research process, and as part of the 'context' of the research. Context is no longer to be seen as something to be tacked on, for it enters into the 'position' of the researcher. Part of that context for social psychological researchers is the structure of academic and professional psychology the psy-complex and, in Britain, its key institutional player is the BPS. It is necessary, before turning to the psy-complex and the BPS, to consider further the nature of subjectivity in research.

Subjectivity

The new paradigm debates in social psychology in the 1970s (e.g. Harré and Secord, 1972), the emergence of discourse analysis during the 1980s (e.g. Potter and Wetherell, 1987), and the discussions of qualitative methods in the early 1990s (e.g. Henwood and Pidgeon, 1992) have given rise to a new climate in the discipline in which it is possible to question traditional views of scientific rigour and reflexivity. New methodological developments have opened a space for alternative conceptions of subjectivity to be explored. Now three distinct ways of grasping the role of subjectivity are apparent in psychology; I will designate these 'uncomplicated', 'blank', and 'complex' subjectivity.

Uncomplicated subjectivity

In spite of, and perhaps because of, the history of positivism in the discipline and its concomitant suspicion of reflexivity, the most tempting, soft, and appealing of objects in psychology is the subject, or the humanist idea of the pure subject as an active reflective agent. The subject is seen as the 'value added' in much qualitative research. When the data speaks for itself it is thought that the uncomplicated subject as researcher need only listen carefully. This is a revival of the assumption that organized knowledge is a 'mirror' of nature (Rorty, 1980), and the nature of the subject who is the reflexive agent is assumed to be pregiven (there before, and independent of social context). Qualitative social psychology which draws on sociology, particularly in 'grounded theory' (Glaser and Strauss, 1967), is founded on this notion of the subject, and it is not surprising that this is so. Humanism has been constructed as an enemy by positivists in the discipline, and so now it is a threat. The notion of 'uncomplicated subjectivity' is one that has been challenged in critical work inspired by post-structuralism, where it has been described as a version of the rational 'unitary subject' of the Cartesian tradition (Henriques *et al.*, 1984; Hollway, 1989). This should not detract from the progressive role that humanist arguments currently play in psychology. We should be aware, though, that there are limitations to this rather naive humanist view of the person.

Blank subjectivity

A rather different reaction to traditional images of the individual in psychology, and one that owes something to structuralist arguments, has entailed a dismissal of individual experience as a fiction. The experience of the individual, in this view, is seen as written through by discourses or other collective resources, such as social representations. Sometimes these resources are conceived of as formal structures that also have a reality inside people's heads, in the form of individual representations (Farr and Moscovici, 1984) or cognitive templates (Harré, 1979). There is also, however, in some writing, a sustained refusal of appeals to individual mental mechanisms or intentions beyond or outside what we can actually read in a text (Edwards and Potter, 1992b), and some understandable worries about the determinism in this position have been expressed (Billig, 1991; Curt, 1994). Insofar as this position takes cultural forms seriously, it deserves serious consideration. However, it should be pointed out that this is the social constructionist flip-side of humanism, a mirror-image of it, and it is not surprising, perhaps, that this obstinate rejection of internal states (individual experience as 'blank subjectivity') can collapse pretty quickly into a simple humanist view of the person (a version of 'uncomplicated subjectivity') through the rhetoric of 'people just do this, why spin more out of it'. Here, what is deliberately unexamined and untheorized at one moment – the human agent – becomes seen as entirely unproblematic the next.

Complex subjectivity

A third approach to this issue is through the figure of 'complex subjectivity' in which a sense of agency is tangled up in cultural forms. This is a mixture of the first and second senses of subjectivity, but one that is complicated further through the particular dominant cultural forms pertaining to self-knowledge that circulate in society at the present time. The figure of 'complex subjectivity' is one that takes seriously both the intentions and desires of the individual and the operation of social structures and discursive forms. A crucial part of this third notion of subjectivity, however, is that the cultural elements out of which a distinct sense of individuality are forged must be attended to. Here the social constructionist position advanced by Harré (1983, 1986b) and Shotter (1984, 1993) on the formation of the self and an inner emotional life through the internalization of shared representations of individuality are relevant. At issue here, and complicating the attempts of social psychological researchers in their search for underlying patterns of behaviour or cognitive mechanisms, is the powerful role played by forms of pop-psychology outside the formal 'psychological' institutions.

Each and every culture complicates research into the social relations that comprize it, and complicates the subjectivity of all who live in it, researchers or not, through religious and ideological mystification, overt coercion, threats and fear, and through orders of discourse which determine what may and may not be said (Foucault, 1969). The 'grounding' of theory is then an endeavour that must involve the researcher in the task of constructing a map of the terrain, one which includes not only the objects of study, but also the researcher themselves. The method a researcher should use, then, also needs to grasp the specific forms of experience lived as culturally constructed resources – resources shared by researcher and researched. Research on social representations has gone some way to addressing this task of cultural analysis (Moscovici, 1976; Farr and Moscovici, 1984), but the contribution of discourse analytic research and psychoanalytic theory is also of value here. Psychoanalytic theory, in particular, is important, for it operates both as topic and resource.

At this point it is necessary to appeal to one of the foundation texts of the social representations tradition, among other studies, to support an argument relating to the nature of shared psychological knowledge in contemporary culture. Moscovici (1976) traced the suffusion of psychoanalysis through popular culture in France, and his detailed study of the social representation of psychoanalysis is paralleled by sociological work in America (Berger, 1965) and Britain (Bocock, 1976), which has traced the 'cultural affinity' of contemporary culture with psychoanalytic categories. It is possible to connect an account of the cultural transmission of psychoanalytic knowledge with social constructionist positions in psychology (Parker, 1993), and the study reported in this chapter is part of a wider project to explore the role of psychoanalytic forms as properties of discourse (Parker, 1997a). For present purposes, it must suffice to point to the way in which 'complex subjectivity' is threaded through with psychoanalytic themes. At the present time, in much of this culture, complex subjectivity is also, to some extent, psychoanalytic subjectivity.

While it may be appropriate simply to employ psychoanalytic theory to understand social phenomena – and there is strong tradition of research now available to social psychologists ranging from the Frankfurt School writings (Elliott, 1992) to Lacanian work (Hollway, 1989) and British object relations theory (Frosh, 1991) – the claim being made here is a little more sceptical of psychoanalysis *per se*. Psychoanalytic theory is used here as an appropriate analytic device because psychoanalytic knowledge helps structure this dominant culture in which the research is being carried out. Reflexivity, then, which is elaborated in the discourse of the culture, also takes on a psychoanalytic character. This reworking of subjectivity also entails the elaboration of specific analytic device, the 'discursive complex'.

Discursive complexes

The notion of the discursive complex is designed to draw upon work on subject positions in discourse analytic research (e.g. Hollway, 1989; Davies and Harré, 1990; Stenner, 1993) and to connect this work with the particular psychodynamic type of culture that hosts subjectivity in the Western world at the present time. Specific examples will be described below in the analysis of the range of subject positions constituted for researchers in the psy-complex, but it is worth specifying some of the general and more abstract properties of a discursive complex first. A discursive complex has two interlinked aspects, concerning social organization and individual reflexive properties of human action. On the one hand, as a first social aspect, it is contained in the network of discourses that are produced in the reading of the texts that comprize the symbolic order. Discourses are seen here as sets of statements that construct objects and an array of subject positions (Foucault, 1969; Parker, 1992), and discursive complexes contain specifications for types of object and shapes of subjectivity. A distinctive feature of the discursive complex, however, is that the shapes they invite the speaking, writing, reading or listening subject to occupy are organized around psychodynamic principles. The theory of self they invite the occupant to elaborate so often now is psychoanalytic.

The second aspect concerns the experiential dimension of language use. A discursive complex is tuned to the complex subjectivity, the psychoanalytic subjectivity that is constituted for culturally competent members and provoked moment by moment in child-rearing practices, self-improvement manuals, therapeutic group settings of every kind, and in versions of psychoanalysis in popular culture. The subject positions that are made available in Western culture are invested with attention and affect that then 'holds' the subject in a particular relation to others. Discursive complexes that operate according to psychoanalytic principles structure locations in the linguistic sphere, on the surface, and simultaneously inscribe psychodynamic forms of feeling on subjects as beings with a sense of 'depth' (Foucault, 1976a).

Where does this leave researchers working in community settings or other social situations who have a background in traditional psychology? A discussion of reflexive research and the grounding of research in discursive and material forms should necessarily, at some point, stop to reflect upon the nature of the discipline that hosts the research enterprize. The account offered here elaborates, in some ways, the call by feminist researchers to engage in 'disciplinary reflexivity' (Wilkinson, 1988). The next empirical and reflexive section of this chapter attempts to do this, and to illustrate how the analytic device of the discursive complex may be employed.

The psy-complex

The psy-complex is the sprawling speculative and regulative network of theories and practices that constitute psychology (Ingleby, 1985; Rose, 1985). 'Psychology' is to be understood here in its broadest sense to include the work of academic social psychologists doing experiments through to general practitioners giving advice and debates over the nature of nursery provision (Riley, 1983; Singer, 1992). Foucauldian historical work sees the psy-complex as all that pertains to the individual, self-monitoring subject and the many practices that subjects employ to survey and improve themselves (Foucault, 1966, 1976a). However, the internal structure of the psy-complex as it is experienced by researchers in psychology, including those who have in interest in Foucauldian work, has been little analysed. How is the psy-complex organized? How are objects distributed across the discipline and how are subject positions ordered within its gaze? How do we function as subjects when we do research and reflexive research in psychology? How might we ground what we do in the network of practices that grounds us? This is not the place for a detailed analysis of the whole of the psy-complex or even, with a narrower focus, of all relevant British Psychological Society documents. The single quotes for each category are simply illustrative of patterns of meaning that have structured the terms of debate in one document, *The Future of the Psychological Sciences* (BPS, 1988). The purpose here is to describe a theoretical position and form of analysis.

The six discursive complexes outlined here are structured into three pairs. Each of the pairs already co-exist in some tension in Freud's (1905, 1914, 1923) writings. The description of discursive complexes may appear, in some respects, to be the simple extension or projection of psychoanalytic categories from an individual level to the collective, and the analysis may also appear to presuppose (as psychoanalysts would) the actual operation of these processes within each individual who participates in the psy-complex. However, no such implication should necessarily be drawn from this account. As the theoretical argument so far as emphasized, discursive complexes operate within the collective, and then position individuals as subjects. The psycho-analytic terminology used to capture these discursive forms here is also designed to capture the dynamic qualities of discourse. These qualities then offer to subjects opportunities for disagreement and spaces for resistance.

The 'ego' versus the 'id'

The first pair consists of the discursive complexes of the 'ego' and the 'id' (Freud, 1923). The 'ego', in this case, refers to the way the institution governing the conduct of the psy-complex in Britain (the BPS) operates as if it were a mental apparatus with a network of 'defences'. The Working Party set up by the Scientific Affairs Board of the BPS notes, for example, that: 'At every meeting of the Board there has been discussion of some new threat to the psychological sciences' (BPS, 1988: 2).

The production of the 'id' as an 'it' is, in psychoanalytic terms, itself the work of repression and, in like form, the attempt of the institution of mainstream psychology to adequately comprehend irrationality precisely produces images of things that seem to lie 'outside', things that operate as if they were irrational and unconscious. An additional fear that motivates the BPS document is that internal dissent could be disruptive and destructive: 'The psychological community could be its own worst enemy ... energies directed at conflict should be diverted to constructive endeavour' (BPS, 1988: 3). Such an image of the institution constitutes specific subject positions for its individual members. Individuals are invited to experience activity outside BPS forums as risky. Overt disagreement over questions of method, for example, could constitute a 'threat' and then a destructive 'conflict', with those responsible seen as breaking the unity of psychology and provoking attack and disorder.

'Working through' versus 'acting out'

Two discursive complexes mark an opposition within psychology that further delegitimizes activity outside or against the institution, and here the point at issue is the type of arena in which rational debate may take place. The complexes of 'working through' and 'acting out' are derived from clinical work (Freud, 1914), but function as specifications of boundaries and proper forums in which certain issues may be explored and changed. To 'work through', understood clinically, is to carry forward the therapeutic work in its proper place, to reflect upon and feel the implications and changes that an interpretation provokes. In the BPS document, there is a similar concern with appropriate arenas for discussion: 'The psychological community should seek to establish mechanisms which ensure mutual communication between such groupings [with common interests within the psychological sciences] and opportunities for synthesis' (BPS, 1988: 7).

Against appropriate working through of disagreement, to 'act out' is to do more than speak, and, usually, to do it outside the therapeutic arena. In this pair of complexes, as it is expressed in the BPS document, an image is reproduced of things as having a proper place in correct channels of communication, and of a necessary dissimulation when talking to outsiders: '[some participants at the Harrogate Conference] insisted that psychologists had better learn to give unequivocal answers. We believe that this is overly simple' (BPS, 1988: 24).

A particular problem is posed here for those engaged in action research, in which the social psychologist should be open about the goals and outcomes of the study (see Goodley and Parker, 2000). Also important, as a general problem, is the way this too cautious view of communication with outsiders seals the inside from the outside. Criteria are then set by the institution to silence those who might be too critical.

'Stages of development' versus 'polymorphous perversity'

Two powerful psychoanalytic themes function as discursive arrangements in psychology's texts, those of 'stages of development' and 'polymorphous perversity' (Freud, 1905). The discursive complex, 'stages of development' is a powerful one in psychology; it structures the way psychologists understand Freud, Piaget, Vygotsky, etc., and the way those who suffer psychology read the progress of their child through normative developmental milestones (Burman, 1994). The BPS Working Party apply this model of development to psychology itself: 'A key purpose of this Report is to identify growth points for the future of the psychological sciences in Britain' (BPS, 1988: 1).

In contrast, the discursive complex 'polymorphous perversity' narrates the past as a state of untutored sensual being that should be left behind, and it functions as a warning to those who lag behind or who may refuse to follow a developmental route towards more rigorous science. These critics may then be seen as wilfully regressing. The state of uncertainty is associated with inadequate development. 'At present, the psychological sciences are in many ways fragmented' (BPS, 1988: 12).

The rhetoric of maturity and responsibility is manifest in the ways in which the BPS then responds to demands it apparently feels to be unprofessional and, by implication, infantile. The cumulative effect of these discursive forms is to position those who are developing hermeneutic, post-structuralist or feminist critiques of positivist methodology as being in favour of fragmentation (and so immature), in favour of sharing the research process with those outside the discipline (and so acting out), and in favour of conflict (and so irrational).

Discussion

The two poles of each pair of these discursive complexes can be understood as working in tension, as would be the polarities of terms uncovered in a deconstructive reading (Parker, 1988; Parker and Shotter, 1990). Each of the three pairs of complexes could also be understood as 'dilemmas' (cf. Billig *et al.*, 1988), which organize the ways in which debates in psychology may be comprehended by participants. In this case, however, the analogy with deconstruction is closer, for in each pair there is one privileged term that dominates the other: The institution of psychology as a rational decision-making collective (its 'ego'), is privileged over the irrational and dangerous forces that might disrupt it (its 'id'); a careful discussion of issues inside the institution ('working through') is privileged over the opening of debate to outside inspection and alliances with those outside ('acting out'); and the attempt to regulate the development of different sections of the discipline ('stages of development') is privileged over infantile and premature clamouring for attention and gratification ('polymorphous perversity'). The link with deconstruction is also perhaps more germane, for it highlights political dimensions of the material, and the ways in which critics may wish systematically to reverse the privilege given to the dominant terms and argue in favour of the subordinate term (as part of a practical deconstruction of the institution of the psy-complex).

The question of political consequences of participation in each of these discursive forms also echoes debates that have already occurred within sectors of the psychoanalytic tradition itself, in the dispute, for example, over the emergence of 'ego psychology' in the United States and the value of the unconscious as a source of resistance. At the very least, that dispute helped structure the ways in which psychologists of different kinds thought about their activity and professional responsibilities, and the debate is still relevant to an understanding of the state of contemporary social psychology (Parker, 1997c).

There is a reflexive issue here that needs to be made explicit, and it bears upon the position of the researcher in relation to the material. I could not produce this analysis as a disengaged scientific researcher, and the reader may disagree with the account presented here, in part, because they engage differently with the texts (perhaps from different subject positions, which flow from their different histories within the discipline). My engagement, for example, is influenced by an involvement with the meetings that led to the formation of one of the oppositional groupings in psychology (see Reicher and Parker, 1993). I realized, in the course of the analysis, that it was necessary to turn to documents written in and against the discipline. The wording of different critical manifestos have slowly and falteringly grasped the symptomological shape of the discipline. They are now, apart from anything else, a valuable resource for critical self-reflection for researchers in the psy-complex. The process of professionalization in the BPS has been discussed with reference to feminism and the Psychology of Women Section (Wilkinson and Burns, 1990), the attempt to persuade the BPS to boycott apartheid institutions in South Africa (Henwood, 1994), and the politics of clinical work (Pilgrim and Treacher, 1992). Such broader reflections on the discipline have been a necessary prerequisite for a discursive analysis of one specific text.

Concluding comments

There is a peculiar reflexive quality to the employment of psychoanalytic theory to comprehend the discipline of psychology: psychoanalysis is the 'repressed other' of psychology (Burman, 1994). Its existence defines and limits what psychologists will allow themselves to say about subjectivity. It is all the more valuable, then, to link it with qualitative research. The issue is not whether psychoanalysis is true or not, rather it is how the theory circulates through culture, and then how the employment of psychoanalytic ideas in the discipline can function as a form of resistance to the routine squashing of human agency. This reflexive research draws, in Foucauldian terms, on experiential and theoretical forms of 'counter-practice' (Foucault, 1977). So it tries to link the personal and the political, and it is grounded in that link.

This is the subjective context against which a researcher in psychology or community psychology attempts, in their everyday practice, to construct an 'objective' account. And the 'grounding' of theory must now be in wider culturally shared theories, including psychoanalytic theories, and in the nature of the enterprize of psychology held within particular institutions, including those that structure the psy-complex. The documents and practices of the psy-complex limit and structure how social psychologists think about objective research, and how they may think about issues of subjectivity. The wider context in the discipline may offer spaces for critiques of science and for action research, but more often the language of psychology inhibits innovation. The BPS text chosen here is but one example of the way that texts in psychology reproduce certain conceptual oppositions and close off certain forms of challenge. The theoretical position described here entails an analysis of the psy-complex that locates our attempts to be 'reflexive' and the concerns of those engaged in reflexive research.

The way that social research is contextualized now will also look a little more complex, for the 'context' is, in this account, not an objective background against which the researcher renders an account of the phenomenon in question. Rather, the context is the network of forms of subjectivity that place contradictory demands on the research. In social psychological research there is an array of competing interests and agendas that frame the production of proposals; the expectations and demands of 'subjects' or co-researchers; and the career investments and projected autobiographies that exist in tension in the academic world. All social psychological research is located in a variety of structures, which bear on the peculiar gendered quality of the research enterprize (Broughton, 1988), the ways in which research questions are structured by assumptions pertaining to race (Phoenix, 1987), and the class divisions that offer career opportunities to some and exclude other sectors of the community (Walkerdine, 1990). Among the structures that frame the experience and reflection of the researcher are those of the psy-complex. If we want to take reflexivity seriously, we have to 'ground' it in the institutional context in which we carry out our research.

8
Tracing Therapeutic Discourse in Material Culture

Approaches to language and subjectivity from post-structuralist theory outside psychology and from deconstructive perspectives within counselling and psychotherapy have questioned the way therapeutic relationships are formed in Western culture. Discourse analysis has been developed as a methodological framework to take this questioning further, and to provide detailed readings of therapeutic patterns of meaning. Foucauldian discourse analytic approaches help us to address how we are made into selves that speak, how we *experience* the self therapeutically. I will elaborate this methodological framework through an analysis of a piece of text – an item of consumer packaging – tracing the contours of therapeutic discourse through a series of twenty methodological steps. Therapeutic discourse draws the reader in as the kind of subject who must feel a relationship at some depth with the (imagined) authors for the text to work. The chapter thus illustrates the value of discourse analytic readings of texts, and helps us to reflect upon our commitment to discourses of counselling and psychotherapy as empowering stories and as culturally specific patterns of subjectivity.

A variety of arguments from post-structuralist theory outside psychology have been brought to bear in recent years upon the activities of counsellors and psychotherapists (e.g., McNamee and Gergen, 1992b). The social construction of therapeutic work in Western culture has been thrown into question, but the 'deconstruction' of therapeutic discourse has been adopted by some practitioners to assist their own critical reflection and to make it possible for counsellors to address patterns of discourse which structure their relationships with clients (e.g., Parker, 1999c). The work of Michel Foucault has been particularly helpful to psychologists here (Parker, 1995a), and forms of discourse analysis have been developed in psychology which draw upon Foucault's (1975a,

1976a) systematic critical analysis of discipline and confession (e.g., Burman and Parker, 1993; Burman *et al.*, 1996). Foucauldian discourse analysis draws our attention to the 'conditions of possibility' for counselling and psychotherapy to work, to the way we *experience* therapeutic relationships when we are positioned as therapeutic subjects in the texts which comprise this culture. This chapter aims to show how Foucauldian discourse analysis may be of relevance to counsellors and psychotherapists, and how this methodological framework functions as part of the broader 'deconstructive' turn in psychology.

I will work through a piece of text which looks, at first glance, to be innocent, but which participates in what Foucault would call a 'regime of truth' that is at one with the 'psy-complex' (Ingleby, 1985; Rose, 1985). It may be thought that the text in question is too trivial to bear the weight of the reading that I weave around it. However, I have chosen this text, in part, precisely because it circulates as a fairly insignificant part of consumer packaging, and we might be tempted to assume that it escapes larger-scale patterns of ideology and power. One of the points we have to keep in mind when we are analysing the discursive construction of knowledge is that such construction operates throughout language, and in the smallest texts. When we are looking for a definition of what a discourse is we cannot do better than start with Foucault's statement that discourses are 'practices that systematically form the objects of which they speak' (Foucault, 1969: 49). I will work through a piece of text following methodological steps that have been derived from this definition (Parker, this volume, Chapter 6, 1992, 1994). The first set of fourteen steps are designed to systematically tease apart the text, identifying objects and subjects, networks of relationships, and the con-tradictions between different images of the world. Also in these first steps, the identification of labels for the discourses – including therapeutic discourse in this case – that run through the text is intended then to open up the way in which certain realities are constructed in the text that enrol us as we read it. Let us now move straight to the text, and take up theoretical issues from Foucault's work in the course of the analysis.

The material

The text is from the cardboard package for 'Silly Strawberry' children's toothpaste. It is mainly marketed, from Maine in North America, through wholefood shops.

The front of the box has the manufacturer's logo 'Tom's of Maine' (in green), the brand name 'Natural Toothpaste for Children' (in red), and the labels 'with Fluoride' (also in red) and 'SACCHARINE FREE' (in green). The name of this version, 'Silly Strawberry', is printed in white (next to the weight) in the bottom red stripe.

The back of the box has a list of ingredients, their purpose and source, and the following lead paragraph:

WHAT MAKES THIS NATURAL? All major brands of toothpaste for children contain saccharin, artificial color, and taste super sweet. We take a simple approach – use natural ingredients to make it taste good and work well. Compare our natural ingredients with any other brand and make your choice.

There is also the statement:

Children under six years of age should be supervised in the use of toothpaste.

One side of the box has a message for parents:

The Story Of Our Children's Natural Toothpaste
Dear Parent,
We think the time is right to make a natural toothpaste just for children. For over 20 years we have committed ourselves to natural oral and body care products.
Many adults have come to trust our natural toothpastes made without saccharin or synthetic flavors, preservatives, dyes or animal ingredients.
We now offer a delicious and effective natural toothpaste with sensible ingredients and natural fruit flavors created with your child's taste in mind. It contains none of the stripes and "sparkles", neon colors and sweet bubble gum flavors you see in other brands. Our gentle formulation is low in abrasivity and contains fluoride to help prevent dental decay.
Try it and let us know what you and your child think.
Your friends, Kate and Tom Chappell
[the signature 'Kate and Tom' follows]

The other side of the box includes messages for children:

JUST foR KiDS by LuKe Chappell (age 8 3/4)
About Animals – Do you like animals? At home we have a dog

Hershey, a bird Eli, and a hamster named Carol. At Tom's of Maine my Mom and Dad make sure our products are safe without testing them on animals. If you have a favorite animal, draw a picture and send it to me.

About Recycling – At home we recycle cans, bottles, newspaper and plastic. Tom's of Maine gave our town green bins so each family can separate and store their recycled things until a special truck picks them up every week. If you do recycling at home, let me know. I'm trying to get recycling news from all the states.

Analytic steps

This text is already in the form of words, but if it were not, we would need to engage in a *first step* to turn it into words and a *second step* to explore connotations through creative free association (which should be understood here as tracing symbolic connections in cultural material rather than delving into any particular individual unconscious). These steps would produce additional text that we could then draw upon to help make sense of the material. I have already selected material from the box, and that selection must itself be reflected upon at some point in the analysis. It is not only the addition of material through a variety of free association, but also the omission of certain bits of text that might be significant to the 'final' reading. I say 'final reading', but the different positions of readers, and changes in meanings over time after the analysis is finished, make every final reading provisional. In the case of interview transcripts, which is the type of material that a qualitative researcher in psychology is most likely to be faced with, this process of selection and omission becomes very important.

In this case, although the text is already in words, we could note typographical differences between the side of the box with the message for parents and the side with the message 'just for kids'. Kate and Tom Chappell's message to the parent is in the form of a letter, and printed in simple type, with a handwritten signature at the end. Luke Chappell's messages, on the other hand, are unsigned, and the header 'JUST foR KiDS by LuKe Chappell (age 8 3/4)' is in children's scrawl. The different typographies, then, signify adult and child forms of communication. The one is formal, and the communication channel also constructs a relationship between writer and reader governed by polite and respectful sharing and accepting of narrative. The other is informal and constructs emotional and playful identification over diverse themes and images. Among the symbolic associations as first thoughts to help the analysis that flooded to my mind were the ways that a personal address was set up to me as reader, and the way the natural character of the toothpaste seemed connected in some way to the simplicity of communication that was assumed to exist between addressor and addressee, between those who supposedly wrote the text(s) and those for whom it was intended. The two types of message also seem to complement each other, and we might want to pick up forms of discourse that could hold those different modes of address together. We will return to these issues below.

If discourses are practices that systematically form 'objects', then we should, as a *third step,* itemize the objects in this text. It is not possible in this brief space of a single chapter to list all the objects that are mobilized here, but it is instructive to select a portion of text in discourse analysis, and to carry out that task. In this case I will select objects that appear to be bound up with specifications of types of relationship. Note that this is a choice, and you as a reader may have other concerns which led you to this text in the first place, as part of a wider sample of texts perhaps. It is a useful exercise to list objects, because it highlights again the interpretative work that goes into even such a simple coding exercise. As we itemize the objects, it is helpful to focus on simple nouns, but it is also useful sometimes to include some more implicit objects produced by word combinations or adjectives. The notes around the different objects assist the drawing of connections and patterns. The list might look like this:

The natural. The term 'natural' is used as an adjective to qualify 'Toothpaste for Children', 'toothpaste just for children', 'toothpaste' (four times), 'ingredients' (twice), 'oral and body care products', and 'fruit flavours'. Also, 'this' (as in 'what makes this natural') may refer to things other than the toothpaste, this message, for example, or this relationship with the reader. 'Natural' is also linked to 'simple' (as in 'simple approach') and 'sensible' (as in 'sensible ingredients');
'taste' (with an opposition between that which tastes 'super sweet' and that which tastes 'good');
'gentle formulation' (as combining absence of 'abrasivity' and presence of 'fluoride');
'commitment' (as in the orientation, 'for over 20 years', to 'natural oral and body care products');
'trust' (as the commitment that 'adults' show, in return for Kate and Tom Chappell's commitment, to natural toothpastes);

'synthetic flavours' (linked metonymically to 'saccharine', 'artificial
    color', 'super sweet' taste, 'preservatives', 'dyes', 'animal ingredients',
    'stripes', '"sparkles"', 'neon colors', and 'sweet bubble gum
    flavors');
'family' (as in 'each family' in 'our town');
'child' (as in 'your child' and in 'kids');
'special truck' (which picks up up the green bins).

This list is incomplete, of course, but the simple notes on the objects
identify some connections, and also start to highlight patterns. It is
important to keep in mind that the objects identified by the text are
constructed within that text, and that it is that construction that concerns
us here. We may know other things about the benefits of saccharine,
say, or the dangers of fluoride, and that may lead us to read certain
statements on the package with a sceptical eye, but it is useful now
to follow a *fourth step* which is to treat the text as our object of study.
If we step outside the text and try to assess the truth claims made by
different statements we may lose sight of the way a particular
construction is operating. We might want to insist, for example, that
'animal ingredients' are actually 'natural ingredients', but we would
then be reading the object 'animal' as separate and apart from the
text itself. This text constructs 'animal' as something that is unnatural as a toothpaste ingredient, and, rather, as something in
nature that should be respected. As Luke Chappell's message indicates, it should be personalized, given a name. It is the *talk* about
what is, and what is not 'natural', and about the other objects, which
is our object of concern.

Subjects in the text

Among the most important objects specified by a text are those objects
which write and read, speak and listen. These are the subjects, and it is
worth being fairly systematic in the *fifth step* of listing the subjects that
appear in the text:

'Tom' (marked as Tom 'of Maine', one of your 'friends', Tom Chappell,
    as 'Dad' to Luke, as provider of 'green bins' and a 'special truck');
'Children' (marked as targets of the natural toothpaste, as needing
    supervision when 'under six years of age', as provided for by
    parents, as owned by adults, as in 'your child', as capable of address
    to other children, who they then call 'kids', who personalize
    animals, and who collect things like 'recycling news');

'Silly Strawberry' (marked as a fruit attributed with human qualities,
  perhaps equivalent to Hershey the dog, Eli the bird and Carol the
  hamster);
'Parent' (marked as the addressee of the letter from Kate and Tom
  Chappell, guardian of the child, here a single child, like Luke);
'Adult' (marked as the category that contains those who have come to
  trust Kate and Tom's natural toothpastes, and as a category equivalent
  here to 'parent');
'Your friends' (marked specifically here as Kate and Tom Chappell, but
  also as a category of subject mirrored in Luke's messages when he
  addresses his friend as 'kids' on the other side of the box);
'Kate Chappell' (marked in the close and signature to the letter, her
  name before 'Tom', as Mom who makes sure, with Dad, that the
  products are safe);
'Kids' (marked as the name that children give themselves, including
  when they have messages marked as 'just for' them);
'Luke Chappell' (marked as of a particular age, '8 3/4', with a range of
  interests in the welfare of animals and recycling which complement
  his parents commitment to 'natural oral and body care products'
  and Dad's gifts to the local community);
'Hershey' (marked as a dog);
'Eli' (marked as a bird);
'Carol' (marked as a hamster);
'Mom' (marked as Luke's);
'Dad' (marked as Luke's);
'Favorite animal' (marked as an equivalent that the 'kid' reader might
  have to Luke's three named animals at home).

In this text the range of subject positions for authors and readers is made
explicit through the naming of these in the headings and signatures,
but although we do not have to engage in such a difficult task of
piecing together exactly who is being addressed here, for it is a 'parent'
and 'kids', we can explore further the ways in which these subject
positions are enrolled through the text into ways of speaking. We can
do this through a *sixth step* of speculating about what they may say
within this system of discourse. We already know something of how
Kate and Tom and Luke speak, but other actors are also put into play
here. A community of subjects is evoked, with the Chappell family and
their three pet animals at the centre, and the rest of the town as
beneficiaries. The town consists of families, which we imagine to be
like Kate, Tom and Luke, and the commitment that Kate and Tom

show to natural oral and body care products is matched by the concern that their son shows to animals and recycling, and then in the participation of the wider town community in recycling. The community is then spread wider through the invitation to send information about recycling in 'all the states', and through the address to the parent as someone like Kate and Tom, as their friend, and to the child by Luke as like Luke, as a fellow kid.

A *seventh step* focuses on the networks of relationships that are conjured up, and many of the statements about the nature of the toothpaste and the associated activities of the Chappells, their animals, and their town with the green bins and special trucks, also enrol the reader as a member of a particular social world. It is worth spending a little time reconstructing what those networks of relationship might be like, and it is helpful to move, in the process, onto the *eighth step* in which we imagine how those implied networks of relationships and pictures of the world might be defended if attacked. Each of the invitations to identify with the Chappells, or to respond to their requests draws the reader into a semiotic system underpinned by a notion of what is 'natural'. We can start to map the types of accusation that might be made against those who refused to participate in this system. One might risk accusations of conformity for buying 'major' brands, of being a dupe by being taken in by 'stripes and "sparkles"', of lack of concern for safety of animals, of ingratitude, and betrayal of trust of the reader's new 'friends'. One might also be accused of lack of awareness. This possible accusation is signalled in the phrase 'we think the time is right', and it holds in it one of the gentlest but most persuasive recriminations that operate in modern popular psychological discourse, that the subject is not yet ready to understand something important about nature, and about their inner needs.

There are a number of rhetorical devices that pin the commitment to nature and simplicity to a particular notion of health and self-awareness, and what seems to be at stake here is a view of what natural mental health entails. A contrast is set up between the 'major brands' of toothpaste for children which contain saccharine and other unnatural ingredients, and this natural toothpaste. To buy and use this toothpaste, then, is to participate in a minority, marginal activity, but it is also to return to 'a simple approach', one which requires a measure of commitment (here on the part of the manufacturers) and trust (here on the part of adults who have bought natural toothpastes before). It is then possible to build up a picture of the type of relationship between manufacturer and consumer as simple, natural and as one of friendship.

Luke is addressing the child, and telling them about the 'special truck' that 'Dad' has provided for other families in their town while a special relationship between Kate and Tom and the parent is being formed. In both cases adult and child are being asked to return the commitment to others that Luke, Kate and Tom show to them. Parents are asked to compare the natural ingredients with other brands, make a choice, and try it. They are then asked to share their views. Children meanwhile are asked to draw a picture of their favourite animal, and send it together with news about recycling.

The comparisons that adults are asked to make between major brands and this toothpaste highlight again the ways in which the text, like any text, is structured around a series of oppositions. Such oppositions can be explored in a *ninth step* which further draws out the patterns of discourse at play in the text by identifying contrasts between ways of speaking. In many cases, of course, an object is identified by a number of intersecting ways of speaking. Toothpaste, for example, is identified as a product that has to 'work well', be 'effective' and 'prevent dental decay'. Talk about the toothpaste in these terms is governed by considerations of function and hygiene. Such preoccupations would then draw other terms in the text, such as 'ingredients', into an interpretative scheme which was concerned with the medical properties of the product. This interpretative scheme is, of course, held together in contemporary modern culture as medical discourse. Talk about toothpaste as containing saccharine, 'stripes and "sparkles"', 'neon colors' and 'sweet bubble gum flavors' is to position the product as one of a realm of sweets. Although this text is distancing itself from that way of appreciating toothpaste as a variety of sweet, it still tries to address some of the lures of what might want to call a 'confectionary discourse' by claiming that this product is 'delicious' and has 'your child's taste in mind'.

While there are points of contrast between different discursive frames for what seems to be the 'same' object, it is also useful to move onto a *tenth step* which looks at the points of overlap between different ways of talking about the 'same' object. Staying with the object 'toothpaste' in this text, we have the object produced both as a medical item and as something that will function as a substitute sweet. The object also functions in a network of relationships and holds that network together across the spread of different realities in different ways of talking. The toothpaste is presented as a natural product and is free of animal ingredients, and so functions as an exemplar of simplicity within an ecological discourse. This ecological discourse holds together the talk about safety and respect for animals and the description of recycling in Luke Chappell's two messages for kids on his side of the packet. The toothpaste also operates as an object that is chosen by adults, although in this 'natural toothpaste' there is also an expectation that the child will be consulted, and that children under a certain age, in this case six years, will be supervised in its use. Here the object is part of the panoply of childcare, and 'works' as part of a childcare discourse, a discourse which also contains within it a developmental notion of supervision, responsibility and rights.

As an *eleventh step* we can now consider how these different discourses speak to different audiences. The talk about the toothpaste in terms of function and hygiene will address a medical audience, but when the talk is of the toothpaste as a natural product it then addresses an audience with ecological concerns. When it is identified as a product that is sometimes wrongly treated as a sweet but which is both delicious and sensible, it addresses an audience of sensible parents, and when the talk is of an item that calls for supervised use it also addresses the parent who is responsible for the development of their child.

Discourses in the text, and therapeutic discourse

I have anticipated the *twelfth step* here in which we choose labels for the discourses that we have identified. It does sometimes seem as if the process of reading a text reveals discourses that have lain hidden within it, but it should be emphasized that a reading is an active interpretative process, and we reconstruct the patterns from our membership in the surrounding culture and our recognition of discourses that play through our subjectivity outside the text. This activity of reconstruction, and the importance of the position from which we make a reading, are particularly evident in the labels we choose to identify discourses. Some of these labels may not seem right to you as reader, and if they do not, then we must explore whether that is because some different patterns are more salient, or whether it is because these patterns have different connotations that can be better captured with another term. These six discourse headings do seem to flow from the steps of analysis presented so far:

'Confectionary' (marked by the likeness to sweets of major brands which have 'neon colors and sweet bubble gum flavors');
'Health' (marked by a concern with the effects of saccharine, synthetic flavours etc., and the emphasis on fluoride as an ingredient to prevent dental decay);

'Childcare' (marked by warnings about the confectionary character of other toothpastes, the note on supervising children, and the letter to parents);

'Childcentred' (marked by the invitation to consult the child, and the message from another child to a child product user);

'Ecological' (marked by the natural ingredients, the descriptions of recycling, the special trucks and green bins, and the care and safety of animals);

'Familial' (marked by the image of the Chappell family, and the address to the parent as guardian of a child).

There is also a strong seventh discourse running through the text that ties the familial, child-centred and ecological discourses together at the point that the parent engages with the text enough to compare the toothpaste with other brands and make their 'choice'. This is also where the childcare discourse is turned from traditional notions of child-training towards notions of autonomous self-driven growth, and the health discourse breaks from a more standard medical discourse and moves into the realm of *mental* health:

'Therapeutic' (marked by the 'story' format, the thought that the 'time is right', the 'commitment' to product lines, the evocation of 'trust' on the part of responsible readers, the 'gentle formulation', and the invitation to respond to addressors positioning themselves as 'friends')

A discourse analytic reading also needs to take this further to a *thirteenth step* which traces how such discourses emerged historically. In the process we can explore how such discourses function to position subjects as the text circulates through culture. At the same time we need to unravel, in a *fourteenth step*, the ways in which the discourses weave their own story of origins and how, in the process they conceal their historical character. Discourses of health, for example, are contradictory blends of medical and mystical notions that exist in contradiction to one another (Stainton Rogers, 1991), and the battle between the two is being continued in this text. The 'prevention of dental decay' participates in a version of health that treats the body as a complicated machine, for example, while the 'simple approach' appeals to the natural abilities of the body to heal itself. Each version of health pretends either that it has discovered a true picture of the body or that it has rediscovered a truth that has been lost.

Childcare discourse is split between hardline developmental notions which resort to empirical observations of ages and stages mostly derived from studies in contemporary Western culture, and humanist visions of autonomy and growth (Burman, 1994). Both are present in this text, and notions of supervision until age six operate alongside and against injunctions to consult the child about their tastes. Again, the one version of the discourse presents itself as discovered rational commonsense and the other as recovered knowledge of natural bonds. The figure of the 'child' as a distinct category of subject with character-istics qualitatively different from those of adults is a fairly recent notion in Western European culture (Ariès, 1962), but child-centred discourse now presents itself as the natural and inevitable recognition of a special kind of being. In this text, the direct mode of address from one child to another in the message 'just for kids' reproduces just such a notion of the child. However, one should note that, at the same moment, it is parents who are addressed as those who may trust in natural toothpastes for their children.

Ecological themes are also contradictory, with different strands of ecological discourse appealing variously to romantic notions of a return to nature or to a more active reflection and practice of community to make a different relationship with nature (Bookchin, 1974). In this case an appeal to what is natural is reinforced by a refusal of what we have termed here 'confectionary discourse'. Such contradictions thread their way through this text, and address the reader variously as an agent driven by commitment and trust or by comparison and choice. Ecology in this text, and more generally in ecological discourse, can appeal to a rational subject who weighs up the advantages and dis-advantages of fluoride and animal testing or to a deeper essentialized subject who experiences themselves in some direct and simple organic relationship to nature (Parker, 1997a).

In each case, in each of these discourses, we are thrown into the realm of the politics of personhood, and this is nowhere more evident than in the paradoxes of therapeutic discourse. To address that, however, we have to turn to Foucault's work again, and so to a theoretical framework that can help us locate these discourses in the operations of institutions, power and ideology.

Therapeutic discourse, subject positions and power

We now move into a further series of six methodological steps to try and read the text with that account in mind. A properly Foucauldian understanding of discourse has to ask, as a *fifteenth step*, what institutions are reinforced by the discourses that have been described in the analysis, and, as a *sixteenth step*, what institutions are subverted by those discourses.

One of the striking things about this text is the way it expresses some of the key concerns in Foucault's writing, and the complex interplay between domination and resistance (Foucault, 1980). The contradictions in each of the discourses we have identified open up the possibility for challenge and debate. Within health, we have a challenge to medical instititutions based on science, and within childcare, we have a challenge to traditional forms of family based on obedience. Notions of growth and autonomy underpin the image of the child, through identification with Luke Chappell, and the parent is invited into a friendship with the manufacturers, Kate and Tom.

When we step back and look at how those notions of growth and autonomy function in the wider political sphere, however, we find two institutions strongly buttressed, and the ecological discourse glues these all the more firmly together. One of these institutions is the *family*, and the text specifies the family as the basic unit of the community through the reference to 'each family' recycling in Luke's home town. The person responsible for making choices is not defined specifically as mother or father (Mom or Dad), but is defined as a generic parent, and they are asked to consult their child, defined here in the singular. The other institution at issue here is the *self*, and the text traces a narrative of appropriate timing for the acceptance of knowledge about needs, and about the importance of trust in order to specify a subject who will not only compare and choose, but will feel, at a simple and natural level, that the product is good and works well. In this context, ecological discourse offers a range of organic metaphors that naturalize each of these two complementary institutions.

Institutions offer to subjects positions in which they enjoy power, and so, as a *seventeenth step*, we should look at what categories of person gain from these discourses. For Foucault (1980), power is not only coercive, but also productive of kinds of relationship and experience. Our own investments in the discourses is emphasized when we consider, as an *eighteenth step*, who would promote and who would oppose these discourses. Foucault's histories of surveillance and confession do not necessarily lead to the view that psychological and psychotherapeutic forms of discourse are bad, but a historical reflection does help us to locate the images of the self that those modern discourses carry with them. The recruitment of readers of this text into an ecological universe is not dangerous as such, but we do need to be able to reflect upon the ways in which it warrants a particular version of subjectivity as something very deep, simple and natural. We need to be able to step back and look at how that knowledge is a discursive construction. Power was transformed, according to Foucault (1975a, 1976a) when culture mutated at around the end of the eighteenth century, and when individuals took responsibility for their own behaviour, became the instruments of the surveillance of themselves and became driven to speak about their innermost desires. A therapeutic discourse is a function of this apparatus of self-regulation and confession, and the text can be interpreted as an instance of that apparatus. It draws the reader in as a subject with depth, and the subject must feel a relationship at some depth with Kate and Tom for the text to work.

If we turn to the ideological functions of the text, we can, as a *nineteenth step*, explore how these discourses interlock with other oppressive discourses. This requires some wider political analysis of, for example, the ways in which paternalism operates in US American culture to gloss over divisions between those who own and those who buy, and how the rhetoric of empowerment and self-help often attaches recipients of welfare all the more firmly to their rich benefactors. In this text, the voice of the child draws another child into a discursive frame which follows the question 'Do you like animals?' with a description of the pets and Mom and Dad's care of them, as if that description was the necessary answer to the question. The description of recycling is then given as a series of activities dependent on the goodwill of Tom's of Maine.

The refusal of that story of goodwill would, in this narrative, also effectively be a statement that we do *not* like animals. A refusal of the friendship offered by Kate and Tom, and by Luke, must also then be a display of meanness, and perhaps of pathology. This would still be pathology even if it were accounted for in this discourse as being a bad response because for us as reader the time is not right. If we consider, as a *twentieth step*, how discourses justify the present, we could look at the ways in which a progressivist narrative operates alongside the ecological and therapeutic discourses such that recycling at home and opposition to animal testing is presented simultaneously as the return to nature and the advance beyond a favour for synthetic major brand toothpastes.

Concluding comments

Not all toothpastes are riddled with therapeutic discourse, and there is evidence that major brands draw upon more mainstream psychological notions of development and rationality (Parker, 1994), and these texts can then be unravelled to show how they carry within them other forms of subjectivity (Parker, 1995b). A discourse analysis does not, however, arrive at the proof or falsification of an hypothesis through the collection and counting of instances of a phenomenon. It would be difficult to arrive at a fixed definition of the phenomenon in the first place, and in this respect discourse analysis participates in a broader critical reflection upon methodological practices in psychology. There are undoubtedly many objections that can be made against discourse analysis, and those working within the Foucauldian tradition have been happy to identify at least thirty-two at last count (Parker and Burman, 1993).

This kind of critical reading complements the arguments of those who have been concerned to display the coercive and profoundly anti-therapeutic patterns of power in the relationship between psychotherapist and patient, or between counsellor and client (e.g., Pilgrim, 1997). However, it is also quite compatible with the internal critiques of counselling and psychotherapy which inspire radical varieties of 'deconstructive', 'discursive', 'Foucauldian', 'narrative' or 'postmodern' work (Parker, 1999c). Discourse analysis of the kind described in this chapter may then function as a methodological and theoretical framework to help counsellors and psychotherapists reflect on what they construct with those who seek help, as empowering stories and as culturally specific patterns of subjectivity.

9
Constructing and Deconstructing Psychotherapeutic Discourse

This chapter reviews recent work on the social construction of the self in counselling and psychotherapy, and argues that we need to attend to the ways in which the therapeutic self is fashioned (a) in relation to the 'psy-complex' as the network of theories and practices concerned with psychological governance and self-reflection in modern Western culture and (b) in the context of 'therapeutic domains' outside the clinic and academe, domains of discursive regulation and self-expression which then bear upon the activities of professional and lay counsellors. Therapeutic domains contain repertoires, templates and complexes within which counsellors and clients fabricate varieties of truth and story a core of experience into being. I then turn to describe and assess some of the various ways in which this kind of critical reflection on therapeutic discourse and counselling practice now already underpins the work of social constructionist 'narrative' therapists. Some attention is given to the different pragmatic and deconstructionist approaches which make the discursive constitution of the problem into the problem, either by dissolving or externalizing the account the client presents. Here I argue that the activities of social constructionist counsellors can be viewed as forms of deconstruction-in-process (a deconstruction of the discursive frames which have been constructed by the client), but that they should not be viewed as stepping outside the discursive conditions of possibility which grounds their work. The psy-complex and therapeutic domains still function as relatively enduring structures which limit the degree to which we may construct and deconstruct psychotherapeutic discourse.

The main argument in this chapter is a simple one, but it does challenge some of the underlying assumptions of counselling psychology: the process of doing counselling or psychotherapy involves the construction of a certain kind of discourse. A discourse is a set of state-ments – words and phrases – that construct objects, that give shape to things outside language so those things become real to us (Parker, 1992). Psychotherapeutic discourse specifies the way we think and feel about problems and solutions and it specifies a kind of self that would be able to appreciate that discourse and act in an appropriate way. This in itself is not a terribly radical or innovative argument. There are a number of writers in counselling and psychotherapy in recent years who have developed an account of the therapeutic process as weaving a certain kind of narrative, as telling a certain kind of story about the self, as engaging in a certain kind of rhetoric which finds a way of performing a new self. Examples here include work from the personal construct tradition (Mair, 1989), from within a psychoanalytic frame-work (Hobson, 1986), and a host of people from a systemic family therapy background (Epston and White, 1989; White and Epston, 1990; Monk *et al.*, 1997) whose work will be discussed in further detail later in this chapter.

These developments draw out some of the implications from, and add their own distinctive theoretical insights to, work on the social construction of the self and emotions. Rom Harré (e.g., 1983, 1986b) has been a key player here in making a case for seeing the formation of the self as requiring the acquisition and idiosyncratic fashioning of a *theory* of the self from culture, and for seeing emotions as embedded in moral orders which are quite different in different cultures. Descriptions and feelings of *accidie*, which arises from a failure to do one's duty to God in medieval England, or *amae*, which expresses a peculiar pleasurable dependency on others in contemporary Japan, for example, raise questions about what counselling psychologists usually assume must be the case for their activity to do good, or for their clients to be better. In North America, Ken Gergen (e.g., 1991, 1994b) has advanced this kind of social constructionist account and added a pragmatic optimistic celebration of postmodernism in psychology and culture in order to challenge narratives of deficit and to encourage new narratives to emerge. If we take these developments seriously, and I think we should, it means that we cannot take for granted either the ability or value of engaging in a rational appraisal of courses of action, of being aware of unconscious meanings, or of nourishing the self. Cognition, affect and the self are functions of discourse; they are not lying under the surface steering, pushing or motivating behaviour.

It would be possible to argue that the creative work that goes on between counsellor and client has *always* required the construction of psychotherapeutic discourse, and that the social constructionists are belabouring a point which makes little odds to the actual process. What does it matter if things are really there making us speak, or exist only in a narrative that frames and reframes experience? It does matter when we augment that main argument – that doing counselling or psychotherapy involves the construction of a certain kind of discourse – with two further interconnected claims: first, that we need to understand how the therapeutic self is fashioned in the context of certain powerful regimes of knowledge; and, secondly, that it may be helpful as part of counselling practice to go about deconstructing psychotherapeutic discourse. It is the link between these two claims that I want to emphasize here, but I will deal with each in turn before exploring the implications of each in relation to the other.

Psychotherapeutic regimes of knowledge

So far I have been slipping between talking about counselling and psychotherapy. This has been fairly deliberate, because although counselling psychology claims to draw upon the distinctive body of knowledge accumulated by the discipline of psychology concerning thinking, development and social behaviour, it is still embedded in wider regimes of knowledge. Some counselling psychologists insist that they operate in their own clearly boundaried professional territory, but there is plenty of theoretical seepage from psychotherapy generally and some unease that counselling may be seen as a lesser, shallower version of psychotherapy. Some psychotherapists have corresponding anxieties, which are evident when they look down on counsellors, that they are only second-rate psychoanalysts. The talk that one hears in counselling circles about the merits of once a week, three times a week or full five times a week personal therapy, and the sense that participants are ratcheting their way up and around a spiral to the 'centre' where they really will find fulfilment, also serves to confirm this poor cousins narrative. This embeddness is worth reflecting on a bit further. We are embedded in what?

The psy-complex

First, in relation to psychology, the therapeutic self can only emerge in a certain discursive climate. If we want to understand who we are and what we want clients to be, we have to look at the 'conditions of possibility' which are structured by psychology as part of a wider set of narratives about the self. I borrow that phrase 'conditions of possibility' from Michel Foucault (e.g., 1980), and the work of Foucauldian scholars has been invaluable in helping us understand our activities as psychologists as part of the 'psy-complex' (Rose, 1985, 1989). The psy-complex is the network of theories and practices concerned with psychological governance and self-reflection in Western culture.

When someone speaks about forms of mental distress to a trained counsellor they have to do so within a set of narratives that will make sense to them, or at least the counsellor must be able to interpret the account and translate it into a set of narratives that help them to locate the distress in already existing categories. The client's speech is filtered and framed by the counsellor's training, supervision and experience, and there is a level of coherence in the talk that the counsellor employs by virtue of the patterns of discourse they have absorbed and negotiated through the course of their professional career.

These patterns of discourse are formalized in theoretical systems, even if the counsellor is eclectic in the use they make of them, and the discourse makes a certain practice – a client sitting, speaking, finding solace and solutions with an other in a defined enclosed social setting – possible. Foucault's concern was with the two sides of power in this kind of psychological work: with the development of psychology as part of the increasing disciplinary surveillance of populations in Western culture from the beginning of the nineteenth century, where the mind becomes the target of professional knowledge (Foucault, 1975a); and with the exacerbation of confessional modes of subjectivity so that each member of the population does that work of surveillance upon themselves, where they believe that the more they speak the happier and healthier they will be (Foucault, 1976a).

Psychology, then, is part of an apparatus of knowledge about the self which not only permits the elaboration of a range of theories about what is going on inside the mind and requires that those who have minds will work with those theories implicitly or explicitly, but also specifies how professionals and clients will be located in relation to one another for the theories to work. These are the 'conditions of possibility' for activities like counselling psychology to make sense to its practitioners. The psy-complex is also imbricated in a range of theories and practices outside classrooms and clinics, and we have to look further into culture to understand the conditions of possibility for counselling discourse generally.

Therapeutic domains

Secondly, then, we need to reflect on the embeddness of the therapeutic self in relation to other therapeutic domains in culture. I want to argue that these therapeutic domains are arenas for discursive regulation and self-expression which bear upon the activities of professional and lay counsellors. These therapeutic domains are constructed and maintained through patterns of discourse so that we are able to make sense to each other as therapeutic subjects, to speak the same language through commonsensical reference to like experiences and responses to events. When we speak through these therapeutic domains we need know nothing about psychology in that we may never have been near a psychology department nor read a psychology textbook, but we know all that we need to know about psychology in that we assume and presume that very web of tacit knowledge that counselling psychologists themselves also need to summon to be able to understand each other.

Because therapeutic discourse contains a variety of different theories of self, it is necessary to describe different characteristics of culturally embedded therapeutic domains in more detail. I am going to focus on three main conceptual frames for the self which are relevant to counselling psychology; psychoanalytic, cognitive and behavioural. Humanist values underpin the way each of these is elaborated in everyday talk and professional practice, and so a separate humanist conceptual frame is not really necessary (see, e.g., Parker, 1995c). Each of these three conceptual frames calls for a distinctive terminology for us to be able to fix upon the relevant sense of self and analyse how it works.

Psychoanalytic discursive complexes. I will start with psychoanalytic notions because my recent work has been on the way psychoanalytic discourse sets out certain subject positions in Western culture (Parker, 1997a). It is also probably worth starting with psychoanalytic senses of self and psychotherapeutic self-work because they still operate as dominant forms of knowledge in this culture, forms which then feed into cognitive and behavioural notions. In this case, I use the term 'discursive complex' to capture the way in which psychoanalytic discourse structures our talk in therapeutic domains. Discursive complexes are patterns of discourse which specify, among other things, how we might understand our distress and find a cure.

Three key discursive complexes seem to be important here, and are elaborated in more detail elsewhere (Parker, 1996b, 1997a). The first is that of *trauma*, in which an event in the past lies inside us and if we can find it we will have found the cause and thereby the solution to our present-day misery. The telling of a story about oneself in informal life-history or in autobiography is now expected to reveal to the reader events that were responsible for a later train of events. The autobiographical novel is a fairly recent narrative form, emerging in the nineteenth century, but one which we can now all follow and so anticipate a certain sequence of childhood events and consequences for the narrator. Even children's films require a quite sophisticated psychoanalytic background knowledge about the effect of the past upon the present. In the *Lion King*, for example, you will remember that Simba the baby prince lion is only able to act against the wicked uncle when he remembers the traumatic moment when the uncle had killed his father, a moment that he had forgotten.

The second discursive complex is *intellectualization*, in which there is an assumption that deeper meanings need to be accessed and touched. Simply speaking about one's experience will not suffice, for there has to be a direct and genuine connection with what is really there. If you look at the proliferation of television talk shows which encourage participants to speak out about their experience – such as *Oprah, Rikki Lake* or *Vanessa* – you quickly discover that a certain kind of *gap* has to be invoked for the talk to work. You watch members of different self-help groups talk about their experiences and you learn that only people who have been through that kind of experience can *really* understand. Think of the way the host succeeds in making them break down and cry. You then become a witness to an account and to an expression of distress that cannot be put into words. As a viewer you realize that there must be a gap between your experience and theirs, and that only those who can access and touch their experience will find relief.

The third discursive complex is that of *transference*, in which we have to assume that patterns of relating to significant others in the past are replayed in relations to others in the present, and that an acknowledgment of this could be helpful. Here, popular images of psychotherapy in the cinema and on television, which are almost always represented as necessarily psychoanalytic, are important in conveying the message that the relationship between client and professional is absolutely crucial.

What is therapeutic about the encounter is the quality of the relationship, and it is vital that the professional boundaries of the relationship be secured to hold in place the transferential affects which well up inside the therapeutic subject. A number of films – with *Final Analysis* as one striking example – have revolved around powerful temptation and disastrous consequences of the relationship being breached. These narratives fascinate their audiences because they know that something peculiarly exciting and dangerous is going to happen, because it is already happening, because it has happened before.

Cognitive discursive templates. Although psychoanalytic discursive complexes of trauma, intellectualization and transference are important, there are other specifications for the self which inhabit therapeutic domains. It would be possible to develop an analysis of the way cognitive models circulate through culture and carry with them certain notions about anxiety and rational self-management. Here, it would be more apposite to refer to the patterns of discourse as clustering around 'discursive templates'.

Among those which may be important would be, first, the discursive template of *interference*, in which there is an assumption that the mind operates as a parallel-processing mechanism in which certain thoughts may stray from their proper place and cause trouble with rational thinking about the self. When students taking computer science and cognitive studies programmes talk about 'debugging' relationships, for example, there is a potent metaphor of viral infection being employed, but it requires us to believe that if it were possible to isolate and screen out inappropriate sequences, then thinking might proceed better.

A second discursive template that seems quite powerful is something we could term *disruption*, in which other kinds of material break into thought and prevent it from operating smoothly. There has been a long-standing role-model for this in the figure of Spock in the original *Star Trek* series, and we now have it available again in Tuvok in *Voyager*. In both cases, these Vulcans are only able to think logically because they are able to shut away emotions, and we are reminded many times over that there is a risk that those emotions may come to the surface and disrupt rational thought, either through the eruption of urges to mate or through reference to the barbaric past of the Vulcans which lives on in the hearts of each of them to the present day.

Behavioural discursive repertoires. If we turn to behavioural notions, we would, perhaps, be better off refering to the relevant clusters of narratives about the self as 'discursive repertoires'. Here, we are concerned with the ways in which distress is configured in discourse in such a way that it is assumed that there is a behavioural problem for which a behavioural solution will be found. Unlike the psychoanalytic and cognitive discursive forms which also draw upon a deep-rooted cultural humanist assumption that we are beings of depth and that some reference to internal affective or reasoning processes must be made to understand distress, these behavioural narratives challenge humanism and so they are not so readily reproduced in their pure state. Often, they must be mixed in with other notions if they are not to appear obstructively anti-therapeutic.

One potent behavioural discursive repertoire would seem to be that of *reinforcement*, in which there is also reference to the gratification that the therapeutic subject gains from being in a self-destructive relationship or situation. Popular representations of a patient's secondary gain from an illness are informed by this kind of narrative, though there is often the implication that they are also engaged in some deliberate manipulation of the situation.

When the patient is thoroughly institutionalized, however, the discursive repertoire of reinforcement is then able to account for the level of collusion that is involved and to explain it without necessarily resorting to attribution of self-deception. Characters suffering from more profound forms of mental disability on film – with examples here ranging from *Rain Man* to *Forrest Gump* – are often rendered into more sympathetic characters – that is, potentially more like us – by reconfiguring the problem as one of behavioural deficit which is remedied by another key character treating them as if they were normal, reinforcing them for doing normal things.

Another discursive repertoire would be that of *social determination*. The notion that someone is locked into a pattern of relationships or into an oppressive and self-oppressive institutional network, and that nothing can be done to help them unless they are removed, is structured by this repertoire. While the social determination of behaviour is a rhetorical device which is sometimes used to explain why nothing can be done to help – because the causes are sedimented too firmly into the history of the individual – it also operates therapeutically when there are calls for people to break from a pattern and thereby release themselves from something that had locked them into a place that they could later recognize they did not at all want to be in.

In this sense, the systemic family therapy tradition is culturally informed by popular behavioural notions of distress and its amelioration if not by explicit theoretical allegiances. The male violence story-line in the BBC Radio 4 soap *The Archers* is one expression of this repertoire. Debbie Archer was able to take action against Simon Pemberton and thus break a vicious circle of silence because of certain sets of precipitating circumstances in which the violence occurred, unlike Shula Hebdon who had also suffered but been unable to break the silence.

These behaviourally informed discursive repertoires not only help us to tell a story about distress that will be understandable to others in this culture, but they also lay out certain subject positions for their objects. People who are trapped in a system of social determination must break from coercive patterns to find a solution, and people who are reinforced must be provided with other kinds of reward and punishment to be made better. The cognitively informed discursive templates of interruption and disruption also call for certain kinds of remedial support, with their therapeutic subjects being taught to focus their thoughts and protect their reason from their emotions. And psychoanalytically informed discursive complexes will also lay out subject positions in which people are encouraged to search for the traumatic cause of the distress, touch it again and do that in a relationship with a professional which may allow it to be replayed.

Therapeutic domains contain complexes, templates and repertoires, then, within which counsellors and clients fabricate varieties of truth and story a core of experience into being. In this view face-to-face counselling or psychotherapy is not a special sealed-off domain which produces its own kind of knowledge about people but is made possible by the ways of speaking about our feelings and our selves that circulate in the wider culture. The kinds of narratives that emerge in counselling will be profoundly shaped by these kinds of complexes, templates and repertoires, and so the construction of psychotherapeutic discourse will always be a construction out of available cultural resources, in the context of powerful regimes of knowledge.

Deconstructing psychotherapeutic knowledge

I will now turn to some of the attempts in recent years to go about *deconstructing* psychotherapeutic discourse. In a way, the account I have been giving so far, which shows how processes that we may take for granted in counselling psychology are constructed in relation to the psy-complex and wider therapeutic domains, is a deconstruction in the loosest sense of the term. If you can show that a psychological phenomenon is a function of discourse rather than having an independent reality that has been discovered by empirical research then you are engaging in a form of de-construction. What has been constructed is revealed to be so. This, at the very least, is what has been accomplished in work by a range of narrative therapists around the world who do claim to be using deconstruction (e.g., White, 1991).

Some of this work has also, at times, referred to itself as being 'narrative', 'discursive' or 'postmodern' therapy, and the variety of different self-descriptive terms is an indication of the *tactical* use of frameworks that might be helpful. The most interesting work has been that which has been accessible enough to be taken up by those working in mental health support services generally – many of whom would be officially designated as counsellors rather than therapists – who want to work with clients in ways that will facilitate challenges to oppression and assist the process of emancipation. It was partly a sensitivity to the intentional and unintentional abuse of power in family therapy, and critical reflection on the unwillingness or inability of practitioners to address this issue that led to an influential current of work which promises something new and genuinely transformative.

Deconstruction

I said that if we can show that something is located in discourse we have thereby effectively deconstructed it, but this is so in the loosest sense of the term 'deconstruction'. I will now describe what deconstruction is in a little more detail, because there are a variety of different discursive or narrative approaches that use the term, and there are important implications in their use of deconstruction for how far they are able to address the fabrication and maintenance of the therapeutic self in the context of the psy-complex and wider therapeutic domains. I will have to proceed negatively here, partly because deconstruction has been oft-caricatured and misunderstood, partly because it developed in relation to other systems of thought, and partly because deconstruction is an exercise in refusal and resistance rather than acceptance and affirmation.

What Derrida meant. The term 'deconstruction' is often associated with the work of Jacques Derrida (e.g., 1973, 1976, 1978), and he has many times insisted on the following points. First, deconstruction is not a method or technique that can be applied arbitrarily to any and every text but it operates as part of a certain conceptual framework asking certain kinds of questions (e.g., Derrida, 1983). Secondly, deconstruction cannot entail the view that there are an infinite number of interpretations of a text because there are constraints on readings by virtue of what he terms 'lines of force' (e.g., Derrida, 1980). Thirdly, deconstruction does not advocate the destruction of subjectivity but instead enables an exploration of the location of the subject (e.g., Derrida, 1981). Fourthly, deconstruction does not entail moral undecidability because it is a moral–political endeavour in which certain key concepts, such as justice, are 'undeconstructible' (e.g., Derrida, 1994). In some ways, deconstruction can be seen as being the latest in series of traditions in Western philosophy concerned with intense examination of meaning and reflection on our presuppositions. This is also why it would be a mistake to see Derrida's work, or that of deconstructive counsellors and psychotherapists for that matter, as breaking with those traditions completely or as being wholly 'postmodern' (cf. Hepburn, 1999).

It rather goes against the spirit of deconstruction to appeal to Derrida's authorial rights to define how the term should and should not be understood, but there are high stakes here, apart from that of accurate scholarship. It means that deconstruction in counselling would start from the particular kinds of questions it would be helpful to pursue, would be attentive to possibilities and constraints on the sense that could be made, would respect and enrich experience as situated, and would be a necessarily ethical endeavour. Let us turn to examples of deconstruction on its home territory.

Deconstruction at home. It is useful to rehearse the development of deconstruction against phenomenology and structuralism, because many of the assumptions that those approaches make about the subject and language are reproduced in contemporary therapeutic discourse and now in counselling psychology.

Derrida took key oppositions in phenomenology, such as that between speech and writing and showed how the privileged term, speech, was dependent on its other, writing; that although speech appeared to be closer, more self-present to thought, it could not operate without pre-existing networks of meaning, without a form of writing (Derrida, 1976). The first phase of a deconstruction, then, is a reversal of the privilege given to the dominant term. But we then need a lever, a lever which will introduce a degree of undecidability into the opposition, which will prevent the opposition from merely reasserting itself, albeit perhaps in reverse. In this case, the sense of term 'writing' is expanded by Derrida to include all webs of difference in signification, and now speech is seen as a form of writing, always in a network of relations, always in relation to others. A corresponding deconstructive operation opens up structuralism such that attempts to restrict uncertainty of signification by appeal to the notion of structure are undermined first by asserting the role of difference in the production of meanings, as the first phase of deconstruction, and then by the notion of *différance* as a lever to prevent structuralism closing down uncertainty again (Derrida, 1978).

The implications of this for counselling practice are two-fold, at least. First, it means that the speech of the client is no longer seen as the expression of an essentially isolated individual but that their story is part of a narrative, part of a process of writing and re-writing which can only be pursued with others. Secondly, it means that the structures that seem to pin the client in place are always mutable, contradictory, and open to movement, to different interpretations and the creation of different meanings. What deconstruction refuses, then, is any temptation to treat the client's self as asocial or as fixed by certain patterns. What it also encourages is the resistance of the client to the power of those who would fix their problem inside them as something for which they then become entirely responsible, or in structures out of their control by which they become entirely powerless.

Deconstruction as refusal and resistance. Deconstruction is concerned with the structuring of power in texts and with the unravelling of the privileged status given to certain terms over others. This is why it has been taken up by feminists who use it to refuse the 'phallogocentric' character of patriarchal discourse (e.g., Weedon, 1987) and by post-colonial literary critics who employ it as part of their resistance to narrative conventions and forms of rationality taken for granted in Western culture (e.g., Said, 1983).

At this point it is worth considering the ways in which deconstruction has been adopted by different writers and the degree to which it has actually functioned as a refusal of power and resistance to authority. Like any other critical system of thought, deconstruction has been recruited into theories and practices which have rubbed off its critical edge. In some variants of deconstructive therapy in North America, there is an emphasis on the 'deconstruction' of problems such that the very use of the term 'problem' is seen as a mistake. The work of Steve de Shazer (1991), for example, has developed through narrative therapy to a 'solution-focused' approach which deconstructs the categories the patient employs. In my view, this approach moves rather too quickly from the hope for a pragmatic pluralist way of talking about issues to the assumption that simply changing the narrative will do the trick right now. It is worth noting that this way of reading deconstruction corresponds quite closely to the development of deconstruction in

North American literary theory, where it is indeed a licence for grandiose methodological imperialism, unlimited interpretation, the complete dispersion of subjectivity and moral relativism (Eagleton, 1983; Norris, 1990). A similar strategy of selective recruitment and pragmatic reinterpretation has also afflicted the reception of Bakhtin's work in North America (Cohen, 1996).

In contrast to this dilute deconstruction, the work of Michael White and David Epston (Epston and White, 1989; White and Epston, 1990) and other colleagues (e.g., Monk *et al.*, 1997) has been concerned with looking at how the 'problem' is constituted in networks of discourse that position the client as helpless and as believing that the problem lies inside them. Here, therapeutic work entails deconstructing categories together *with* the client. This version of deconstruction in the arena of mental health, which has developed in Australia and New Zealand, is closer to European uses of deconstruction in literary theory and to attempts to combine Derrida's work with Foucault's analyses of knowledge, self-knowledge and power (Parker *et al.*, 1995).

Deconstructing psychotherapy

Now we come to the link between our understanding of how the therapeutic self is fashioned in the context of certain powerful regimes of knowledge – something we learn from Foucault – and how far it is possible to go about deconstructing psychotherapeutic discourse in counselling practice – something we learn from Derrida. Just as deconstruction emphasizes the in-between – writing, *différance* – which constitutes those things which usually seem so fixed and self-sufficient, so we now need to emphasize that link.

We can make the link by viewing this kind of critical work as a *deconstruction-in-process* which has three aspects: first, deconstruction could be used *in* counselling as part of the process of exploring problems and reconstructing how they function in the stories people tell; secondly, deconstruction could be used *as* counselling in the reworking of the relationship between therapist and client to address issues of power; and, thirdly, deconstruction could be developed *of* counselling to reflect critically upon the role of this disciplinary confessional enterprise of helping and expertise applied to the distress in people's lives (Parker, 1999c). Deconstruction-in-process is concerned with the way in which we unravel and reconstruct who we are as perpetual reflexive labour rather than with arriving at a point of health or well-being and stopping there.

The development of this current of work raises once again the possibility, oft dreamt about in the feminist and socialist movements, of an approach to *individual* and *social* distress which links the two, a view of relationships which understands the 'personal' as 'political' without reducing one to the other, and an account of discursive complexes, templates and repertoires as sites for subjectivity. These would thus be viewed as sites for subjectivity in the psy-complex and therapeutic domains which function as relatively enduring structures which will *always* limit the degree to which we may want to participate in constructing and deconstructing psychotherapeutic discourse.

10
Critical Reflections

This book is assembled within certain conditions of possibility. It is viable to say certain kinds of things about psychology and theory and critique, and for those things to be accepted or contested. In the most part, the things said in this book have been contested for various reasons by writers inside and outside the terrain of critical and discursive research. All the better, for the debate between different positions is necessary for all of us to sharpen our thinking about the problematic character of psychology, a discipline that thinks that it knows all about thinking but usually does not engage in it very self-critically. The conditions of possibility for statements about psychology also impose certain constraints, and one of the running themes in the book has been that critical discursive research must take seriously the parameters within which we speak. Those parameters limit what will be understood as lawful things to say and what will be ruled out of court. Any analysis of discourse must entail an analysis of the operations of power, power that runs through the texts we study and power that frames how texts are produced.

Discipline

It is indeed possible to speak about psychology from outside the boundaries that mark it off from other disciplines, and some of most important historical work on the development of the 'psy-complex', for example, has been carried out from within sociology (e.g., Rose, 1985, 1989, 1996). Some of the writers I have used as theoretical resources, roughly and inaccurately grouped together under the rubric of 'post-structuralism' in this book, are hardly 'psychologists', though the point has been made that Foucault was trained as a psychologist and that might explain why he had an abiding suspicion of the discipline (Parker, 1995a). And Marx, whose spirit hovers over this book and whose work informs the way I read the 'post-structuralists', was engaging in a different project of interpretation and transformation than that which defines contemporary psychology.

This book is written *in and against* psychology, and so it bears the marks of the disciplinary parameters that structure what can be said and understood in the discipline. The specific engagement with psychoanalysis, psychotherapy and counselling in the third part of the book is with a view to transforming the way we understand those endeavours by discursively situating them. This means that at the very moment that psychoanalysis is taken seriously as a critical theoretical resource to analyse the forms of subjectivity that appear in discourse in Western culture it must also be located as a *story* within that culture. Psychoanalysis claims to speak the truth, and it may indeed help us to speak something of the truth of how we have come to be the way we are in this culture, but its truth is *specific* not universal. The risk is that this disciplinary location for critical work, inside psychology, leads us to unwittingly frame what we say in psychological terms. One of the remits of 'critical psychology' must be to attend to the way psychological assumptions are carried in 'psychological culture'. Critical psychology must include:

> the study of forms of surveillance and self-regulation in everyday life and the ways in which psychological culture operates beyond the boundaries of academic and professional practice.
>
> (Parker, 1999a: 12)

This means that we also need to be aware that psychological culture inhabits the speech of even those who speak against psychology when they have chosen to remain within it (Gordo-López, 2000).

Culture

There is another set of parameters, which is just as easy to overlook when we are framed by it and assume it as our commonsense. These parameters define the local cultural preoccupations that we take for granted as being as fascinating to everyone else as they are to ourselves. Another aspect of critical psychology should serve to alert us to the problems with this. Here, critical psychology includes:

> the study of the ways in which all varieties of psychology are culturally historically constructed, and how alternative varieties of

psychology may confirm or resist ideological assumptions in mainstream models.

(Parker, 1999a: 11)

The debates over 'discourse analysis' and the formation of different 'schools' of discourse analysis in psychology are a case in point, and are as misleading as they are illuminating (e.g., Burr, 1995; Nikander, 1995). The difference between theoretical positions over the role of discourse in the second part of the book can sometimes seem a little parochial, and could serve to limit the options for readers as much as the debates have limited the room for manoeuvre of the writers concerned. Discourse analysis is very different in other disciplines, and the disputes between those who choose conversation analysis and those who prefer Foucault do seem as stupid to outsiders as they seem necessary to those who think they are inside one school or another. Unfortunately, the perceived divisions between local groups of discourse analysts in British psychology have actually tended to obscure the critical and cross-cutting character of key theoretical debates. Within each of the local groups there are those who use Foucault and Garfinkel or Derrida and Sacks, say, in strange and innovative combinations.

The theoretical debates over psychology and politics cut across these particular theoretical allegiances. Furthermore, most of the critical, discursive and theoretical work done now is outside the old 'groups' (e.g., Edley and Wetherell, 1995; Hollway and Jefferson, 2000) and outside Britain (e.g., Davies, 2000; Walkerdine, 2001). Traditional and alternative are constructed within certain cultural parameters, and critical analysis needs to reflect on the locations within which we speak (e.g., Sloan, 2000).

History

There are also some powerful limits set by the time in which we speak. This is particularly evident in the first part of the book, where a concern with 'postmodernism' governs the way we think about where we are in psychology and where we think critical work in the discipline is going. Again, it is worth noting one of the claims of critical psychology to highlight what might be going on here. It is said that critical psychology must include:

the exploration of the way everyday 'ordinary psychology' structures academic and professional work in psychology and how everyday activities might provide the basis for resistance to contemporary disciplinary practices.

(Parker, 1999a: 13)

One of the most striking characteristics of contemporary social constructionism in psychology is that it promises to link its reading of Wittgenstein to a form of relativism that is at one with a certain kind of culture. Here, the 'postmodern' does not merely signify a theoretical option but it marks a form of life which we are invited to embrace because it is already around us (e.g., Gergen, 1991).

The chapters 'against' postmodernism, relativism and Wittgenstein then risk looking like they are refusing to fall in line with a historical shift that has already been accomplished, and of harking back to a time when old enlightened truths about reality served us well. In one sense, of course, postmodern subjectivity *is* a form of resistance, and, like psychoanalysis, it is unbearable to old modern psychology. In this sense it is important to emphasise that to be 'against' a theoretical position must be to work in and against it *dialectically*. In each case, then, the analysis of the limits of postmodernism, relativism and Wittgenstein opens a space for us to work with those frameworks, to re-read them so that we can find ways of being 'for' them.

Institutions

Every text that appears in an academic setting adheres to certain conventions, and there are overarching parameters that bear on every publication to ensure that it is clean and healthy enough to pass through to the reader (Cameron, 1995). We need to bear that assessment process in mind when we read the injunction that critical psychology should include:

> the systematic examination of how some varieties of psychological action and experience are privileged over others, how dominant accounts of 'psychology' operate ideologically and in the service of power.

(Parker, 1999a: 11)

Dominant accounts do not only enjoy their privilege over other subordinate accounts because they are more persuasive, but also because they conform to styles of argument that are acceptable to journal editors or publishers. This book opened with a chapter on 'Theoretical

Discourse, Subjectivity and Power', for example, that was once submitted to a journal (*Science & Society*) and rejected by it. Referee reports for journals sometimes serve to sharpen an argument, and the to and fro between submission and publication can be very helpful, but they sometimes serve to block the appearance of an argument. I report one reviewer's comment so that this process might be made a little more public (though I do not in this case know who the reviewer was), and so that you can make your own assessment. Perhaps you agree that:

> This exercise in post-modern anti-scientism has no place in a Marxian journal. I will pass over the author's posturing as a 'revolutionary' and the bizarre manner in which this claim is 'proven', and go right to the horses, the psychology article he cites on stroking horses. The author makes no attempt to examine or replicate the horse and human heart-beat data ...

That much is true, but you might now take it as an instructive paradox that my anti-relativism is not as hard-line as many discourse analysts in psychology think it to be.

Reflections

The reviewing process for a book like this is also one that can be opened out a little and made useful for the reader as well as the writer. This book has a shape that is a little different from that intended at the outset. It changed its shape in response to reviewer's comments, and these comments (by Alexa Hepburn, who gave her permission to include them here in full) are from just one stage in the process:

> This is a revised proposal for a book of essays on critical psychology written from the particular brand of committed discourse work underpinned by critical realism developed and promoted by Ian Parker and his colleagues over the past ten years or so. The book consists of thirteen chapters, the majority previously published in journals (especially *Theory and Psychology*) or edited collections, and four of which contain responses from other authors with whom Parker has taken issue. These chapters are organised into four Parts, on context, theory, discursive research and psychoanalysis. The book is aimed at a broad range of undergraduate and graduate students.

The proposal is strong in several ways. Ian Parker is a well known figure in the field of critical psychology and the group he and Erica Burman gathered around themselves in Manchester is energetic and quite influential, particularly amongst graduate students using discourse analysis. He is very well travelled and politically committed, which again contributes to his renown, and he is immensely energetic in publishing his own work and that of students. He has also ploughed a particular furrow in the rather confusing world of critical psychology, drawing on discursive psychology, Marxism, feminism and (recently, especially Lacanian) psychoanalysis in ways which resist the simplifications which sometimes arise from each of these positions taken singly. While many Parkerphiles will have read these papers (the sources for them are not that disparate), having them together in one volume is likely to be helpful and give each of the papers a new lease of life.

The book itself has much of interest in it, from Parker's attempt to offer a kind of manifesto for critical psychology, through debates on language and method to a use of psychoanalysis as a reading tool. This means that the book addresses some issues central to the development of critical thinking in psychology, as well as 'critical psychology' itself, in terms of philosophical base, adaptation and employment of qualitative research methodology, and aspiration to offer an account of subjectivity and its relations to social positioning. As such, it is likely to be of considerable interest to students struggling to make sense of this area. How many of these will be undergraduates is a moot point: social psychology teaching at BSc level nowadays is much more open to qualitative methods and critical discursive work than ever before, but this still forms a relatively small part of the psychology curriculum. Given the specificity of the work, it is unlikely that undergraduate students in the cognate areas mentioned in the proposal (sociology, cultural studies, philosophy) will pick this up, and at postgraduate level outside psychology it is most likely to be read by research students interested in methodology or in what is happening in psychology rather than as a key text in their fields of study. So the main readership is likely to be postgraduate psychologists involved in qualitative, discursive and/or critical work, plus some more advanced undergraduates on relatively enlightened courses.

I still have some doubts on the content of the proposed book (which, incidentally, looks like it will be tediously long). Although the title is careful and accurate, explaining that the book is about critical *discursive* research, it seems to me that the book rather encourages a slippage between critical psychology and discursive psychology in which the latter becomes the only or at least main way to do the former – an unreasonable slippage given the range of positions called 'critical' around the world. This is aggravated by a slightly omnipotent tendency to suggest (even if this is shorthand) that the history of Parker's thinking is the history of critical psychology, particularly in Part 1 ('In the first chapter there is a personal story and an account of how a range of ideas that have become so important in critical psychology were accumulated'). I do not think I am expressing a minority view by suggesting that there is much more to critical psychology than the work of Parker and his colleagues at MMU, and that they have no copyright either on the term or on the correct way to set about doing critical work, discursive or otherwise. Parker's liking for polemic and argument is also not really to my taste, and the inclusion of the various 'debates' in this, his own, book is really specious. Basically, the impression is that he allows others to speak for themselves against him in order to show how right he is: 'in line with a dialectical analysis of their arguments, the positions they take are revealed to be untenable *even on their own terms.*' Poor things … This is not really debate, but a rather conventional and uncritical trick, in which the author is the one who actually knows. I would be interested to see if Parker thinks that anything written by his interlocutors changed his own views at all.

That said, I think the collection is generally worthy of publication and the quality of the individual pieces as well as Parker's reputation should enable it to pick up a decent readership amongst graduate students in psychology committed to, or interested in, discursive and qualitative analysis with a critical edge. So long as Parker can guard against presenting his work as the sole truth of the critical approach, it is likely to be a good intervention in this complex field.

I hope this is some safeguard against you reading this book as the sole truth of the critical approach. The book is clearly set in certain limited institutional, historical, cultural and disciplinary debates, in discourses that are also practices, and the question now is whether the debates will help you question where you stand in relation to critical discursive psychology.

References

Abrams, D. (1989) 'How social is social identity theory?', *European Congress of Psychology, Symposium on Intergroup Relations*, July 3, Amsterdam.

Abrams, D. (1990) 'How do group members regulate their behaviour? An integration of social identity and self-awareness theories', in D. Abrams and M. A. Hogg (eds) *Social Identity Theory: Constructive and Critical Advances*. London: Harvester-Wheatsheaf.

Abrams, D. and Hogg, M. A. (1988) 'Comments on the motivational status of self-esteem in social identity and intergroup discrimination', *European Journal of Social Psychology*, 18: 317–334.

Abrams, D. and Hogg, M. A. (1990) 'Social identification, self-categorization, and social influence', in W. Stroebe and M. R. C. Hewstone (eds) *European Review of Social Psychology, Vol. 1*. Chichester: Wiley.

Abrams, D., Wetherell, M., Cochrane, S., Hogg, M. A. and Turner, J. C. (1990) 'Knowing what to think by knowing who you are: self-categorization and the nature of norm formation, conformity and group polarization', *British Journal of Social Psychology*, 29: 97–119.

Adlam, D., Henriques, J., Rose, N., Salfield, A., Venn, C. and Walkerdine, V. (1977) 'Psychology, ideology and the human subject', *Ideology and Consciousness*, 1: 5–56.

Adorno, T. (1967) 'Sociology and psychology I', *New Left Review*, 46: 67–80.

Ahmad, A. (1994) 'Reconciling Derrida: "Spectres of Marx" and deconstructive politics', *New Left Review*, 208: 88–106.

Althusser, L. (1971) *Lenin and Philosophy, and Other Essays*. London: New Left Books.

Anderson, P. (1968) 'Components of the national culture', *New Left Review*, 50: 3–57.

Anderson, P. (1983) *In the Tracks of Historical Materialism*. London: Verso.

Anderson, P. (1984) 'Modernity and revolution', *New Left Review*, 144: 96–113.

Anderson, P. (1990a) 'A culture in contraflow – I', *New Left Review*, 180: 41–78.

Anderson, P. (1990b) 'A culture in contraflow – II', *New Left Review*, 182: 85–137.

Antaki, C. (1994) *Explaining and Arguing: The Social Organization of Accounts*. London: Sage.

Ariès, P. (1962) *Centuries of Childhood*. London: Cape.

Armistead, N. (ed.) (1974) *Reconstructing Social Psychology*. Harmondsworth: Penguin.

Aron, H. (1978) 'Wittgenstein's impact on Foucault', *Wittgenstein and his Impact on Contemporary Thought: Proceedings of the Second International Wittgenstein Symposium*. Vienna: Holder-Pichler-Tempsky.

Ashmore, M. (1989) *The Reflexive Thesis: Wrighting Sociology of Scientific Knowledge*. Chicago: Chicago University Press.

Atkinson, J. M. and Heritage, J. C. (eds) (1984) *Structures of Social Action: Studies in Conversation Analysis*. Cambridge: Cambridge University Press.

Austin, J. L. (1962) *How to Do Things with Words*. Oxford: Clarendon Press.

Banister, P., Burman, E., Parker, I., Taylor, M. and Tindall, C. (1994) *Qualitative Methods in Psychology: A Research Guide*. Buckingham: Open University Press.

Banton, R., Clifford, P., Frosh, S., Lousada, J. and Rosenthall, J. (1985) *The Politics of Mental Health*. London: Macmillan.

Barrett, M. and McIntosh, M. (1982) *The Anti-social Family*. London: Verso.

Barthes, R. (1973) *Mythologies*. London: Paladin.

Barthes, R. (1975) *The Pleasure of the Text*. London: Jonathan Cape.

Barthes, R. (1977) *Image-Music-Text*. London: Colins.

Bates, B. (1983) *The Way of Wyrd*. London: Century.

Baudrillard, J. (1983) 'The ecstasy of communication', in H. Foster (ed.) (1985) *Postmodern Culture*. London: Pluto Press.

Begelman, D. A. (1975) 'Wittgenstein', *Behaviourism*, 4, 201–207.

Bell, D. (1965) *The End of Ideology: On the Exhaustion of Political Ideas in the Fifties*. New York: Free Press.

Bell, D. (1973) *The Coming of Post-Industrial Society*. New York: Doubleday.

Berger, P. L. (1965) 'Towards a sociological understanding of psychoanalysis', *Social Research*, 32, 26–41.

Berger, P. L. and Luckmann, T. (1971) *The Social Construction of Reality: A Treatise in the Sociology of Knowledge*. Harmondsworth: Penguin.

Berman, M. ([1982]1983) *All That Is Solid Melts Into Air: The Experience of Modernity*. London: Verso.

Bhaskar, R. (1978) *A Realist Theory of Science*, 2nd edn. Brighton: Harvester Press.

Bhaskar, R. (1986) *Scientific Realism and Human Emancipation*. London: Verso.

Bhaskar, R. (1989) *Reclaiming Reality: A Critical Introduction to Contemporary Philosophy*. London: Verso.

Bhavnani, K. K. (1990) 'What's power got to do with it? Empowerment and social research', in I. Parker and J. Shotter (eds) *Deconstructing Social Psychology*. London: Routledge.

Billig, M. (1976) *Social Psychology and Intergroup Relations*. London: Academic Press.

Billig, M. (1978) *Fascists: A Social Psychological View of the National Front*. London: Academic Press.

Billig, M. (1979) *Psychology, Racism and Fascism*. Birmingham: Searchlight Publications.

Billig, M. (1985) 'Prejudice, categorization and particularization: from a perceptual to a rhetorical approach', *European Journal of Social Psychology*, 15: 79–103.

Billig, M. (1987) *Arguing and Thinking: A Rhetorical Approach to Social Psychology*. Cambridge: Cambridge University Press.

Billig, M. (1988a) 'Rhetorical and historical aspects of attitudes: the case of the British monarchy', *Philosophical Psychology*, 1: 83–104.

Billig, M. (1988b) 'Social representation, objectification and anchoring: a rhetorical analysis', *Social Behaviour*, 3: 1–16.

Billig, M. (1988c) 'Methodology and scholarship in understanding ideological explanation', in C. Antaki (ed.) *Analysing Everyday Explanation: A Casebook of Methods*. London: Sage.

Billig, M. (1988d) 'Common-places of the British royal family: a rhetorical analysis of plain and argumentative sense', *Text*, 8: 91–110.

Billig, M. (1989a) 'The argumentative nature of holding strong views: a case study', *European Journal of Social Psychology*, 19: 203–223.

Billig, M. (1989b) 'Psychology, rhetoric, and cognition', *History of the Human Sciences*, 2: 289–307.

Billig, M. (1990a) 'Collective memory, ideology and the British royal family', in D. Middleton and D. Edwards (eds) *Collective Remembering*. London: Sage.

Billig, M. (1990b) 'Studying the thinking society: social representations, rhetoric and attitudes', in G. Breakwell and D. Canter (eds) *Empirical Approaches to Social Representations*. Oxford: Oxford University Press.

Billig, M. (1991) *Ideology and Opinions: Studies in Rhetorical Psychology*. London: Sage.

Billig, M., Condor, S., Gane, M., Middleton, D. and Radley, A. (1988) *Ideological Dilemmas: A Social Psychology of Everyday Thinking*. London: Sage.

Bloor, D. (1983) *Wittgenstein: A Social Theory of Knowledge*. New York: Columbia University Press.

Bocock, R. (1976) *Freud and Modern Society*. London: Van Nostrand Reinhold.

Bogen, D. and Lynch, M. (1989) 'Taking account of the hostile native: plausible deniability and the production of conventional history in the Iran-Contra hearing', *Social Problems*, 36: 197–224.

Bond, C. F. and Titus, U. (1983) 'Social facilitation: a meta-analysis of 241 studies', *Psychological Bulletin*, 94: 265–292.

Bookchin, M. (1974) *Post-Scarcity Anarchism*. London: Wildwood House.

Bourdieu, P. and Passeron, J.-C. (1977) *Reproduction in Education, Society and Culture*. London: Sage.

Bowers, J. (1988) 'Essay review of *Discourse and Social Psychology*', *British Journal of Social Psychology*, 27: 185–192.

British Psychological Society (1988) *The Future of the Psychological Sciences: Horizons and Opportunities for British Psychology*. Leicester: British Psychological Society.

Broughton, J. (1988) 'The masculine authority of the cognitive', in B. Inhelder (ed.) *Piaget Today*. Hillsdale, NJ: Lawrence Erlbaum.

Brown, G., and Yule, G. (1983) *Discourse Analysis*. Cambridge: Cambridge University Press.

Bulhan, H. A. (1981) 'Psychological research in Africa', *Race and Class*, 23 (1): 25–81.

Burbach, R. (1994) 'Roots of the postmodern rebellion in Chiapas', *New Left Review*, 205: 113–124.

Burbach, R., Nuñez, O. and Kagarlitsky, B. (1996) *Globalization and its Discontents: The Rise of Postmodernism Socialisms*. London: Pluto Press.

Burman, E. (1990) 'Differing with deconstruction: a feminist critique', in I. Parker and J. Shotter (eds) *Deconstructing Social Psychology*. London: Routledge.

Burman, E. (1994) *Deconstructing Developmental Psychology*. London: Routledge.

Burman, E., Aitken, G., Alldred, P., Allwood, R., Billington, T., Goldberg, B., Gordo-López, A. J., Heenan, C., Marks, D. and Warner, S. (1996) *Psychology Discourse Practice: From Regulation to Resistance*. London: Taylor and Francis.

Burman, E., Alldred, P., Bewley, C., Goldberg, B., Heenan, C., Marks, D., Marshall, J., Taylor, K., Ullah, R. and Warner, S. (1995) *Challenging Women: Psychology's Exclusions, Feminist Possibilities*. Buckingham: Open University Press.

Burman, E. and Parker, I. (eds) (1993) *Discourse Analytic Research: Repertoires and Readings of Texts in Action*, London: Routledge.

Burnham, J. ([1941]1962) *The Managerial Revolution*. Harmondsworth: Penguin.

Burr, V. (1995) *An Introduction to Social Constructionism*. London: Routledge.

Butler, J. (1990) *Gender Trouble: Feminism and the Subversion of Identity*. London: Routledge.

Callinicos, A. (1989) *Against Postmodernism: A Marxist Critique*. Cambridge: Polity Press.

Callinicos, A. (1995) *Theories and Narratives: Reflections on the Philosophy of History*. Cambridge: Polity Press.

Cameron. D. (1995) *Verbal Hygiene*. London: Routledge.

Cohen, T. (1996) 'The ideology of dialogue: the Bakhtin/De Man (dis)connection', *Cultural Critique*, 33: 41–86.

Collier, A. (1981) 'Scientific realism and the human world: the case of psycho-analysis', *Radical Philosophy*, 29: 8–18.

Collier, A. (1994) *Critical Realism: An Introduction to Roy Bhaskar's Philosophy*. London: Verso.

Collier, A. (1998) 'Language, practice and realism', in I. Parker (ed.) *Social Constructionism, Discourse and Realism*. London: Sage.

Condor, S. (1987) 'From sex categories to gender boundaries: reconsidering sex as a "stimulus variable" in social psychological research', *BPS Social Psychology Section Newsletter*, 17: 48–71.

Condor, S. (1988) '"Race stereotypes" and racist discourse', *Text*, 8: 69–90.

Condor, S. (1997) 'And so say all of us?: Some thoughts on "experiential demo-cratization" as an aim for critical social psychologists', in T. Ibáñez and L. Íñiguez (eds) *Critical Social Psychology*. London: Sage.

Conway, G. D. (1989) *Wittgenstein on Foundations*. Atlantic Highlands, NJ: Humanities Press International.

Costall, A. and Still, A. (1987) *Cognitive Psychology in Question*. Hassocks, Sussex: Harvester Press.

Coulter, J. (1979) *The Social Construction of Mind*. Ottowa, NJ: Rowman and Littlefield.

Coulter, J. (1985) 'Two concepts of the mental', in K. Gergen, and K. Davis (eds) *The Social Construction of the Person*. New York: Springer.

Coulthard, M. (1977) *An Introduction to Discourse Analysis*. London: Longman.

Coulthard, M. and Montgomery, M. (eds) (1981) *Studies in Discourse Analysis*. London: Routledge and Kegan Paul.

Crawford, M. (1995) *Talking Difference: On Gender and language*. London: Sage.

Crosby, F. and Crosby, T. L. (1981) 'Psychobiography and psychohistory', in S. L. Long (ed.) *The Handbook of Political Behaviour*. New York: Plenum.

Curt, B. (1994) *Textuality and Tectonics: Troubling Social and Psychological Science*. Buckingham: Open University Press.

Dalal, F. (1988) 'The racism of Jung', *Race and Class*, 29 (1): 1–22.

Danziger, K. (1990) *Constructing the Subject: Historical Origins of Psychological Research*. Cambridge: Cambridge University Press.

Davies, B. (1998) 'Psychology's subject: a commentary on the relativism/realism debate', in I. Parker (ed.) *Social Constructionism, Discourse and Realism*. London: Sage.

Davies, B. (2000) *A Body of Writing 1990–1999*. Walnut Creek, CA: Altamira Press.

Davies, B. and Harré, R. (1990) 'Positioning: the discursive production of selves', *Journal for the Theory of Social Behaviour*, 19 (4): 43–63.

Deaux, K. and Wrightsman, L. S. (1984) *Social Psychology in the 80s*, 4th edn. Monterey, CA: Brooks/Cole.

Debord, G. (1977) *Society of the Spectacle*. Detroit: Black and Red.

Derrida, J. (1973) *Speech and Phenomena, and Other Essays on Husserl's Theory of Signs*. Evanston, ILL: Northwestern University Press.

Derrida, J. (1976) *Of Grammatology*. Baltimore: Johns Hopkins University Press.

Derrida, J. (1978) *Writing and Difference*. London: Routledge and Kegan Paul.

Derrida, J. (1980) 'An interview', *The Literary Review*, 14: 21–22.

Derrida, J. (1981) *Positions*. London: Athlone Press.

Derrida, J. (1983) 'Letter to a Japanese friend', in D. Wood and R. Bernasconi (eds) *Derrida and Différance*. Evanston, ILL: Northwestern University Press.

Derrida, J. (1994) 'Spectres of Marx', *New Left Review*, 205: 31–58.

Descombes, V. (1980) *Modern French Philosophy*. Cambridge: Cambridge University Press.

De Shazer, S. (1991) *Putting Difference to Work*. New York: W. W. Norton and Company.

Dews, P. (1987) *Logics of Disintegration: Post-structuralist Thought and the Claims of Critical Theory*. London: Verso.

Dominguez, R. (1998) 'The Zapatista electronic movement: clogging up the pipelines of power', *Crash Media*, 1: 5.

Drew, P. (1989) 'Recalling someone from the past', in D. Roger and P. Bull (eds) *Conversation*. Clevedon: Multilingual Matters.

During, S. (1987) 'Postmodernism or post-colonialism today', *Textual Practice*, 1 (1): 32–47.

Eagleton, T. (1981) *Walter Benjamin, or, Towards a Revolutionary Criticism*. London: Verso.

Eagleton, T. (1983) *Literary Theory: An Introduction*, Oxford: Blackwell.

Eagleton, T. (1986) 'Wittgenstein's friends', in *Against the Grain: Selected Essays*. London: Verso.

Eagleton, T. (1991) *Ideology: An Introduction*. London: Verso.

Eagleton, T. (1993) 'Introduction to Wittgenstein', in British Film Institute (ed.) *Wittgenstein: The Terry Eagleton Script, the Derek Jarman Film*. London: British Film Institute.

Easthope, A. (1990) '"I gotta use words to talk to you": deconstructing the theory of communication', in I. Parker and J. Shotter (eds) *Deconstructing Social Psychology*. London: Routledge.

Easthope, A. (1999) *Englishness and National Culture*. London: Routledge.

Easton, S. M. (1983) *Humanist Marxism and Wittgensteinian Social Philosophy*. Manchester: Manchester University Press.

Edley, N. and Wetherell, M. (1995) *Men in Perspective: Practice, Power and Identity*. London: Prentice-Hall.

Edwards, D. (1985) *Language Society and Identity*. Oxford: Blackwell.

Edwards, D. (1995) 'A commentary on discursive and critical psychology', *Culture and Psychology*, 1: 55–63.

Edwards, D. (1997) *Discourse and Cognition*. London: Sage.

Edwards, D., Ashmore, M. and Potter, J. (1995) 'Death and furniture: the rhetoric, politics, and theology of bottom-line arguments against relativism', *History of the Human Sciences* 8 (2): 25–9.

Edwards, D. and Middleton, D. (1986) 'Joint remembering: constructing an account of shared experience through conversational discourse', *Discourse Processes*, 9: 423–459.

Edwards, D. and Middleton, D. (1988) 'Conversational remembering and family relationships: how children learn to remember', *Journal of Social and Personal Relationships*, 5: 3–25.

Edwards, D. and Potter, J. (1992a) 'The Chancellor's memory: language and truth in discursive remembering', *Applied Cognitive Psychology*.

Edwards, D. and Potter, J. (1992b) *Discursive Psychology*. London: Sage.

Edwards, D. and Potter, J. (1993) 'Language and causation: a discursive action model of description and attribution', *Psychological Review*, 100 (1): 23–41.

Edwards, J. (1985) *Language, Society and Identity*. Oxford: Blackwell.

Elliott, A. (1992) *Social Theory and Psychoanalysis in Transition: Self and Society from Freud to Kristeva*. Cambridge: Polity Press.

Epston, D. and White, M. (1989) *Literate Means to Therapeutic Ends*. Adelaide: Dulwich Centre Publications.

Essed, P. (1988) 'Understanding verbal accounts of racism: politics and heuristics of reality construction', *Text*, 8: 5–40.

Esteva, G. and Prakesh, M. S. (1997) *Grassroots Postmodernism*. London: Zed.

Evans, E. P. ([1906] 1987) *The Criminal Prosecution and Capital Punishment of Animals: The Lost History of Europe's Animal Trials*. London: Faber and Faber.

Farr, R. M. and Moscovici, S. (eds) (1984) *Social Representations*. Cambridge: Cambridge University Press.

Ferrara, K. W. (1994) *Therapeutic Ways with Words*. Oxford: Oxford University Press.

Fodor, J. (1975) *The Language of Thought*. New York: Crowell.

Fodor, J. (1983) *The Modularity of Mind*. Cambridge, MA: MIT Press.

Forbes, P. (1995))A new empire of absurdity', *The Guardian OnLine*, 27 April: 13.

Foucault, M. ([1961] 1971) *Madness and Civilization: A History of Insanity in the Age of Reason*. London: Tavistock.

Foucault, M. (1966) *The Order of Things*. London: Tavistock.

Foucault, M. ([1969] 1972) *The Archaeology of Knowledge*. London: Tavistock.

Foucault, M. (1971) 'Orders of discourse', *Social Science Information*, 10: 7–30.

Foucault, M. (1973) *Birth of the Clinic*. London: Tavistock.

Foucault, M. ([1975a] 1976) *Discipline and Punish: The Birth of the Prison*. London: Allen Lane.

Foucault, M. ([1975b] 1977) *I Pierre Rivière, Having Slaughtered my Mother, my Sister, and my Brother ...* New York: Random House.

Foucault, M. ([1976a] 1981) *The History of Sexuality, Vol. I: An Introduction*, Harmondsworth: Penguin.

Foucault, M. (1976b) 'The politics of crime', *Partisan Review*, 43, 453–459.

Foucault, M. (1977) *Language, Counter-Memory, Practice: Selected Essays and Interviews*. Oxford: Blackwell.

Foucault, M. (1980) *Power/Knowledge: Selected Interviews and Other Writings 1972–1977*. Brighton: Harvester Press.

Foucault, M. (1982) 'The subject and power', *Critical Inquiry*, 8: 777–795.

Foucault, M. ([1984] 1986) *The Care of the Self: The History of Sexuality, Vol. III*. Harmondsworth: Penguin.

Fowers, B. J. and Richardson, F. C. (1996) 'Individualism, family ideology and family therapy', *Theory and Psychology*, 6 (1): 121–151.

Fox, D. and Prilleltensky, I. (eds) (1997) *Critical Psychology: An Introduction*. London and New York: Sage.

Frazer, E. (1988) 'Teenage girls talking about class', *Sociology*, 22: 343–358.

Freud, S. (1905) 'Three essays on the theory of sexuality', in A. Richards (ed.) (1977) *On Sexuality*, Pelican Freud Library Vol. 7. Harmondsworth: Pelican.

Freud, S. (1914) 'Remembering, repeating and working-through', in S. Freud (1953–1973) *The Standard Edition of the Complete Psychological Works of Sigmund Freud (24 vols)*, Vol. XII. London: Hogarth Press.

Freud, S. (1923) 'The Ego and the Id', in A. Richards (ed.) (1984) *On Metapsychology: The Theory of Psychoanalysis*, Pelican Freud Library, Vol. II. Harmonsworth: Pelican.

Frosh, S. (1991) *Identity Crisis: Modernity, Psychoanalysis and the Self.* London: Macmillan.

Fukuyama, F. (1992) *The End of History and the Last Man.* Harmondsworth: Penguin.

Furnham, A. (1997) 'Defending science against postmodernism and irrationalism', paper delivered at the European Congress of Psychology, Dublin, Ireland.

Garfinkel, H. (1967) *Studies in Ethnomethodology.* New York: Prentice-Hall.

Gauld, A. O. and Shotter, J. (1977) *Human Action and its Psychological Investigation.* London: Routledge and Kegan Paul.

Gay, P. (1988) *Freud: A Life for Our Time.* New York: Norton.

Geras, N. (1995) 'Language, truth and justice', *New Left Review*, 209: 110–135.

Gergen, K. J. (1985) 'The social constructionist movement in modern psychology', *American Psychologist*, 40, 266–275.

Gergen, K. J. (1988) 'If persons are texts', in S. B. Messer, L. A. Sass, and R. L. Woolfolk (eds), *Hermeneutics and Psychological Theory: Interpretive Perspectives on Personality, Psychotherapy, and Psychopathology.* New Brunswick, NJ: Rutgers University Press.

Gergen, K. J. (1989a) 'Social psychology and the wrong revolution', *European Journal of Social Psychology*, 19: 463–484.

Gergen, K. J. (1989b) 'Induction and construction: teetering between worlds', *European Journal of Social Psychology*, 19: 431–438.

Gergen, K. J. (1991) *The Saturated Self.* New York: Basic Books.

Gergen, K. J. (1992) 'Toward a postmodern psychology', in S. Kvale (ed.) *Psychology and Postmodernism.* London: Sage.

Gergen, K. J. (1994a) 'Exploring the postmodern: perils or potentials?', *American Psychologist*, 49 (5): 412–416.

Gergen, K. J. (1994b) *Realities and Relationships: Soundings in Social Construction.* Cambridge, MA: Harvard University Press.

Gergen, K. J. (1997) 'On the poly/tics of postmodern psychology', *Theory and Psychology*, 7 (1): 31–36.

Gergen, K. J. (1998) 'Constructionism and realism: how are we to go on?', in I. Parker (ed.) *Social Constructionism, Discourse and Realism.* London: Sage.

Gilbert, N. and Mulkay, M. (1984) *Opening Pandora's Box: A Sociological Analysis of Scientists' Discourse.* Cambridge: Cambridge University Press.

Giles, H. and Robinson, P. (1990) *Handbook of Language and Social Psychology.* Chichester: Wiley.

Gill, R. (1990) 'Ideology and popular radio: a discourse analytic examination of disc jockey's talk', unpublished PhD thesis, Loughborough University of Technology.

Gill, R. (1995) 'Relativism, reflexivity and politics: interrogating discourse analysis from a feminist perspective', in S. Wilkinson and C. Kitzinger (eds) *Feminism and Discourse*. London: Sage.

Gilligan, C. (1982) *In a Different Voice: Psychological Theory and Women's Development*. Cambridge, MA: MIT Press.

Gilroy, P. (1987) *There Ain't No Black in the Union Jack*. London: Hutchinson.

Glaser, B. G. and Strauss, A. L. (1967) *The Discovery of Grounded Theory: Strategies for Qualitative Research*. New York: Aldine.

Goodley, D. and Parker, I. (2000) 'Critical psychology and action research', *Annual Review of Critical Psychology*, 2: 3–18.

Gordo-López, A. (2000) 'On the psychologization of critical psychology', *Annual Review of Critical Psychology*, 2: 55–71.

Gordo-López, A. and Parker, I. (eds) (1999) *Cyberpsychology*. London: Macmillan.

Gott, R. (1996) 'No future for rebels trapped in past', *The Guardian*, 21 December: 11.

Gouldner, A. (1971) *The Coming Crisis of Western Sociology*. London: Heinemann.

Greenwood, J. D. (1989) *Explanation and Experiment in Social Psychological Science: Realism and the Social Constitution of Action*. New York: Springer.

Greenwood, J. (1991) *Relations and Representations: An Introduction to the Philosophy of Social Psychological Science*. London: Routledge.

Greenwood, J. D. (1994) *Realism, Identity and Emotion: Reclaiming Social Psychology*. London: Sage.

Greer, S. (1997) 'Nietzsche and social construction', *Theory and Psychology*, 7 (1): 83–100.

Gross, P. R. and Levitt, N. (1994) *Higher Superstition*. Baltimore: Johns Hopkins, University Press.

Gross, P. R., Levitt, N. and Lewis, M. W. (eds) (1996) *The Flight from Science and Reason*. New York: New York Academy of Science.

Gustafson, D. F. (1984) 'Wittgenstein and a causal view of intentional action', *Philosophical Investigations*, 7 (3): 225–243.

Halliday, M. A. K. (1978) *Language as Social Semiotic*. London: Edward Arnold.

Hama, H., Yoga, M. and Matsuyama, Y. (1996) 'Effects of stroking horses on both human's and horses' heart rate responses', *Japanese Psychological Research*, 38: 47–64.

Harper, D. (1994) 'The professional construction of "paranoia" and the discursive uses of diagnostic criteria', *British Journal of Medical Psychology*, 67: 131–143.

Harré, R. (1979) *Social Being: A Theory for Social Psychology*. Oxford: Blackwell.

Harré, R. (1983) *Personal Being: A Theory for Individual Psychology*. Oxford: Blackwell.

Harré, R. (1986a) *Varieties of Realism: A Rationale for the Natural Sciences*. Oxford: Blackwell.

Harré, R. (ed.) (1986b) *The Social Construction of Emotion*. Oxford: Blackwell.

Harré, R. (1989a) 'Language games and texts of identity', in J. Shotter and K. J. Gergen (eds) *Texts of Identity*. London: Sage.

Harré, R. (1989b) 'Metaphysics and methodology: some prescriptions for social psychological research', *European Journal of Social Psychology*, 19: 439–454.

Harré, R. and Gillett, G. (1994) *The Discursive Mind*. London: Sage.

Harré, R. and Secord, P. F. (1972) *The Explanation of Social Behaviour*. Oxford: Blackwell.

Harvey, D. (1989) *The Condition of Postmodernity: An Enquiry into the Origins of Cultural Change*. Oxford: Blackwell.

Harvey, K. (1995) 'Zapatistas: the "first postmodernist guerilla group"?', *Trotskyist International*, 18: 11–15.

Hassan, I. (1987) *The Postmodern Turn*. Columbus, OH: Ohio State University Press.

Hawkes, T. (1977) *Structuralism and Semiotics*. London: Methuen.

Hearse, P. (1994) 'You can hear the jackboots marching: "deep' postmodernism shows its nasty side [review of S. G. Meštrovič, *The Balkanisation of the West*]', *Socialist Outlook*, 67: 14.

Heaton, J. and Groves, J. (1994) *Wittgenstein for Beginners*. London: Icon.

Henriques, J., Hollway, W., Urwin, C. Venn, C., and Walkerdine, V. (1984) *Changing the Subject: Psychology, Social Regulation and Subjectivity*. London: Methuen.

Henwood, K. L. (1994) 'Resisting racism and sexism in academic psychology: A personal political view', *Feminism and Psychology*, 4 (1): 41–62.

Henwood, K. L. and Pidgeon, N. F. (1992) 'Qualitative research and psychological theorizing', *British Journal of Psychology*, 83: 97–111.

Hepburn, A. (1999) 'Derrida and psychology: deconstruction and its ab/uses in critical and discursive psychologies', *Theory and Psychology*, 9: 641–647.

Hepburn, A. (2000) 'On the alleged incompatibility between relativism and feminist psychology', *Feminism and Psychology*, 10 (1): 91–106.

Heritage, J. (1978) 'Aspects of the flexibilities of natural language use', *Sociology*, 12: 79–105.

Heritage, J. (1984) *Garfinkel and Ethnomethodology*. Cambridge: Polity Press.

Heritage, J. (1988) 'Interactional accountability: a conversation analytic perspective', in C. Antaki (ed.) *Analysing Everyday Explanation: A Case Book of Methods*. London: Sage.

Hobson, R. (1986) *Forms of Feeling: The Heart of Psychotherapy*. London: Tavistock.

Hogg, M. A. and McGarty, C. (1990) 'Self-categorization and social identity', in D. Abrams and M. A. Hogg (eds) *Social Identity Theory: Constructive and Critical Advances*. London: Harvester-Wheatsheaf.

Hogg, M. A. and Turner, J. C. (1987) 'Social identity and conformity: a theory of referent informational influence', in W. Doise and S. Moscovici (eds) *Current Issues in European Social Psychology*, Vol. 2. Cambridge: Cambridge University Press.

Hollway, W. (1989) *Subjectivity and Method in Psychology: Gender, Meaning and Science*. London: Sage.

Hollway, W. and Jefferson, T. (2000) *Doing Qualitative Research Differently: Free Association, Narrative and the Interview Method*. London: Sage.

Holzman, L. (1995) '"Wrong", said Fred: a response to Parker', *Changes: An International Journal of Psychology and Psychotherapy*, 13 (1): 23–26.

Holzman, L. (1997) *Schools for Growth: Radical Alternatives to Current Educational Models*. Mahwah, NJ: Erlbaum.

Holzman, L. (ed.) (1999) *Performing Psychology: A Postmodern Culture of the Mind*. New York: Routledge.

Howitt, D. and Owusu-Bempah, J. (1994) *The Racism of Psychology: Time for Change*. New York: Harvester Wheatsheaf.

Hugill, B. (1995) 'Truce declared in bitter war of couch gurus', *The Observer*, 10 September: 11.

Hyland, M. (1981) *Introduction to Theoretical Psychology*. London: Macmillan.

Ibáñez, T. (1990) 'Henri, Serge ... and the next generation', *BPS Social Psychology Section Newsletter*, 24: 5–14.

Ibáñez, T. and Íñiguez, L. (eds) (1997) *Critical Social Psychology*. London: Sage.

Ingleby, D. (1985) 'Professionals as socializers: the "psy-complex"', *Research in Law, Deviance and Social Control*, 7: 79–109.

Iser, W. (1974) *The Act of Reading*. London: Methuen.

Jameson, F. (1984a) 'Postmodernism, or the cultural logic of late capitalism', *New Left Review*, 146: 53–92.

Jameson, F. (1984b) 'Foreword', in J.-F. Lyotard, *The Postmodern Condition: A Report on Knowledge*. Manchester: Manchester University Press.

Jameson, F. (1991) *Postmodernism, or the Cultural Logic of Late Capitalism*. London: Verso.

Jarman, D. (Dir.) (1993) *Wittgenstein*. London: British Film Institute.

Jost, J. T. (1995) 'Toward a Wittgensteinian social psychology of human development', *Theory and Psychology*, 5 (1): 5–25.

Jost, J. T. and Hardin, C. (1994) 'A Marxian critique of Gergen's postmodernism', unpublished manuscript, Yale University.

Kagan, C. and Lewis, S. (1990) 'Transforming psychological practice', *Australian Psychologist*, 25 (3): 270–280.

Kendall, G. and Michael, M. (1997) 'Politicizing the politics of postmodern social psychology', *Theory and Psychology*, 7 (1): 7–29.

Kinder, D. R. and Sears, D. O. (1981) 'Symbolic racism vs threats to the good life', *Journal of Personality and Social Psychology*, 40: 414–430.

Kitching, K. (1988) *Karl Marx and the Philosophy of Praxis*. London: Routledge.

Klein, J. (1994) 'A postmodern president', *Newsweek*, 17 January: 21–23.

Kruglanski, A . W. (1992) 'Social constructionism and experimental social psychology: Why don't the cousins kiss?' Paper presented at the Annual Meeting of the Society for Experimental Social Psychology, October, San Antonio, TX.

Kvale, S. (ed.) (1992a) *Psychology and Postmodernism*. London: Sage.

Kvale, S. (1992b) 'Postmodern psychology: a contradiction in terms?', in S. Kvale (ed.) *Psychology and Postmodernism*. London: Sage.

Kvale, S. (1992c) 'Introduction: from the archaeology of the psyche to the architecture of cultural landscapes', in S. Kvale (ed.) *Psychology and Postmodernism*. London: Sage.

Latour, B. ([1991] 1993) *We Have Never Been Modern*. New York: Harvester Wheatsheaf.

Levett, A., Kottler, A., Burman, E. and Parker, I. (eds) (1997) *Power and Discourse: Culture and Change in South Africa*. London: Zed Books.

Litton, I. and Potter, J. (1985) 'Social representations in the ordinary explanation of a "riot"', *European Journal of Social Psychology*, 15: 371–388.

Lovibond, S. (1989) 'Feminism and postmodernism', *New Left Review*, 178: 5–28.

Lynch, M. and Woolgar, S. (eds) (1988) 'Representational practices in science', special issue of *Human Studies*, 11: 99–359.

Lyotard, J.-F. ([1979] 1984) *The Postmodern Condition: A Report on Knowledge*. Manchester: Manchester University Press.

Lyotard, J.-F. (1984) 'Answering the question: what is postmodernism?', in. J.-F. Lyotard *The Postmodern Condition: A Report on Knowledge*. Manchester: Manchester University Press.

MacDonnell, D. (1986) *Theories of Discourse: An Introduction*. Oxford: Blackwell.

Mair, M. (1989) *Between Psychology and Psychotherapy: A Poetics of Experience*. London: Routledge.

Malcolm, N. (1982) 'Wittgenstein and idealism}, in G. Vesey (ed.) *Idealism Past and Present*. Cambridge: Cambridge University Press.

Mama, A. (1995) *Beyond the Masks: Race, Gender and the Subject*. London: Routledge.

Mandel, E. (1971) *The Formation of the Economic Thought of Karl Marx*. London: New Left Books.

Mandel, E. (1974) *Late Capitalism*. London: New Left Books.

Mandel, E. (1978) *From Stalinism to Eurocommunism*. London: Verso.

Mandel, E. (1979) *Revolutionary Marxism Today*. London: New Left Books.

Mandel, E. (1986) *The Place of Marxism in History*. Amsterdam: Notebooks for Study and Research.

Manicas, P. T. and Secord, P. F. (1983) 'Implications for psychology of the new philosophy of science', *American Psychologist*, 38: 399–413.

Mao Tse Tung (1967) *On Contradiction*. Peking: Foreign Languages Press.

Marcos (1995a) 'Mexico: penthouse, ground floor and basement', *International Viewpoint*, 263: 7–9.

Marcos (1995b) 'Subcomandante Marcos' three interpretations of the election results', *International Viewpoint*, 263: 8.

Marglin, F. A. and Marglin, S. A. (eds) (1990) *Diminishing Knowledge: Development, Culture and Resistance*. Oxford: Oxford University Press.

Marin, L. (1983) 'Discourse of power: power of discourse: Pascalian notes', in A. Montefiore (ed.) *Philosophy in France Today*. Cambridge: Cambridge University Press.

Marks, D., Burman, E., Burman, L. and Parker, I. (1995) 'Collaborative research into education case conferences', *Educational Psychology in Practice*, 11 (1): 41–49.

Marshall, H. and Wetherell, M. (1989) 'Talking about career and gender identities: a discourse analysis perspective', in S. Skevington and D. Baker (eds) *The Social Identity of Women*. London: Sage.

Marx, K. ([1845] 1975) 'Concerning Feuerbach', in *Karl Marx: Early Writings*. Harmondsworth: Penguin.

Marx, K., and Engels, F. ([1846] 1970) *The German Ideology*. New York: International Publishers.

Marx, K. and Engels, F. ([1848] 1965) *Manifesto of the Communist Party*. Peking: Foreign Languages Press.

McKenzie, W. and Monk, G. (1997) 'Learning and teaching narrative ideas', in G. Monk, J. Winslade, K. Crocket and D. Epston (eds) *Narrative Therapy in Practice: The Archaeology of Hope*. San Francisco: Jossey-Bass Publishers.

McKinlay, A. and Potter, J. (1987) 'Model discourse: interpretative repertoires in scientist's conference talk', *Social Studies of Science*, 17: 443–463.

McKinlay, A., Potter, J. and Wetherell, M. (1990) 'Discourse analysis and social representations', in G. Breakwell and D. Cantor (eds) *Empirical Approaches to Social Representations*. Oxford: Oxford University Press.

McNamee, S. and Gergen, K. J. (1992a) 'Introduction', in S. McNamee and K. J. Gergen (eds) *Therapy as Social Construction*. London: Sage.

McNamee, S. and Gergen, K. J. (eds) (1992b) *Therapy as Social Construction*. London: Sage.

Mead, G. H. (1934) *Mind, Self and Society*. Chicago: Chicago University Press.

Messer, D. (1996) 'The rising tide of psychology: annual conference report', *The Psychologist*, 9 (6): 252.

Meštrovič, S. G. (1994) *The Balkanisation of the West*. London: Routledge.

Michael, M. (1994) 'Discourse and uncertainty: postmodern variations', *Theory and Psychology*, 4 (3): 383–404.

Michael, M. and Kendall, G. (1997) 'Critical thought, institutional contexts, normative projects: a reply to Gergen', *Theory and Psychology*, 7 (1): 37–41.

Middleton, D. and Edwards, D. (eds) (1990) *Collective Remembering*. London: Sage.

Miles, R. (1989) *Racism*. London: Routledge.

Miller, M. (1998) *Freud and the Bolsheviks: Psychoanalysis in Imperial Russia and the Soviet Union*. New Haven, CT: Yale University Press.

Millet, K. (1977) *Sexual Politics*. London: Virago.

Milner, M. (1950/1971) *On Not Being Able to Paint*. London: Heinemann.

Mitter, S. (1994) 'What women demand of technology', *New Left Review*, 205: 100–110.

Monk, G., Winslade, J., Crocket, K. and Epston, D. (eds) (1997) *Narrative Therapy in Practice: The Archaeology of Hope*. San Francisco: Jossey-Bass Publishers.

Monk, R. (1990) *Ludwig Wittgenstein: The Duty of Genius*. London: Cape.

Montag, W. (1988) 'What is at stake in the debate on postmodernism?', in E. A. Kaplan (ed.) *Postmodernism and its Discontents: Theories, Practices*. London: Verso.

Montefiore, A. (ed.) (1983) *Philosophy in France Today*. Cambridge: Cambridge University Press.

Moran, J. (1972) 'Wittgenstein and Russia', *New Left Review*, 73: 85–96.

Morgan, M. (1996) 'Qualitative research: a package deal?', *The Psychologist*, 9 (1): 31–32.

Morrow, R. A. with Brown, D. D. (1994) *Critical Theory and Methodology*. London: Sage.

Moscovici, S. (1976) *La Psychanalyse: Son image et son public* (2nd edn). Paris: Presses Universitaires de France.

Mudge, L. S. (1987) 'Thinking in the community of faith: towards an ecclesial hermeneutic', in L. S. Mudge and J. N. Poling (eds) *Formation and Reflection: The Promise of Practical Theology*. Philadelphia, PA: Fortress Press.

Mulkay, M. (1985) *The Word and the World: Explorations in the Form of Sociological Analysis*. London: Allen & Unwin.

Mulkay, M., Potter, J. and Yearley, S. (1983) 'Why an analysis of scientific discourse is needed', in K. Knorr-Cetina and M. Mulkay (eds) *Science Observed: Perspectives on the Social Study of Science*. London: Sage.

Myers, G. (1990) 'Writing Biology: texts in the construction of scientific knowledge', Madison, WI: University of Wisconsin Press.

Newman, F. and Gergen, K. J. (1995) 'Diagnosis: the human cost of the rage to order', paper delivered at the 103rd Annual Convention of the American Psychological Association, New York, August.

Newman, F. and Holzman, L. (1993) *Lev Vygotsky: Revolutionary Scientist*. London: Routledge.

Newman, F. and Holzman, L. (1996) *Unscientific Psychology: A Cultural-Performatory Approach to Understanding Human Life*. Westport, CT: Praeger.

Newman, F. and Holzman, L. (1997) *The End of Knowing (and a New Developmental Way of Learning)*. London: Routledge.

Ng, S. H. (1980) *The Social Psychology of Power*. London: Academic Press.

Nietzsche, F. (1977) *A Nietzsche Reader*. Harmondsworth: Penguin.

Nightingale, D. J. (1999) '(Re)theorising constructionism', in W. Maiers, B. Bayer, B. Duarte Esgalhado, R. Jorna and E. Schraube (eds) *Challenges to Theoretical Psychology*. Toronto: Captus University Publications.

Nightingale, D. J. and Cromby, J. (eds) (1999) *Social Constructionist Psychology: A Critical Analysis of Theory and Practice*. Buckingham: Open University Press.

Nikander, P. (1995) 'The turn to the text: the critical potential of discursive social psychology', *Nordiske Udkast*, 2: 3–15.

Nissen, M., Axel, E. and Bechmann Jensen, T. (1999) 'The abstract zone of proximal conditions', *Theory and Psychology*, 9 (3): 417–426.

Norris, C. (1990) *What's Wrong With Postmodernism: Critical Theory and the Ends of Philosophy*. Hemel Hempstead: Harvester Wheatsheaf.

Norris, C. (1996) *Reclaiming Truth: Contribution to a Critique of Cultural Relativism*. London: Lawrence and Wishart.

North, D. (1995) 'The twentieth century has substantiated the historical conception outlined by Marx', *The International Workers Bulletin*, 30 January: 17.

Novack, G. (1971) *An Introduction and the Logic of Marxism*. New York: Pathfinder Press.

Novack, G. (1975) *Pragmatism versus Marxism: An Appraisal of John Dewey's Philosophy*. New York: Pathfinder Press.

Osbeck, L. M. (1993) 'Social constructionism and the pragmatic standard', *Theory and Psychology*, 3: 337–349.

Parker, I. (1987) 'The social status of mentalistic constructs', in W. Baker, M. Hyland, H. V. Rappard and A. Staats (eds) *Current Issues in Theoretical Psychology*. Amsterdam: Elsevier.

Parker, I. (1988) 'Deconstructing accounts', in C. Antaki (ed.) *Analysing Everyday Explanation: A Case-book of Methods*. London: Sage.

Parker, I. (1989) *The Crisis in Modern Social Psychology, and How to End it*. London: Routledge.

Parker, I. (1992) *Discourse Dynamics: Critical Analysis for Social and Indvidual Psychology*. London: Routledge.

Parker, I. (1993) 'Social constructionist psychoanalysis and the real', in B. Kaplan, L. Mos, H. Stam and W. Thorngate (eds) *Recent Trends in Theoretical Psychology*, Vol. III. New York: Springer Verlag.

Parker, I. (1994) 'Discourse analysis', in P. Banister, E. Burman, I. Parker, M. Taylor and C. Tindall (eds) *Qualitative Methods in Psychology: A Research Guide*. Buckingham: Open University Press.

Parker, I. (1995a) 'Michel Foucault, psychologist', *The Psychologist*, 8 (11): 214–216.

Parker, I. (1995b) '"Right" said Fred "I'm too sexy for bourgeois group therapy"': The case of the Institute for Social Therapy. *Changes: An International Journal of Psychology and Psychotherapy*, 13 (1): 1–22.

Parker, I. (1995c) 'Discursive complexes in material culture', in J. Haworth (ed.) *Psychological Research: Innovative Methods and Strategies*. London: Routledge.

Parker, I. (1996a) 'The Revolutionary Psychology of Lev Dowidovich Bronstein', in I. Parker and R. Spears (eds) *Psychology and Society: Radical Theory and Practice*, pp. 184–194. London: Pluto Press.

Parker, I. (1996b) 'Postmodernism and its discontents: Therapeutic discourse', *British Journal of Psychotherapy*, 12 (4): 447–460.

Parker, I. (1997a) *Psychoanalytic Culture: Psychoanalytic Discourse in Western Society*. London: Sage.

Parker, I. (1997b) 'Discursive psychology', in D. Fox and I. Prilleltensky (eds) *Critical Psychology: An Introduction*. London: Sage.

Parker, I. (1997c) 'The unconscious state of social psychology', in T. Ibáñez and L. Íñiguez (eds) *Critical Social Psychology*. London: Sage.

Parker, I. (1999a) 'Critical psychology: critical links', *Annual Review of Critical Psychology*, 1: 3–18.

Parker, I. (1999b) 'Psychology and Marxism: dialectical opposites?', in W. Maiers, B. Bayer, B. Duarte Esgalhado, R. Jorna and E. Schraube (eds) *Challenges to Theoretical Psychology*. Toronto: Captus University Publications.

Parker, I. (ed.) (1999c) *Deconstructing Psychotherapy*. London: Sage.

Parker, I. (in press) 'Discursive practice: analysis, context and action in critical research', *International Journal of Critical Psychology*.

Parker, I. and the Bolton Discourse Network (1999) *Critical Textwork: An Introduction to Varieties of Discourse and Analysis*. Buckingham: Open University Press.

Parker, I. and Burman, E. (1993) 'Against discursive imperialism, empiricism and constructionism: thirty-two problems with discourse analysis', in E. Burman and I. Parker (eds) *Discourse Analytic Research: Repertoires and Readings of Texts in Action*. London: Routledge.

Parker, I., Georgaca, E., Harper, D., McLaughlin, T. and Stowell-Smith, M. (1995) *Deconstructing Psychopathology*. London: Sage.

Parker, I. and Shotter, J. (eds) (1990) *Deconstructing Social Psychology*. London: Routledge.

Parker, I. and Spears, R. (eds) (1996) *Psychology and Society: Radical Theory and Practice*. London: Pluto Press.

Pears, D. (1971) *Wittgenstein*. London: Collins.

Perez, J. A. and Mugny, G. (1990) 'Minority influence: manifest discrimination and latent influence', in D. Abrams and M. A. Hogg (eds) *Social Identity Theory: Construction and Critical Advances*. London: Harvester Wheatsheaf.

Perry, R. E. and Cacioppo, J. T. (1981) *Attitudes and Persuasion: Classic and Contemporary Approaches*. Dubuque, IA: W. C. Brown.

Peters, D. P. and Ceci, S. J. (1982) 'Peer-review practices of psychological journals: the fate of published articles, submitted again', *The Behavioural and Brain Sciences*, 5: 187–255.

Phillips, D. L. (1977) *Wittgenstein and Scientific Knowledge: A Sociological Perspective*. London: Macmillan.

Phoenix, A. (1987) 'Theories of gender and black families', in G. Weiner and M. Arnot (eds) *Gender Under Scrutiny: New Inquiries in Education*. London: Hutchinson.

Phoenix, A. (1990) 'Social research in the context of feminist psychology', in E. Burman (ed.) *Feminists and Psychological Practice*. London: Sage.

Pilgrim, D. (1997) *Psychotherapy and Society*. London: Sage.

Pilgrim, D. and Treacher, A. (1992) *Clinical Psychology Observed*. London: Routledge.

Potter, J. (1987) 'Reading repertoires: a preliminary study of some techniques scientists use to construct readings', *Science and Technology Studies*, 5: 112–121.

Potter, J. (1988a) 'Cutting cakes: a study of psychologists' social categorisations', *Philosophical Psychology*, 1: 17–33.

Potter, J. (1988b) 'What is reflexive about discourse analysis?: The case of reading readings', in S. Woolgar (ed.) *Knowledge and Reflexivity: New Frontiers in the Sociology of Knowledge*. London: Sage.

Potter, J. (1996) *Representing Reality: Discourse, Rhetoric and Social Construction*. London: Sage.

Potter, J. (1997) 'Discourse and critical social psychology', in T. Ibáñez and L. Íñiguez (eds) *Critical Social Psychology*. London: Sage.

Potter, J. (1998) 'Fragments in the realization of relativism', in I. Parker (ed.) *Social Constructionism, Discourse and Realism*. London: Sage.

Potter, J. and Collie, F. (1989) '"Community care" as persuasive rhetoric: a study of discourse', *Disability, Handicap and Society*, 4: 57–64.

Potter, J. and Edwards, D. (1990) 'Nigel Lawson's tent: discourse analysis, attribution theory and the social psychology of fact', *European Journal of Social Psychology*, 20: 405–424.

Potter, J. and Halliday, Q. (1990) 'Community leaders: a device for warranting versions of crowd events', *Journal of Pragmatics*. 14: 225–241.

Potter, J. and Litton, I. (1985) 'Some problems underlying the theory of social representations', *British Journal of Social Psychology*, 24: 81–90.

Potter, J. and Mulkay, M. (1985) 'Scientists' interview talk: interviews as a technique for revealing participants' interpretative practices', in M. Brenner, J. Brown and D. Canter (eds) *The Research Interview: Uses and Approaches*. London: Academic Press.

Potter, J. and Reicher, S. (1987) 'Discourses of community and conflict: the organisation of social categories in accounts of a "riot"', *British Journal of Social Psychology*, 26: 25–40.

Potter, J., Stringer, P. and Wetherell, M. (1984) *Social Texts and Context: Literature and Social Psychology*. London: Routledge and Kegan Paul.

Potter, J. and Wetherell, M. (1987) *Discourse and Social Psychology: Beyond Attitudes and Behaviour*. London: Sage.

Potter, J. and Wetherell, M. (1988a) 'Accomplished attitudes: fact and evaluation in racist discourse', *Text*, 8: 51–68.

Potter, J. and Wetherell, M. (1988b) 'The politics of hypocrisy: notes on the discrediting of apartheid's opponents', *BPS Social Psychology Section Newsletter*, 19: 30–42.

Potter, J. and Wetherell, M. (1989) 'Fragmented ideologies: accounts of educational failure and positive discrimination', *Text*, 9: 175–190.

Poulantzas, N. (1978) *State Power, Socialism*. London: New Left Books.

Prilleltensky, I. (1994) *The Morals and Politics of Psychology: Psychological Discourse and the Status Quo*. Albany, NY: State University of New York Press.

Psychotherapists and counsellors for social responsibility (1996) 'Psychotherapists and counsellors for social responsibility', *Free Associations*, 4 (3): 125–128.

Rantzen, A. J. (1993) 'Constructivism, direct realism and the nature of error', *Theory and Psychology*, 3 (2): 147–171.

Reason, P. and Rowan, J. (eds) (1981) *Human Inquiry: A Sourcebook of New Paradigm Research*. Chichester: Wiley.

Reed, E. (1996) 'The challenge of historical materialist epistemology', in I. Parker and R. Spears (eds) *Psychology and Society: Radical Theory and Practice*. London: Pluto Press.

Reeves, W. (1983) *British Racial Discourse: A Study of British Political Discourse about Race and Race-related Matters*. Cambridge: Cambridge University Press.

Regis, E. (1995) 'His dreams were unusual, even for dreams [review of P. Feyerabend, *Killing Time: The Autobiography of Paul Feyerabend*]', *London Review of Books*, 17 (11): 26.

Reicher, S. (1982) 'The determination of collective behaviour', in H. Tajfel (ed.) *Social Identity and Intergroup Relations*. Cambridge: Cambridge University Press.

Reicher, S. (1984) 'The St Pauls' riot: an explanation of the limits of crowd action in terms of a social identity model', *European Journal of Social Psychology*, 14: 1–21.

Reicher, S. (1988) 'Essay review of *Arguing and Thinking*', *British Journal of Social Psychology*, 27: 283–288.

Reicher, S. and Parker, I. (1993) 'Psychology politics resistance – the birth of a new organization', *Journal of Community and Applied Social Psychology*, 3: 77–80.

Reicher, S. and Potter, J. (1985) 'Psychological theory as intergroup perspective: a comparative analysis of "scientific" and "lay" accounts of crowd events', *Human Relations*, 38: 167–189.

Richard, N. (1987) 'Postmodernism and periphery', *Third Text*, 2: 6–12.

Richards, B. (1989) *Images of Freud*. London: Dent.

Ricoeur, P. (1971) 'The model of the text: meaningful action considered as a text', *Social Research*, 38: 529–562.

Riley, D. (1983) *War in the Nursery: Theories of the Child and the Mother*. London: Virago.

Roberts, H. (ed.) (1981) *Doing Feminist Research*. London: Routledge and Kegan Paul.

Roiser, M. (1991) 'Post-modernism and social psychology, a critique', *British Psychological Society Social Psychology Section Newsletter*, 25: 6–13.

Roiser, M. (1997) 'Postmodernism, postmodernity and social psychology', in T. Ibáñez and L. Íñiguez (eds) *Critical Social Psychology*. London: Sage.

Rorty, R. (1980) *Philosophy and the Mirror of Nature*. Oxford: Blackwell.

Rorty, R. (1989) *Contingency, Irony, and Solidarity*. Cambridge: Cambridge University Press.

Rose, N. (1985) *The Psychological Complex: Psychology, Politics and Society in England 1869–1939*. London: Routledge and Kegan Paul.

Rose, N. (1989) *Governing the Soul: The Shaping of the Private Self*. London: Routledge.

Rose, N. (1996) *Inventing Ourselves: Psychology, Power and Personhood*. Cambridge: Cambridge University Press.

Rosenthal, R. (1966) *Experimenter Effects in Behavioral Research* New York: Appleton-Century-Crofts.

Roudinesco, E. (1990) *Jacques Lacan and Co.: A History of Psycho-Analysis in France 1925–1985*. London: Free Association Books.

Rowbotham, S., Segal, L. and Wainwright, H. (1979) *Beyond the Fragments: Feminism and the Making of Socialism*, NSC/ICP, Newcastle and London.

Rubinstein, D. (1981) *Marx and Wittgenstein: Social Praxis and Social Explanation*. London: Routledge and Kegan Paul.

Rushkoff, D. (1994) *Cyberia: Life in the Trenches of Hyperspace*. London: Flamingo.

Rustin, M. (1987) 'Psychoanalysis, philosophical realism, and the new sociology of science', *Free Associations*, 9: 102–136.

Ryan, M. (1982) *Marxism and Deconstruction: A Critical Articulation*. Baltimore: Johns Hopkins, University Press.

Ryle, G. (1949) *The Concept of Mind*. London: Hutchinson.

Sachdev, I. and Bourhis, R. Y. (1990) 'Language and social identification', in D. Abrams and M. A. Hogg (eds) *Social Identity Theory: Constructive and Critical Advances*. London: Harvester Wheatsheaf.

Sacks, H. (1974) 'On the analyzability of stories by children', in R. Turner (ed.) *Ethnomethodology*. Harmondsworth: Penguin.

Sacks, H., Schegloff, E. A. and Jefferson, G. A. (1974) 'A simplest systematics for the organization of turn-taking in conversation', *Language*, 50: 697–735.

Said, E. (1983) *The World, the Text, the Critic*. London: Faber and Faber.

Sampson, E. E. (1993) *Celebrating the Other: A Dialogical Account of Human Nature*. New York: Harvester Wheatsheaf.

Samuels, A. (1993) *The Political Psyche*. London: Routledge.

Saussure, F. de (1974) *Course in General Linguistics*. London: Collins.

Sawacki, J. (1991) *Disciplining Foucault: Feminism, Power and the Body*. London: Routledge.

Scott-Fox, L. (1997) 'Diary', *London Review of Books*, 23 January: 29.

Searle, J. R. (1969) *Speech Acts*. Cambridge: Cambridge University Press.

Searle, J. R., Kieffer F. and Bierwisch, M. (eds) (1979) *Studies in Semantics and Pragmatics*. Dordrecht: Reidel.

Sears, D. O. (1986) 'College sophomores in the laboratory: influences of a narrow data base on social psychology's view of human nature', *Journal of Personality and Social Psychology*, 15 (3): 515–530.

Seidel, G. (1986a) Right-wing discourse', in R. Levitas (ed.) *The Ideology of the New Right*. Oxford: Polity Press.

Seidel, G. (1986b) *The Holocaust Denial: Anti-Semitism, Racism and the New Right*. Leeds: Beyond the Pale Collective.

Sennett, R. and Cobb, J. (1972) *The Hidden Injuries of Class*. London: Faber and Faber.

Sève, L. (1978) *Man in Marxist Theory*. Hassocks, Sussex: Harvester Press.

Sharrock, W. and Anderson, B. (1987) 'Epilogue: the definition of alternatives: some sources of confusion in interdisciplinary discussion', in G. Button and J. R. E. Lee (eds) *Talk and Social Organisation*. Clevedon: Multilingual Matters.

Sherif, M. (1936) *The Psychology of Social Norms*. New York: Harper and Row.

Shotter, J. (1975) *Images of Man in Psychological Research*. London: Methuen.

Shotter, J. (1984) *Accountability and Selfhood*. Oxford: Blackwell.

Shotter, J. (1987) 'Cognitive psychology, Taylorism. and the manufacture of unemployment', in A. Costall and A. Still (eds) *Cognitive Psychology in Question*. Hassocks, Sussex: Harvester Press.

Shotter, J. (1990) '"Getting in touch": the metamethodology of a postmodern science of mental life', *The Humanistic Psychologist*, 18: 7–22.

Shotter, J. (1991) 'Wittgenstein and psychology: on our "hook up" to reality', in A. P. Griffiths (ed.) *Wittgenstein Centenary Essays*. Cambridge: Cambridge University Press.

Shotter, J. (1993) *Cultural Politics of Everyday Life: Social Constructionism, Rhetoric and Knowing of the Third Kind*. Buckingham: Open University Press.

Shotter, J. and Gergen, K. J. (eds) (1989) *Texts of Identity*. London: Sage.

Silverman, D. and Torode, B. (1980) *The Material Word: Some Theories of Language and its Limits*. London: Routledge and Kegan Paul.

Sinclair, J. M. and Coulthard, R. M. (1975) *Towards an Analysis of Discourse: The English used by Teachers and Pupils*. Oxford: Oxford University Press.

Singer, E. (1992) *Child Care and the Psychology of Development*. London: Routledge.

Sloan, T. (ed.) (2000) *Critical Psychology: Voices for Change*. London: Macmillan.

Smith, B. H. (1988) *Contingencies of Value: Alternative Perspectives for Critical Theory*. Cambridge, MA: Harvard University Press.

Smith, B. H. (1997) *Belief and Resistance: Dynamics of Contemporary Intellectual Controversy*. Cambridge, MA: Harvard University Press.

Smith, D. (1974) 'Theorizing as ideology', in R. Turner (ed.) *Ethnomethodology*. Harmondsworth: Penguin.

Smith, D. (1978) 'K is mentally ill: the anatomy of a factual account', *Sociology*, 12: 23–53.

Smith, J. (1987) 'Making people offers they can't refuse: a social psychological analysis of attitude change', in J. Hawthorn (ed.) *Propaganda, Persuasion and Power*. London: Edward Arnold.

Smith, M. B. (1994) 'Selfhood at risk: postmodern perils and the perils of postmodernism', *American Psychologist*, 49 (5): 405–411.

Spivak, G. C. (1990) *The Post-Colonial Critic*. London: Routledge.

Stainton Rogers, R., Stenner, P., Gleeson, K. and Stainton Rogers, W. (1995) *Social Psychology: A Critical Agenda*. Cambridge: Polity Press.

Stainton Rogers, W. (1991) *Explaining Health and Illness: An Exploration of Diversity*. Hemel Hempstead: Harvester Wheatsheaf.

Stainton Rogers, W. and Stainton Rogers, R. (1997) 'Does critical social psychology mean the end of the world?', in T. Ibáñez and L. Íñiguez (eds) *Critical Social Psychology*. London: Sage.

Stam, H.J. (1990) 'Rebuilding the ship at sea: the historical and theoretical problems of constructionist epistemologies in psychology', *Canadian Psychology*, 31: 239–253.

Stanley, L. and Wise, S. (1983) *Breaking Out: Feminist Consciousness and Feminist Research*. London: Routledge and Kegan Paul.

Stenner, P. (1993) 'Discoursing jealousy', in E. Burman and I. Parker (eds) *Discourse Analytic Research: Repertoires and Readings of Texts in Action*. London: Routledge.

Stenner, P. and Eccleston, C. (1994) 'On the textuality of being: towards an invigorated social constructionism', *Theory and Psychology*, 4 (1): 85–103.

Stern, D. N. (1985) *The Interpersonal World of the Infant: A View from Psychoanalysis and Developmental Psychology*. New York: Basic Books.

Stich, S. (1983) *From Folk Psychology to Cognitive Science: The Case against Belief*. Cambridge, MA: MIT Press.

Stoke Newington 8 Defence Group (1972) *Armed Resistance in West Germany: Documents from the Red Army Fraction*. London: Stoke Newington 8 Defence Group.

Stroebe, W. and Kruglanski, A. (1989) 'Social psychology at epistemological cross-roads: on Gergen's choice', *European Journal of Social Psychology*, 19: 485–489.

Sykes, M. (1985) 'Discrimination in discourse', in T. A. Van Dijk (ed.) *Handbook of Discourse Analysis*, Vol. 4. London: Academic Press.

Tajfel, H. (1972) 'Experiments in a vacuum', in J. Israel and H. Tajfel (eds) *The Context of Social Psychology: A Critical Assessment*. London: Academic Press.

Taylor, C. (1988) 'Wittgenstein, empiricism, and the question of the "inner": commentary on Kenneth Gergen', in S.B. Messer, L. A. Sass, and R. L. Woolfolk (eds) *Hermeneutics and Psychological Theory: Interpretive Perspectives on and Personality, Psychotherapy, and Psychopathology*. New Brunswick, NJ: Rutgers University Press.

Terre Blanche, M. (1996) 'A spanner in the works of the factory of truth', *Psychology in Society*, 21: 78–80.

Therborn, G. (1976) *Science, Class, Society: On the Formation of Sociology and Historical Materialism*. London: Verso.

Timpanaro, S. (1976) *The Freudian Slip*. London: New Left Books.

Tolman, C. (1994) *Psychology, Society and Subjectivity: An Introduction to German Critical Psychology*. London: Routledge.

Tolman, C. and Maiers, W. (eds) (1991) *Critical Psychology: Contributions to an Historical Science of the Subject*. Cambridge: Cambridge University Press.

Trotsky, L. ([1936] 1973) *The Revolution Betrayed: What is the Soviet Union and Where is it Going?* London: New Park Publications.

Trotsky, L. (1973) *In Defense of Marxism*. New York: Pathfinder Press.

Tunney, S. (1991) 'Post-modernism – what it is and how to fight it', *Socialist Outlook*, 6: 11.

Turner, B. S. (1987) *Medical Power and Social Knowledge*. London: Sage.

Turner, J. C., Hogg, M. A., Oakes, P. J., Reicher, S. D. and Wetherell, M. (1987) *Rediscovering the Social Group: A Self-categorisation Theory*. Oxford: Blackwell.

Vanaik, A. (1997) *The Furies of Indian Communalism: Religion, Modernity and Secularization*. London: Verso.

Van Dijk, T. A. (1984) *Prejudice in Discourse: An Analysis of Ethnic Prejudices in Cognition and Conversation*. Amsterdam: John Benjamins.

Van Dijk, T. A. (ed.) (1985) *Handbook of Discourse Analysis* (4 Vols). London: Academic Press.

Van Dijk, T. A. (1987) *Communicating Racism: Ethnic Prejudice in Thought and Talk*. London: Sage.

Van Dijk, T. A. and Kintch, W. (1983) *Strategies of Discourse Comprehension*. London: Academic Press.

Von Wright, G. (1982) *Wittgenstein*. Oxford: Basil Blackwell.

Vygotsky, L. S. (1978) *Mind in Society*. Cambridge, MA: Harvard University Press.

Vygotsky, L. S. (1987) *The Collected Works of L. S. Vygotsky*, Vol. 1. New York: Plenum.

Walkerdine, V. (1981) 'Sex, power and pedagogy', *Screen Education*, 38, 14–24.

Walkerdine, V. (1988) *The Mastery of Reason*. London: Routledge and Kegan Paul.

Walkerdine, V. (1990) *Schoolgirl Fictions*. London: Verso.

Walkerdine, V. (ed.) (2001) *Critical Psychology: The International Journal of Critical Psychology 1*. London: Lawrence and Wishart.

Waller, B. (1977) 'Chomsky, Wittgenstein, and the behaviorist perspective on language', *Behaviourism*, 5: 43–59.

Walsh, D. (1995a) 'Social progress and contemporary culture, part I: why is the notion of progress under attack?', *The International Workers Bulletin*, January 2: 16–17.

Walsh, D. (1995b) 'Social progress and contemporary culture, part II: Marxism and the Enlightenment', *The International Workers Bulletin*, January 16: 16–17.

Weedon, C. (1987) *Feminist Practice and Post-structuralist Theory*. Oxford: Blackwell.

Wetherell, M. (1986) 'Linguistic repertoires and literary criticism: new directions for the social psychology of gender', in S. Wilkinson (ed.) *Feminist Social Psychology*. Milton Keynes: Open University Press.

Wetherell, M. and Potter, J. (1986) 'Discourse analysis and the social psychology of racism', *BPS Social Psychology Section Newsleader*, 15: 24–29.

Wetherell, M. and Potter, J. (1988) 'Discourse analysis and the identification of interpretative repertoires', in C. Antaki (ed.) *Analysing Everyday Explanation: A Case Book of Methods*. London: Sage.

Wetherell, M. and Potter, J. (1992) *Mapping the Language of Racism: Discourse and the Legitimation of Exploitation*. Hemel Hempstead: Harvester Wheatsheaf.

Wetherell, M., Stiven, H. and Potter, J. (1987) 'Unequal egalitarianism: a preliminary study of discourses concerning gender and employment opportunities', *British Journal of Social Psychology*, 26: 59–71.

White, M. (1991) 'Deconstruction and therapy', *Dulwich Centre Newsletter*, 3, 21–40.

White, M. (1995) *Re-Authoring Lives: Interviews and Essays*. Adelaide: Dulwich Centre Publications.

White, M. and Epston, D. (1990) *Narrative Means to Therapeutic Ends*, Adelaide: Dulwich Centre Publications.

Widdicombe, S. (1995) 'Identity, politics and talk: a case for the mundane and the everyday', in S. Wilkinson and C. Kitzinger (eds) *Feminism and Discourse: Psychological Perspectives*. London: Sage.

Widdicombe, S. and Wooffitt, R. (1990) '"Being" Versus "doing" punk (etc.): on achieving authenticity as a member', *Journal of Language and Social Psychology*, 9 (3): 1–21.

Wieder, L. (1974) 'Telling the code', in R. Turner (ed.) *Ethnomethodology*. Harmondsworth, Penguin.

Wilkinson, S. (1988) 'The role of reflexivity in feminist psychology', *Women's Studies International Forum*, 11 (5): 493–502.

Wilkinson, S. and Burns, J. (1990) 'Women organizing within psychology', in E. Burman (ed.) *Feminists and Psychological Practice*. London: Sage.

Wilkinson, S. and Kitzinger, C. (eds) (1995) *Feminism and Discourse*. London: Sage.

Williams, M. (1985) 'Wittgenstein's rejection of scientific psychology', *Journal for the Theory of Social Behaviour*, 15 (2): 203–223.

Willig, C. (1998) 'Social constructionism and revolutionary socialism – a contradiction in terms?', in I. Parker (ed.) *Social Constructionism, Discourse and Realism*. London: Sage.

Wittgenstein, L. (1953) *Philosophical Investigations*, Oxford: Blackwell.

Wittgenstein, L. (1961) *Tractatus Logico-Philosophicus*. London: Routledge and Kegan Paul.

Wittgenstein, L. (1965) *The Blue and Brown Books*. New York: Harper.

Wittgenstein, L. (1967) *Zettel*. Berkeley, CA: University of California Press.

Wittgenstein, L. (1969) *On Certainty*. New York: Harper and Row.

Wittgenstein, L. (1973) 'Conversations on Freud', in F. Cioffi (ed.) *Freud: Modern Judgements*. London: Macmillan.

Wittgenstein, L. (1979) 'Remarks on Frazer's "The golden bough"', in C. G. Luckhardt (ed.), *Wittgenstein: Sources and Perspectives*. Ithaca, NY: Cornell University Press.

Wittgenstein, L. (1980) *Remarks on the Philosophy of Psychology*, (Vol. 1–2). Oxford: Blackwell.

Wooffitt, R. (1989) '(Telling) tales of the unexpected: a sociological analysis of accounts of the paranormal', unpublished DPhil thesis, University of York.

Woolgar, S. (1988) *Science: The Very Idea*. London: Ellis Horwood/Tavistock.

Yardley, L. (1996) 'Reconciling discursive and materialist perspectives on health and illness: a reconstruction of the biopsychosocial approach', *Theory and Psychology*, 6 (3): 485–508.

Young, N. (1992) 'Postmodern self-psychology mirrored in science and the arts', in S. Kvale (ed.) *Psychology and Postmodernism*. London: Sage.

Young, R. M. (1988) 'Biography: the basic discipline for human science', *Free Associations*, 11: 108–130.

Zajonc, R. B. (1989) 'Styles of explanation in social psychology', *European Journal of Social Psychology*, 19: 345–368.

Zimmermann, W. (1978) 'The later Wittgenstein and historical materialism', *Wittgenstein and his Impact on Contemporary Thought: Proceedings of the Second International Wittgenstein Symposium*. Vienna: Holder-Pichler-Tempsky.

Žižek, S. (1989) *The Sublime Object of Ideology*. London: Verso.

Žižek, S. (1996) *The Indivisible Remainder: An Essay on Schelling and Related Matters*. London: Verso.

Žižek, S. (1999) *The Ticklish Subject: The Absent Centre of Political Ontology*. London: Verso.

Index

Note: Contributors to multi-authored works, who are not named in the text, are listed with the name of the first author in brackets.

Abrams, Dominic: discourse 172–86
absent centres 5, 16
academia *see* disciplines
academic position 48–9, 55–6; relativism and 70, 71, 75, 83–4
accidie 221
'acting out' 200–1
action research 201; discourse as variety of 157
actions: collective and individual 193–4; discourse and 166; language research and 162
Adlam, D. 125, 126
Adorno, Theodor 1–2, 13, 18
All Stars Talent Show Network 48–9, 55, 56
Althusser, Louis 152, 169
amae 221
amoralism: postmodernism and 21, 41–2, 45, 53
analytic philosophy 10, 143
analytic practice 165–6
Anderson, Perry 5, 14, 33
'anything goes': relativism 63, 74–5, 82
Archers, The (radio programme) 76, 227–8
argument, evaluation of 76
Ashmore, Malcolm: (Edwards) 64, 71, 74, 75; relativism 73–81
audiences: for discourses 214
author, death of the 136–7, 148
authoritarianism: of individuals 193–4
autobiographical novels 225
autonomy: postmodernism and 21, 43–4, 45
AVEPSO 8

Bakhtin, Mikhail 112, 118, 232
balance: in psychology 58–60
Barnes, Barry 80
Barthes, Roland 132, 136–7, 144, 148, 170
behavioural discursive repertoires 226–8
behaviourism 170
Bell, D. 33
Berman, M. 27, 33
Bhaskar, R. 181
bias: institutionalized 48–9; researcher 192
Billig, M. 127–8, 163
British Psychological Society 6, 189, 191, 199–203, 204
broadcasting: relativism and 63, 75; *see also* television
Burnham, J. 33

capitalism: postmodernism and 27, 30, 33, 36, 53–4; systemization in 47–8
caution: relativism and 65–6
change: Wittgenstein 94, 95
childcare discourse 214, 215, 216, 217
childcentred discourse 215, 216
Chomsky, N. 91
class, social 3–4; reflexive research 190; Wittgenstein 87, 103–4, 114–15
Clinton, Bill 38
cognition and cognitivism 135; Wittgenstein 89–91
cognitive discursive templates 226
collective action 193–4
collectivism: postmodernism and 21, 42–3, 45, 48–50
Collier, A. 67, 68

common sense: discourse and 139–40, 166–8, 184; tolerance and 95, 97, 98
community repertoire   169
computers   25; in discourse analysis 136, 137
Condor, S.   69
confectionary discourse   213, 214, 216
connotation: in language   132
conservatism: Wittgenstein   97, 115
constitution: in discourse   130
construction: in discourse   129–30, 163
contexts: in discourse   180, 182–4; objectivity and   194; in research 204; Wittgenstein   103–4
contingent repertoire: science   127
contradictions: in dialectics   59–60; in discourse   129, 148–9, 150, 158, 164, 215–16
conversation analysis   9, 62, 129–30, 133, 161, 162; interpretative repertoire   170–1
conversational turns   61–2, 64, 66, 75, 129–30
counselling   235; deconstruction in 230, 231, 232; discourse analysis and   205–6, 219; psychotherapeutic discourse 220–2, 229
counter-discourses   126
counter-practice   203
critical distance   43, 49, 52, 53, 54, 55
critical psychology   4, 5, 18, 133–4, 235–6, 236–7; described   58; discourse analysis   9–10; other disciplines and   68–9; postmodernism and   30–1; reflexivity and   2–3; relativism and   66
critical realism   60; discourse and 138–9; psychology and   13, 78–9; relativism and   66–71, 74, 75–6, 77, 80, 82, 84; use of   57, 58
Critical Theory   22
cultural capital: Wittgenstein   103
cultural forms: subjectivity and   196–7
culture   15–16, 235–6

cyberpsychology   15–16
Davies, Bronwyn   79
De Shazer, Steve   231

deconstruction   202; objectivity and 194; of psychotherapeutic discourse 220, 228–33; in psychotherapy 232–3; texts   129, 138, 191, 231; use of term   23–4
deconstruction-in-process   220, 232
denotation: in language   132
Derrida, Jacques   87, 95, 106; critique of philosophy   76; deconstruction   10, 94, 191, 229–30; discourse   136; feminism and   11; post-structuralism   119, 144; power   115
development, stages of   201–2
deviance   133
Dewey, J.   112, 118
dialectical critique   19, 237; of postmodernism   23, 39–40, 46, 53
dialectics   46–8, 55, 59–60, 87
dilemmas   193, 202
disciplines, academic: psychology and 68–9, 79, 234–5; relationships amongst   5–6
discourse   76, 83; context and   180, 182–4; criteria   145–56, 164–8, 172–5; defined   123–5, 142–3, 145; empirical   8–10, 127; escape from   157, 175; Foucauldian 125–6; historical locations   145, 153–4, 174; object status   181–2; political   12–13; power of 176–7, 180; practice and   184–6; scientific   167; social and motivational processes   177; theoretical   10–12; therapeutic 205–19; *see also* interpretative repertoires
discourse analysis   62, 83, 119, 123, 219; historical location   157–8; methodology   175–6; objectivity 192–3; in psychology   128–41, 143–5, 160, 162–8; schools of 236; strands of   161

Discursive Action Model 127
discursive complexes 197–8,
    199–202; psychoanalytic 224–6
discursive practices 154–5;
    classroom 97–9
discursive psychology 76, 123–41
discursive repertoires, behavioural
    226–8
discursive templates, cognitive
    226
dispersion 23–4
disruption: as discursive template
    226, 228
distance, critical *see* critical distance
dominance 237–8

Eagleton, Terry 106, 115;
    Wittgenstein 89, 96–7
East Side Institute 48, 55, 56
ecological discourse 213–14, 215,
    216, 217
ecology 44
Edwards, Derek 64, 71, 74, 75;
    discourse 160–71; relativism
    73–81
ego 200
embodiment 2, 68
emotions 6; disruptive 226; social
    construction of 221
empirical discourse 8–10; science
    127
empiricism 5, 72, 74, 83, 102
empowerment 177–8, 185
Engels, F. 109
Enlightenment: postmodernism and
    35, 37–8, 38–40
epistemes 130
Epston, David 232
essentialism: defined 135;
    Wittgenstein 99–100, 108, 111,
    113–14, 117, 119
ethnomethodology 9, 129, 133,
    143, 162, 186; feminism and 134;
    interpretative repertoire 170–1;
    relativism and 62
European psychology 3
experimenter effects 192
extravagence: relativism and 65–6
Eysenck, Hans 5

familial discourse 215
family therapy 44, 229;
    postmodernism and 32; systemic
    227–8
Faurisson, Robert 63, 64, 77
feminism 11, 17, 158, 203; common
    sense 140; deconstruction 231;
    discourse 134; objectivity 192;
    postmodernism 43; reflexivity
    190, 198; relativism 70, 79, 138;
    subjectivity 194; Wittgenstein
    111
Feyerabend, Paul 40–1
Fodor, J. 90
force, lines of 229
Foucault, Michel 136, 165, 232;
    conditions of possibility 223;
    discourse 125–6, 128, 129, 146,
    154–5, 161, 205–6; epistemes
    130; feminism and 11; ideology
    132, 156; post-structuralism 144;
    power 99, 115, 131, 218; psy-
    complex 7, 199; as psychologist
    234–5; regimes of truth 10, 98;
    silence 95; Wittgenstein and
    87, 105, 106, 119
Freud, Sigmund 14, 18, 74, 91, 148,
    201; discursive complexes 199,
    200
Frosh, S. 27–8
Fukuyama, F. 33
function: in discourse analysis 130–1,
    162–3
fundamentalism: postmodernism and
    21, 42, 44, 45, 53; psycholanalysis
    17

Gekko, Gordon 81
gender: in psychology 3, 4, 11, 12;
    Wittgenstein and 104
genealogy 130
Geras, N. 64, 77–8
Gergen, Ken 82; postmodernism
    22, 29, 221; Wittgenstein 111,
    112–13, 118, 119
Germany: postmodern racism 42
Gill, Ros: discourse 160–71
Gilroy, P. 167
globalization: postmodernism and 36

grammar   169–70
Gross, P.R.   41

Hall, Stuart   80
Halliday, M. A. K.   168
Hardin, Curtis D.: Marx and
   Wittgenstein   108–16
Harré, Ron   70, 113, 143, 181, 221
health discourse   214, 215, 217
Henriques, J.   125, 126
Hepburn, Alexa   238–40
hermeneutics   149
historical materialism: Wittgenstein
   87, 94
history   236–7; relativism and   63–4
Hogg, Michael A.: discourse   172–86
Hollway, W.   130; (Henriques)
   125, 126
Holocaust   62, 63, 64, 65, 77, 78, 138
Holzman, Lois: postmodernism
   46–51
homosexuality: Wittgenstein   104
humanism   195; postmodernism
   and   26; Wittgenstein   105–6

id   200
idealism   110
identity: discourse and   178
identity crises   27–8
identity politics: postmodernism and
   42
ideology: discourse and   132, 134,
   156, 174, 175; psychology and   1;
   relativism and   58, 61, 74, 80;
   Wittgenstein   91
Ideology and Consciousness   10, 125,
   126
India: postmodernism   42
individual action   193–4
individualism   110; postmodernism
   and   21, 43, 44, 45, 50, 53
individuals and individuality   57, 195
inside–outside: in discourse   134–6
institutionalized bias   48–9
institutions   237–8; discourse and
   154–5, 174, 217; *see also* British
   Psychological Society
intellectualization: as discursive
   complex   225

interference: discursive template of
   226
interpretative repertoires   126–8,
   129, 146, 165, 168–71
interrelationships: discourses   150
interruption: as discursive template
   228
intertextuality   124
interview transcripts: discourse
   analysis of   208
intuition   148

Jameson, Fredric   10, 11, 25, 26
Jarman, Derek: *Wittgenstein*   89, 96–7
Jost, John T.: Marx and Wittgenstein
   108–16
journals, psychology   8
Jungian movement: nature   44

Kleinian analysis   5, 14–15
knowing: end of   28, 42–3, 47, 50–1,
   52, 54–6, 61; fetishization of
   50–1, 53–4; of a third kind   28, 61
Kraus, Karl   18
Kuhn, T. S.   163

Lacan, Jacques   10, 11
language   2, 5; inside   100–1;
   outside   101–2; research   162;
   turn to   85, 143–5; Wittgenstein
   85–107; *see also* discourse
language games   25, 101, 106, 115;
   defined   98, 100
languages: primitive   101–2
Latin America: postmodernism   37;
   psychology journals   8
Latour, Bruno   21, 34–6
Levitt, N.   41
linguistics, structural   132
Lion King (film)   225
literary criticism: deconstruction in
   231–2
literary texts   136–7; post-colonial
   36; *see also* autobiographical novels
logic: Wittgenstein   92–6
Luria, A. R.   14
Lyotard, Jean-François   63;
   postmodernism   11, 24–5, 26, 27,
   28–9, 33; post-structuralism   144

Marx, Karl 235; Wittgenstein and
108–10, 111–12, 113, 117–19
Marxism: dialectics 93–4;
postmodernism and 23, 24, 25,
27, 33–4, 35–6, 38, 42–3, 47, 53–4;
psychology and 12–13, 17;
relativism and 60, 80–1, 84;
Wittgenstein and 87–8, 105, 106,
116, 120
Mead, G. H. 112, 118
meaning(s): in discourse 145–7;
hidden 149; layers of 149
medical discourse 144, 213
mental health: deconstruction in
232
mentalism 110
metaphysicalism 110
methodology: discourse analysis
175–6
Mexico: postmodernism 37–8, 55
micro–macro: in discourse 133–4
microsociology 10, 133, 143
modernity and modernism:
postmodernism and 21, 23–36,
47
Moore, G. E. 104
moral–political critique: relativism
71–2
Morgan, M. 31
Moscovici, S. 197
motivational processes: discourse
177
myth 132, 148

narrative therapy 44, 220, 221, 223,
228–9, 231
nature: postmodernism and 44
neurophysiology 90, 102
New Age movements 44
new paradigm psychology 25–6,
127, 143, 190
Newman, Fred 119; postmodernism
46–51
Nietzsche, Friedrich 41, 43, 50
Norris, C. 63
North American Free Trade
Agreement (NAFTA) 38, 55
North American psychology 3
novels, autobiographical 225

objectivity: relationship with
subjectivity 191–4, 203
objects: in discourse analysis 151–2,
174, 181–2, 209–10
omission: in discourse analysis 208
opportunity: postmodernism and
28–30
oppressive discourses 218
organicism: postmodernism and 21,
43–4, 45, 53
orientalism 17
Outlines 8

Papadopoulos, Renos 44
perspectivism: relativism and 63–5,
75
perturbation, climate of 29–30
phenomenology 230
Piaget, Jean 14, 201
play, dialectics as 48
polarities: postmodernism and
28–9; relativism and 71, 75, 83
political discourse 12–13
politics: of discourse 158;
postmodernism and 22;
relativism and 62–3;
Wittgenstein 114–15
polymorphous perversity 201–2
Popper, K. 163
popular psychology 6–7
positivism 190–1, 195
possibility: conditions of 206, 220,
222–3, 234
postcolonial writing 36
postcolonialism 11–12, 231
postmodernism 11, 63, 236, 237;
modernism and 21, 23–36, 47;
Newman and Holzman on 46–51;
Parker on 21–45, 52–6;
psychology and 21–3, 25–6,
27–8, 29–32, 35, 39, 45
post-structuralism 10, 153;
discourse and 130, 143–4, 186;
interpretative repertoires 170–1;
language and 132, 149–50;
postmodernism and 22;
subjectivity 195; Wittgenstein
87, 119

Potter, Jonathan   74, 176; (Edwards)
   64, 71, 75; discourse   142–3, 145,
   160–71; New Zealand culture
   128–9, 149; relativism   73–81
power: in discourse   131–2, 155–6,
   174–5, 176, 180, 217–18, 234;
   postmodernism and   50;
   psychology and   1, 134; in
   psychotherapy   223; psy-complex
   and   7; relativism and   58, 60,
   61, 74; in texts   231; Wittgenstein
   85, 87, 91, 92–100, 103–4, 105,
   106–7, 108–9, 115; *see also*
   empowerment
practice: in discourse   180, 184–6
presuppositions   86–7
primitive languages   101
problematization, climate of   29–30
progression: postmodernism and
   24–6
psychiatry   7
psychoanalysis   235; discourse and
   126; postmodernism and   24–5;
   psychology and   5–6, 14–18, 68,
   69–70, 197–202
psychoanalytic discursive complexes
   224–6
psychology: critical realism and   13,
   78–9; discourse in   8–13;
   discourse analysis in   128–41,
   143–5, 160, 162–8; discursive   76,
   123–41; location of   5–7; popular
   6–7; postmodernism and   21–3,
   25–6, 27–8, 29–32, 35, 39, 45;
   psychoanalysis and   5–6, 14–18,
   68, 69–70, 97–202; scientific
   89–90, 102, 167; traditional
   10–11, 90, 124–5; Wittgenstein and
   88–92, 100–2; *see also* critical;
   research; researchers
Psychology Politics Resistance group
   13
Psychology in Society   8
psychotherapeutic discourse
   220–33; deconstruction of
   228–33
psychotherapy   205–6, 219, 222, 235
psy-complex   59, 74, 78, 190; critical
   realism and   57, 58; described   7,

126, 199–202; Foucauldian   130;
   postmodernism and   22;
   psychotherapy and   220, 222–3
publication   237–8; class and   4;
   reviewing process   238–40
purification   34

qualitative research: reflexivity in
   2–3, 190
quantitative research   141
quantitative–qualitative: in discourse
   136–7
Quayle, Dan   146–7
queer theory   12

race   3, 140, 167; reflexive research
   190
racism, postmodern   42
rationality: collective action and
   193–4
reader reception   137
realism   57, 75; in discourse
   138–9; relativism and   61, 67–71,
   82–4
reality   60; discourse and   151, 152,
   180, 183–4, 185; relativism and
   65; Wittgenstein   88–9, 92
recuperation   1
reflection: in discourse   148–9;
   postmodernism and   26–8
reflexivity: in discourse   144, 149,
   157–8, 166, 173–4; in research
   189–204
Regis, E.   40–1
registers   168
reification   134, 164–5
reinforcement: as discursive repertoire
   227, 228
relativism   237; critical realism and
   57, 58, 66–71, 75–6, 77, 80, 82, 84;
   in discourse   138–9;
   moral–political critique   71–2;
   Parker on   57–72, 82–4;
   postmodernism and   21, 30–1, 40,
   45, 53; Potter, Edwards and
   Ashmore on   73–81; Wittgenstein
   85–6, 91–2, 99–100, 108, 111–13,
   117, 119
repression   16–17

research: class and 4; reflexivity and
189–204; subjects 3, 192, 195, 204
researchers: bias 192; location of
189, 190, 202–3; psy-complex
199; reflexivity 7; situated
knowledge 2–4
reviewing process: publication
238–40
revolutionary activity 47–8
rhetoric: in discourse analysis
212–13; relativism and 57, 72,
76, 83
Rorty, Richard 29, 157
Rose, Nik 74, 78; (Adlam) 125, 126
Rubinstein, D. 112

Salfield, A. (Adlam) 125, 126
Sampson, E. E. 28
Sartre, Jean-Paul 87
Saussure, Ferdinand de 124, 132
science: discourse and 127, 136,
139, 178–9; relativism and 67–8,
70–1, 80
scientific discourse 167
scientific psychology 89–90, 102, 167
scientism: postmodernism and 21,
40–1, 44, 45, 53
selection: in discourse analysis 208
self: discourse and 129, 135–6;
postmodernism and 22; social
construction of 220–2
self-help groups 7, 225
semiology 124, 143
semiotics 124
Shotter, John 22, 143
silence: Wittgenstein 95, 98
Silverman, D. 92
situational factors 2–4, 184
Situationism 1, 18
Skinner, B. F. 91
Smith, Barbara Herrnstein 74, 75
Smith, M. B. 30–1, 36
social: individual and 193–4
social construction 2, 59; Marxism
106; relativism and 61–2, 68, 74,
91–2; self 220–2; Wittgenstein
85–6, 93–4, 105, 112–13, 118
social determination 228; as
discursive repertoire 227

social materialism: Wittgenstein
108–16, 118, 120
social networks: in discourse analysis
212
social processes: in discourse 177
social psychology: discourse and
172–3, 173–4, 178–9, 183, 185
Soros, George 81
South Africa: discourse analysis 140;
psychology journals 8
Soviet Union 12; postmodernism
37; Wittgenstein 103–4
spectacle, society of the 1
speech act theory 131, 143, 161,
162
Sraffa, Piero 96
Stalin, Joseph 93, 103–4
Star Trek (television series) 226
starting points 86
Stich, S. 90–1
structural linguistics 132
structuralism 132, 230–1
subject positions 169, 193, 197–8,
217–18, 211–12, 228; described
131–2
subjectivism 110
subjectivity 233; blank 195–6;
complex 14–18, 196–7; role in
psychology 194–7, 203;
uncomplicated 195; use of term
135
subjects: in discourse analysis
152–3, 174, 210–11; in research
3, 192, 195, 204; unitary 158,
195
surveillance 223, 235
symbolic associations: in discourse
analysis 209; in text 208–9
systemization 47–9

Taylor, Charles 112
television talk shows 225
texts: analysis 161; discourse and
147–8, 173; example of discourse
analysis 206–19; of experiments
8–9; literary 136–7, 225; readerly
and writerly 137; *see also*
deconstruction
theoretical discourse 10–12

theory 8; discourse and 132,
140–1; psychology 102;
reflexivity and 189, 191, 195,
196–7, 203
therapeutic discourse 205–19
therapeutic domains 220, 224–8
therapy: discourse in 136
tolerance, dialectical 95, 97
toothpaste packaging; discourse
analysis 206–19
Torode, B. 92
traditional psychology 10–11;
Wittgenstein and 90
transference 225–6
translation 34
trauma 224–5, 228
Trotsky, L. 93–4, 95, 113
truth: regimes of 6, 10, 98, 126, 206;
relativism and 65
truth effects 86

uncertainty: postmodernism and
28, 32
undecidability: relativism and 61–3
unitary subjects 158, 195
Urwin, C. (Henriques) 125, 126
usage, rules of: Wittgenstein
96–100
variability and variation: in discourse
analysis 128–9, 163–4

Venn, C. (Henriques) 125, 126
Vygotsky, L. S. 52, 112, 118, 201

Walderdine, V. 131; (Henriques)
125, 126
war crimes 138; relativism and 62,
63, 64, 77–8
Wetherell, Margaret 176; discourse
142–3, 145, 160–71; New Zealand
culture 128–9, 149
White, Michael 232
Williams, M. 89, 90, 91
Wittgenstein, Ludwig 52, 53, 237;
class 103–4; Jost and Hardin on
108–16; language 11, 100–2, 131;
Parker on 85–107, 117–20;
Philosophical Investigations 92, 96;
psychology and 88–92; rules of
logic 92–6; rules of usage
96–100; *Tractatus
Logico-Philosophicus* 92, 93, 95, 96,
104, 113
Wittgenstein (film) 89, 96–7
'working through' 200–1

Yugoslavia, former: postmodernism
37

Zapatistas 37–8, 55
Zizek, Slavoj 17, 42